Body Language

Advanced 3D Character Rigging

PLEASE CHECK FOR I DISC in back

BEFORE AND AFTER EACH CIRCULATION

Body Language

Advanced 3D Character Rigging

Eric Allen and Kelly L. Murdock
with contributing authors Jared Fong and Adam G. Sidwell

WILEY PUBLISHING, INC.

Acquisitions Editor: Mariann Barsolo
Development Editor: Mary Ellen Schutz
Technical Editor: Geordie Martinez
Production Editor: Christine O'Connor
Copy Editor: Kim Wimpsett
Production Manager: Tim Tate
Vice President and Executive Group Publisher: Richard Swadley
Vice President and Executive Publisher: Joseph B. Wikert
Vice President and Publisher: Neil Edde
Media Associate Project Manager: Laura Atkinson
Media Assistant Producer: Josh Frank
Media Quality Assurance: Kit Malone
Compositors: Chris Gillespie and Kate Kaminski at Happenstance Type-O-Rama
Proofreader: Nancy Bell
Indexer: Nancy Guenther
Cover Designer: Ryan Sneed
Cover Images: Eric Allen
Cover image "Rosie" by Jan Jureczko. Copyright © 2007 by DAZ Productions Inc. www.daz3d.com

Library of Congress Cataloging-in-Publication Data

Allen, Eric M., 1976–
  Body language advanced 3D character rigging / Eric Allen and Kelly Murdock ; with contributing authors Jared Fong and Adam G. Sidwell.
     p. cm.
  ISBN-13: 978-0-470-17387-9 (paper/cd-rom)
  ISBN-10: 0-470-17387-4 (paper/cd-rom)
  1. Computer animation. 2. Characters and characteristics—Computer simulation. 3. Three-dimensional imaging. I. Murdock, Kelly. II. Title.
  TR897.7.A455 2008
  006.6'96—dc22
                          2008008484

Dear Reader

Thank you for choosing *Body Language: Advanced 3D Character Rigging*. This book is part of a family of premium quality Sybex books, all written by outstanding authors who combine practical experience with a gift for teaching.

Sybex was founded in 1976. More than thirty years later, we're still committed to producing consistently exceptional books. With each of our titles we're working hard to set a new standard for the industry. From the paper we print on, to the authors we work with, our goal is to bring you the best books available.

I hope you see all that reflected in these pages. I'd be very interested to hear your comments and get your feedback on how we're doing. Feel free to let me know what you think about this or any other Sybex book by sending me an email at nedde@wiley.com, or if you think you've found a technical error in this book, please visit http://sybex.custhelp.com. Customer feedback is critical to our efforts at Sybex.

Best regards,

NEIL EDDE
Vice President and Publisher
Sybex, an Imprint of Wiley

This book is dedicated to my wife and kids for supporting my efforts of turning my dreams into reality.

—Eric

There are bodies of water and bodies of air
And bodies of knowledge of which we can share.
There are heavenly bodies that shine from afar,
Like galaxies and nebulas and a distant shining star.
Courtrooms often see, bodies of evidence and law,
From which there are conclusions that you can draw.
There are bodies of doctrine and bodies of time,
And bodies of art with contents sublime.
There are bodies of civilians and bodies of state
That keep bodies of rules first on their slate.
Of all of these bodies, we each have just one,
That enables us to walk, to jump and to run.
And the body that we most often curse and bless,
Is the one in the mirror we daily assess.
This book is dedicated to my dynamic cousins, Chad and Randy.

—Kelly

Acknowledgments

Huge thanks to my wife for allowing all of this work to take place and for being one of the best editors on the planet. Thanks to Jared Fong and his *huge* contributions to the technical aspects of this work. His late night discussions were lifesaving. Thank you, Geordie Martinez, for the amazing technical editing. He polished the rough edges in a way I wasn't even expecting. Thank you to Adam Sidwell, who brought the great chapter on referencing into the work. Adam's knowledge and skill is legendary. A big thank you goes out to Seth Hippen, Enrique Gato, Adam Sidwell, and Stephen Candell for their time helping with the interviews. Thank you to Jacob Speirs and Taylor Eshelman for their rigging discussions and contributions. Thank you to all of the artists whose artwork is showcased in this work. You inspire me. A big thank you to Kelly L. Murdock for working alongside me all through this process.

A huge thank you goes out to Phil Dench, creator of UVLayout, for his editing help in this work. Thank you to Daz3D for allowing the use of the Victoria 4 character in this book. Thank you to BYU for allowing some of their great work to be shown here before their short *Pajama Gladiator* is even available.

A special thank you to my family, who supported me and even sacrificed to get this book here. A big thank you to God for blessing me with an amazing family and a profession that I love.

—*Eric Allen*

Huge thanks to my co-author, Eric Allen. This book is really his vision and he's been wonderful to work with. Thanks as always to my dear wife, Angela, and my sons, Eric and Thomas, without whose support I wouldn't get very far.

Thanks also to Eric's wife, who really pitched in and helped us out of a tight spot. Thanks also to Geordie Martinez, who handled the technical editing.

—*Kelly Murdock*

Eric and Kelly would both to thank Mariann Barsolo, acquisitions editor, and Mary Ellen Schutz, developmental editor, for their help with the editing and their patience in coordinating with the authors. Thank you to Phil Dench, creator of UVLayout, for his editing of Chapter 16. Phil has single-handedly made the best UV software to date. Thanks also to Kim Wimpsett, copyeditor, who made sure grammar and spelling were picture perfect; Nancy Bell, proofreader, for catching those last little "oops," and Christine O'Connor, production editor, who also had to work with the authors and made sure everything flowed through the production process. Thanks also to our compositors, Chris Gillespie and Kate Kaminski at Happenstance Type-O-Rama, and the indexer, Nancy Guenther. The book couldn't happen without them.

—*The Authors*

About the Authors

Eric Allen is currently the Modeling Lead at Daz3d. Besides creating and managing the creation of the figures, he is in charge of the creation of hundreds of deformer and viseme morphs for the Daz3d figures. He also oversees the creation of the joint controlled corrective morphs. These can add up to hundreds of shapes that work with each other to produce realistic deformations. He helped create Victoria 4 (Daz3D female model found in the book) and rigged her in Maya for this title. He also built and rigged the "Runner" character which is used for most of the advanced examples. His figures are used in everything from movie content to graphic art. They have been used for the covers of *3D User*, *Popular Science* and *Scientific American* and have been used in the digital art Exotique publications. He has also worked as a freelance commercial animator where he has created medical and other types of animation using mainly Maya. He has studied Maya rigging and experimented with various techniques for years.

Eric graduated from BYU and worked on the first short film "Lemmings" to win both a student emmy and bronze student academy award.

www.ericmatthewallen.com

Kelly L. Murdock has been authoring computer books for many years now and still gets immense enjoyment from the completed work. His book credits include various 3D, graphics, multimedia, and Web titles, including seven previous editions of his book, *3ds Max Bible*. Other major accomplishments include *Edgeloop Character Modeling for 3D Professionals Only* (also with Eric Allen), *Maya 6 and 7 Revealed*, *LightWave 3D 8 Revealed*, *Poser 6 and 7 Revealed*, *3D Game Animation for Dummies*, *gmax Bible*, *Adobe Atmosphere Bible*, *Master VISUALLY HTML and XHTML*, *JavaScript Visual Blueprint*, and co-authoring duties on two editions of the *Illustrator Bible* (for versions 9 and 10) and three editions of the *Adobe Creative Suite Bible*.

With a background in engineering and computer graphics, Kelly has been all over the 3D industry and still finds it fascinating. He's used high-level CAD workstations for product design and analysis, completed several large-scale visualization projects, created 3D models for feature films and games, worked as a freelance 3D artist, and even done some 3D programming. Kelly's been using 3D Studio since version 3 for DOS. Kelly has also branched into training others in 3D technologies. He teaches at the local university and is a frequent speaker at various conferences.

In his spare time, Kelly enjoys the outdoors while rock climbing, mountain biking, or skiing.

Contributing Author Jared Fong has a profound ability for Maya rigging. He brought us Chapters 15 and 17 as well as many of the scripts included on the CD. He has been a major influence on the rigging of the projects at BYU and part of the thinking that went into this book. Jared is currently working at Pixar as a TD resident.

Contributing Author Adam Sidwell has traveled the world spreading his 3D talents. He has worked at such studios as Digital Domain, ILM, Sony Imageworks, and Weta. He has presented at Siggraph and is very proficient in the studies and methods of the "back end" of the production pipeline. Adam contributed the brilliance of Chapter 19, the "Pipeline in a Box."

Contents

Chapter 10 **What Are You Looking At? Realistic Eyes** **165**

Chapter 11 **Show Your Teeth: Creating the Mouth and Jaw** **189**

Chapter 12   **Can't You See What I'm Saying? Logical Viseme Creation**   **217**

Chapter 13   **Control That Face of Yours: Working with Expressions
and Facial User Interfaces**   **241**

Introduction

Character rigging is one of the most difficult tasks in the production pipeline. It is also one of the most essential. Failure to correctly rig a character will frustrate animators and lead to delays or, even worse, unrealistic results.

Although the rigging tools are getting better all the time, it still takes a lot of patience and know-how to be able to make a complex rig work well. There are a multitude of effective rigging techniques and it can often be confusing to know when to use which one. The goal of this book is to cut through all the clutter and present a clear path to follow when rigging characters. Along the way, we'll share the wealth of information on the subject that we've gathered.

What You Will Learn from This Book

Whether you aspire to create your own animation or work in the animation industry, *Body Language: Advanced 3D Character Rigging* will be a tremendous resource for multiple parts of the production process that goes into 3D animation. Mainly focusing on the foundation and more advanced concepts of character rigging, this work will give you a secure base setup as well as teaching some interesting and unique ways to deform a 3D character.

Some of the more difficult aspects of the 3D pipeline are also discussed. Adam Sidwell joins us with his "Pipeline in a Box" method of referencing. This self-contained workflow is perfect for small projects to large productions. Phil Dench helped with the editing of a chapter covering UVLayout. The new Maya Muscle systems are covered, as well as some great beginning and advanced scripting techniques. *Body Language: Advanced 3D Character Rigging* is a great resource for anyone creating and learning about effective 3D character setup.

Who Should Read This Book

Body Language: Advanced 3D Character Rigging will hone the beginner to advanced artist by teaching standard as well as unique principles about the more intricate parts of 3D character setup.

This book is really geared toward the intermediate to advanced rigger. It assumes that you are comfortable with the basic rigging tasks and jumps right into several advanced techniques.

Although the book uses Maya for its examples, you can apply the principles in the book equally to other software packages.

How to Use This Book

This book is intended to follow the typical production pipeline. If you follow the chapters in order, you'll be taken through the entire process of rigging a character.

How This Book Is Organized

The first three chapters of the book cover the basic concepts of rigging and show some of the basics of Maya that are used throughout the examples.

Next, we present all of the rigging techniques to rig an entire character from start to finish. Chapter 4 begins the rig with coverage of the spine and we then continue in the subsequent chapters to cover the pelvis, arms, legs, feet, hands, neck, head, eyes and jaw.

We then look at the details of working with visemes and facial expressions that enable the character to speak and show emotions.

The last chapters conclude with some specialized miscellaneous chapters on MEL scripting, efficient UV layout, building control interfaces, skinning, and finally referencing.

The Book's CD

The included CD has many examples and files to glean from. It includes a fully rigged figure which you can pick apart to see how the advanced figure techniques actually work.

You can also utilize the many mel scripts that are covered in this book.

There is also a digital copy of this book in the files.

Lastly, Adam's "Pipeline in a Box" is there as well. It is a valuable resource for those looking to create a referencing pipeline or those just looking to study industry procedures.

The Vehicle to Get You There: Applications and Approaches

1

Rigging *is the process of endowing a character with a set of controls that make it easy to animate. These controls can consist of simple joints, handles, or even separate character selection windows. A character's animation is going to be only as good as the rig that controls it.*

As you approach the rigging process, you will find that there are different ways to rig each different body part. Some are simple; some are rather complex. The rigging method you choose depends on the type of motion you want to convey with your character.

Chapter Contents
Planning your rig
Considering your time and needs
Choosing an application
Preparing for character creation
Making your wish list
Discovering what the animators need

Rosie

The opening image for this chapter is Rosie, originally created by Jan Jureczko, which is now owned by DAZ Productions Inc. Victoria 4, the character who is the base figure used in this image, has a morph-based facial rig and joint-controlled morphs for more realistic deformations.

Planning Your Rig

Setting up a rig can be a time-consuming process. But time spent planning the rig prior to the building cycle will save time when you actually start the rigging process. During the planning phase, you should identify the following:

- The types of movement the character needs to perform
- The look of the character
- The body parts that need to move
- Any specialized body parts

If your character is a female action character, then the work you do will be very different than it would be if you were animating a very soft cartoon character. Good planning allows you to predict the needs of your rig before you get there. Figure 1.1 shows a runner character and his controls.

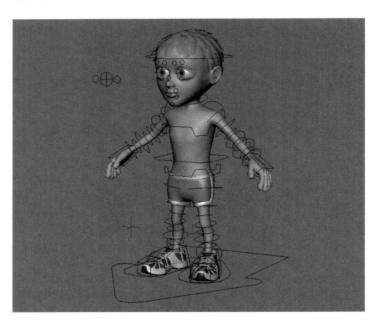

Figure 1.1
Runner character
and his controls

What Constitutes Advanced Rigging?

Throughout the book we'll be walking you through a variety of rigging techniques. Some of these techniques are considered basic—they enable the most common types of motion, such as walking, bending at the waist, and reaching out to grab a weapon. Other techniques are considered advanced—they are more complex and enable specific motions that aren't as common, such as acrobatic or ballistic movement, or something even more specialized, such as swinging from a vine.

We'll show how to build an advanced character rig that includes some complex controls. For example, we will show you how to build a double compression wave spine that can be animated to squash and stretch portions of the torso, and we'll show you how to build an advanced wrist control that enables forearm deformations. We will also show you how to break that arm without breaking the IK chain.

Planning for Advanced Rigging

You will want to address those advanced rigging features that will be needed for your character early in your plan. When considering the advanced rigging features, be sure to consider the following additions which we will add to our rig in this book:

- Stretchy spline IK spine
- FKIK stretchable arms
- FKIK stretchable legs
- Advanced arm and leg with rivet-based deformation
- Facial deformation with influence objects
- Hand-based finger controls
- World and figure orient switch for feet, hands, pole vectors, and focus point
- Making it so controls are the only thing visible and can even be turned off
- An intuitive selection UI
- Organizing and building for referencing

Going Beyond the Normal and Becoming Unique

Even the simplest character can have some advanced rigs added to it. The deciding factor depends on the type of motion you want to create. For example, a snooty butler character might have a specialized control that raises his nose in the air. For these advanced controls, it is important that the rig control is intuitive so that the animator can figure out quickly how to use it without any trouble.

Considering Time and Needs

One of the rigs that we will create in this book is an advanced rig with many controls and switches. Although an advanced rig is the ideal, you might not always have the time to complete a full-featured rig for all your project's characters.

One way to improve your efficiency is to include only the rigging you know your character will use. Most projects include a full-featured rig for the animation's main characters, while the ancillary and background characters use a simple rig. Here are some tips to help you sort out the details:

Prioritizing rigging tasks You need to figure out what you need to do and what you can achieve in the given time. If you have a good plan, it will be easy to determine which rigging procedures are most important and which would be nice, if you have the time. You can then prioritize and start working on the most important rigging tasks first.

Reusing rigs One way to save some time is to reuse rigs. When the characters are fairly similar, you can save time by using the same rig with slight modifications. However, if the characters are different, then tweaking the rig to fit a unique character may take more time than creating a new rig. Reusing rigs is especially useful for background characters that aren't the focus of the scene.

Scripting Scripting is by far the best way to save time building a rig. Scripts will save you countless hours, once you learn how to control Maya Embedded Language (MEL). Many of the advanced setups we'll be creating use a script.

Scripting may take a little more time than actually running through the rigging steps the first time, but in the end it will save you time. The great thing about scripting is you know exactly what you are creating. Each process is broken into small steps. If you rig something once, great. If you need to do it twice, script it. After the initial creation, scripts can save an amazing amount of time.

 Note: Maya has just introduced Python as an alternative method of scripting. Now, the power of Python scripts are available to you.

Choosing an Application

You can use a number of good off-the-shelf 3D software packages to build a rig for a character. But to have the rig control the motions of a bound character, you'll need a 3D package that can handle a skinned mesh. When looking for an application to rig and skin a character, consider the following:

- Maya
- 3ds Max
- Softimage XSI
- LightWave 3D

Maya has become the standard for film and game creation in many studios. Its rigging and skinning tools offer an amazing array of flexibility for creating any possible rig you can imagine. Maya also includes the MEL scripting language that allows you to automate a lot of rigging tasks.

In this book, we'll use Maya for all our examples and tutorials. This decision was based on familiarity with the product and its popularity in the industry. Although we'll use Maya exclusively throughout this book for rigging, you can apply many of the same concepts and techniques to other software packages. In Chapter 2, "Getting to Know You: Maya's Interface and Basics," we'll cover some of the basic functionality that is unique to Maya.

Many of the other 3D applications have similar workflows and approaches for rigging. For example, we'll use a character, Tadeo Jones, in some of the examples in this book, and Tadeo was created and rigged in 3ds Max by Enrique Gato. The setups Enrique used are similar to those we'll show you using Maya.

Creating a Character

Whether you are creating the character's mesh yourself or using one that was built by someone else, one of the first issues to consider when rigging is the character's default pose. There are many default positions for characters; however, we recommend using a pose similar to the standard T-pose but in a more relaxed state.

The standard T-pose The standard T-pose has the character facing forward with its arms extended out to its sides and its palms down. The character's legs are about shoulder-width apart. Although this is a common pose for many characters, this position isn't natural and might cause some problems when rigging the character. For example, when the characters joints are straight, it makes it more difficult to assign an IK chain and pole vector to it. Also, the character's shoulders are in a fully flexed position, which could introduce some muscle bulging. However, it is easier to create and see how morphs are going to look in this upstanding pose.

A relaxed T-pose We recommend dropping the arms to a 45-degree angle from the body. Most of your character's arm movement will likely be from straight out horizontally from the shoulder (like the standard T-pose) down to the side of the body. Placing the arms at a 45-degree angle from the body puts them in the middle of where the majority of the movement will be.

You will also want to keep the hands relaxed. The character should be posed with the fingers separated from one another and not rigid. If you have the fingers and hands relaxed in the default pose, it will look more natural when you animate the rig.

We also suggest making the elbows and knees slightly relaxed so that it's easier to assign an IK chain and pole vector to it. Figure 1.2 shows the character Tadeo Jones, which was created by Enrique Gato. Notice how this character's shoulder and hands are in a relaxed state. This relaxed state is ready for rigging.

Figure 1.2 Tadeo Jones's default position by Enrique Gato

Introducing Our Players

Throughout the book, we will use two main characters in the tutorials to show the rigging concepts. Other characters, such as the Tadeo Jones character, will be featured to show specific concepts.

Runner character The first character we'll be working with is a cartoony runner character. His proportions aren't realistic. His head is abnormally large, his arms are long compared to the rest of his body, and his legs are short, as shown in Figure 1.3. He is a good character to show how rigging concepts can be applied to nonrealistic, unique characters.

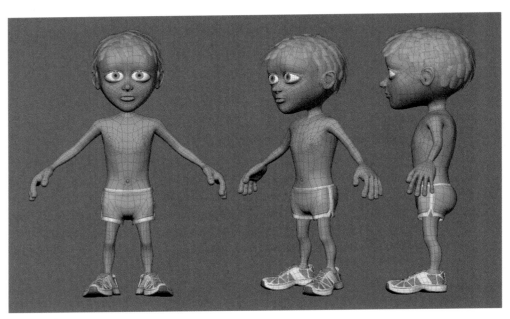

Figure 1.3 Runner

Victoria 4 The second character you'll see in this book is Victoria 4, created by Daz3D. We'll use this character to show you how to rig a realistic character. Notice in Figure 1.4 how Victoria is positioned in the standard T-pose, with the ankles and fingers relaxed. The elbows are also slightly relaxed. Although her arms aren't at a 45-degree angle, this is the default position that the team used.

With these two characters, we'll be able to show how you can apply rigging concepts to different types of characters.

Making Your Wish List

When planning a character rig, it is often helpful to create a wish list of available rigging components from which you can choose. Such a wish list helps you to consider the motions that the character may need.

Variants of rig What type of spine do you need to have? Does it need to stretch? Do the arms need to stretch? What about the fingers and toes? Can movement be built with morphs that are linear, or do they need to be built with joints? When considering the elements that need to be rigged, try your best to outline all the possible combinations and connections.

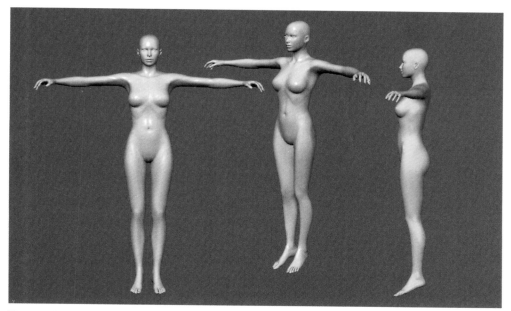

Figure 1.4 Daz3D Victoria 4

Variants of controls A rig works best if there are controls to drive the joint rotation. When considering the controls to use, be sure to choose a control that is easy to select, easy to read, and intuitive to use. Do you want controls that surround the body part or that are located near the body part?

Variants of UIs You have several choices to make regarding the user interface. You could build a group of buttons for selecting specific rigs, or you could build sliders for moving between extreme values. The decision of which type of UI to use, like the controls, needs to be intuitive and easy to access for the animator.

Seth Hippen's Wish List

Take a look at this rig wish list we received from Seth Hippen. Seth has worked on films at Sony Imageworks and has experience in animating traditionally for film and for games. Here is his wish list for a 3D character rig final setup:

Alternative Means of Selection

(I prefer seeing no selection flags in the viewport.)

- Shelves
- GUIs
- Channel box (especially with foot, hand, and facial controls)

Continues

Seth Hippen's Wish List *(Continued)*

Selection Groups

- All
- Spine
- Head/Neck
- Head/Neck/Spine
- All fingers or toes
- Individual fingers or toes
- And so on

Ability to Choose and Key (in Channel Box) Object or World Space For

- Eye target
- Arms, including IK in shoulder, COG, or world space
- Legs

FK Spine

- With ability to move the pivot from the bottom to the top of the spine

IK/FK Switching

- Arms
- Legs
- Head/neck

Facial

- Expression sliders, divided to allow asymmetry
- Phoneme sliders ("The quick brown fox jumped over the lazy dog.")
- Finite control to push and pull expressions beyond the default slider:
  - Brows: Four control points on each eyebrow
  - Nose: Sneers, flares, stretch
  - Mouth: Corners in/out/forward/back/up/down:
    - Four or five controls on each lip (not including corners)
    - Whole mouth up/down/roll/side to side
    - Individual lip up/down/in/out
    - Eyelid shape controls: four or five on each lid/six to eight per eye
    - Cheeks: full/gaunt/smile/puff
    - Ear controls
    - Squash and stretch controls

Finding What the Animators Need

One of the most important aspects of creating a rigging plan is to find out what the animator needs. Animators who can find and quickly understand the rig controls will be able to better do their jobs. However, if they can't find or access the controls, then they'll be hunting you down to help them figure it out.

Ease of use and great organization Animators like a rig that works as they expect. Animators don't like to have to click extra buttons to get to the rig controls. Make the controls available and organized in a logical manner, and the animator will be happy.

Controls Placing the controls near the parts they control is helpful for animators. If an animator has to search to find a control, then they'll get frustrated. It is important to build a rig that has all the controls that an animator will need to do their job. If a rig is lacking, then the animator will send the rig back to the rigger and request that the needed controls be added.

Interfaces It is helpful to learn the type of interface the animator likes to work with. If you can place all the interface controls together, such as in a floating panel, the animators can position it where they want.

Controls vs. interfaces vs. both Some animators like to work with rigs that use only controls, but other animators like to use interfaces that let you access the various rigs. Still other animators like a combination of both. Find out from the animator who will be working with the rig what their preferences are. We will talk about these approaches in more detail throughout the book.

> **Tadeo head rig** One alternative is to place the interface within the scene using graphical controls, like the facial controls for the Tadeo character, as shown in Figure 1.5. Using these controls, you can select and move the character's face without having to actually manipulate the face's surface.

Figure 1.5 Tadeo head rig by Enrique Gato

Selection controls Another technique is to create a series of selection overlays that make it easy to choose a specific part of the body, like the controls shown in Figure 1.6.

Joystick controls Still another method is to control the expressions using a joystick interface, like the one shown in Figure 1.7.

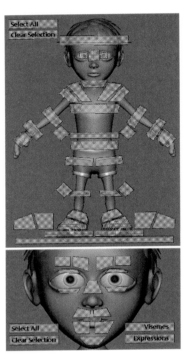

Figure 1.6 Selection controls

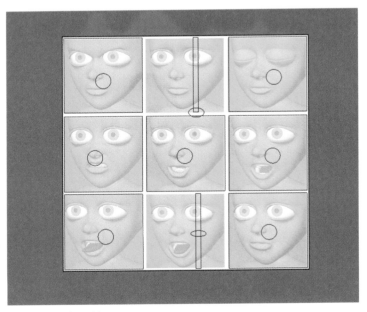

Figure 1.7 Head joystick setup

Introducing Seth Hippen

What is your background?

Animation has been in my blood since I was a young tyke. I have been drawing my whole life in anticipation of a career as an animator. While I was a student at Brigham Young University, I decided to learn computer animation, and most of my career since then has been involved with it in some form or another. I began my career with an internship at Film Roman, working on *The Simpsons*, and after that had a few years at the Waterford Institute, where I was animating for children's  educational software. From there, I went to work at Sony Pictures Imageworks as a character animator for *The Polar Express*, *Monster House*, *Surf's Up*, and *Beowulf*. Now I'm working at Avalanche Software making Disney video games.

As an animator, what are the major things you like/dislike in rigs?

A lot of rigs I've worked with have been so heavy they were too cumbersome to scrub in the timeline. That can be very frustrating, but I would rather have an overengineered rig as opposed to an underengineered one. The best solution I've seen to a heavy rig is the ability to load only the parts of the rig that you need for the particular stage of animation you are working in.

An underdeveloped facial rig can be one of the most exasperating things to try to animate. Just try to get a coy expression out of a rig with eyebrows that only go up and down! Ideally, there should be some set poses for the brows and mouth that are generally split up between quadrants of the face to allow for asymmetrical expressions and then allow for further tweaking beyond that with more precise controls. For example, besides the general expression controls for the eyebrows (such as up, down, angry, sad, worried, surprised, in and out), four controls per eyebrow have been optimal for more precise control. More than that can start to feel cumbersome.

Rigs that are disconnected from themselves can be very aggravating, meaning when I move a part of the body that naturally affects the position of another part, that other part doesn't move. In most cases, that's great for the legs, but torso movements almost always need the arms, neck, and head to be moved to compensate for it. I really like it when I can choose to have the IK handles in world or object space. Most of the time, I want the arms to come along with the torso twists but occasionally stay where they are.

I love it when I have a rig that gives me a quick and clear means of selection. I hate when I have to move the camera around to find a control that I need, either because it's hiding behind geometry or because there is such a jumble of controls in close proximity to each other that I have a hard time picking the right controls. Selection groups are a big time-saver, whether in a shelf or a GUI. When you have an FK spine, neck, and head, for example, that is a group that I often pose together, and it's nice to push one button to get those controls instead of seven. Whatever can be done to keep the animator in a constant train of thought in regards to where they are going with their animation is a big help. It may seem like a small thing if the animator has to click four times to get a specific control, but if you can take that down to one click, the flow of animation will be smoother, and the results will be faster and better.

Continues

Another advantage to selection through shelves and GUIs is the clear view you can get of the character. I've gone back many times to fix animation that I thought was done until I turned off the control flags and saw what the shot really looked like without them.

What has been your hardest rig to animate and why?

The actual house in *Monster House* was, in fact, a monster to animate. There were thousands of controls on that thing, and we had control of everything down to each individual broken piece of siding. The rig was amazing, but there was so much to keep track of that it was easy to feel over-whelmed by it. It took a very long time to load and unload specific parts of the rig. That could be frustrating, but it was better than loading the entire rig at once, which would make it too heavy to animate.

What is the most common thing you had to send a rig back to the riggers for?

Facial controls and poses seem to be the hardest thing to get right.

What advice would you give future 3D artists about getting into the field?

Choose what you love to do, and do it better than anything else out there. Don't just pick a discipline and do it because you think you'll have a better chance of getting your foot in the door at your dream company. If you're modeling in hopes of someday animating, you're going to be spending a lot more time as a modeler than you would have if you would just push yourself in animation now.

Don't compare yourself to your classmates; compare yourself to the professionals working in the field you hope to be in someday. Don't make excuses for yourself by saying that you are just a student and you will learn to be as good as the professionals someday; learn now. Your potential employers won't be making those excuses for you either.

Be the best in your discipline, but don't be cocky about it. Too many students come out of school thinking they are going to show everyone how to do it right. Respect the talents you have, but don't discount the years of experience that other highly talented people have on you. You'll get a lot further, a lot faster, with the right attitude.

Becoming employed usually happens when three things come together:

- Professional-level skill set
- Who you know
- Timing

First you have to be good enough to get employed in the first place, but that alone is not enough. Get to know professionals you hope to work with someday. Don't be annoying, but stay within their line of sight. That way, you will have enough of a relationship with them that they will clue you in to the right times to submit your reel. They will also help you get your reel in front of the right people instead of having your reel get lost in the crowd; it would be even better if the people you knew in the industry were the right people (that is, the ones making the hiring decisions).

Good luck! You can do it!

Conclusion

After considering all the aspects you desire for your rig, the final planning step is to put the plan down on paper. This plan should then guide you through the process. You will be able to efficiently build your rig because you'll know exactly what you want your character to be able to do and where you want your character to end up when you are done.

Figure 1.8 shows the final rigging setup for the runner character.

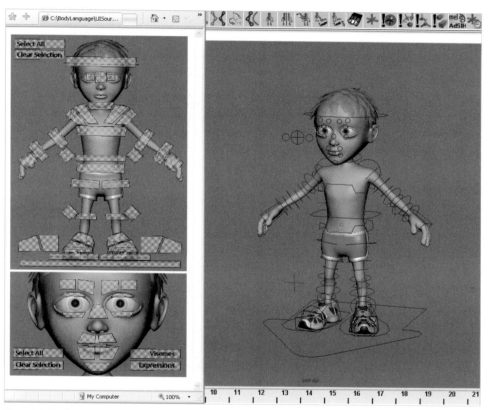

Figure 1.8 Final setup

In the next chapter, you'll take a closer look at the features specific to the tool that we'll use to do the rigging throughout this book. Our look at the Maya features focuses specifically on those features that are unique to rigging. If you're using a different tool, then look for similar features in the package you are using.

Getting to Know You: Maya's Interface

2

You can use any 3D animation package as you work through the tutorials in this book, but if you work with a package other than Maya, you will need to be familiar enough with your own package to translate the concepts we present. If you choose to use Maya, you will need to be familiar with the basic process of skeletal creation in Maya. Regardless of the package you are using, if you understand the basics of using Maya, then you'll be able to navigate the tutorials better than if you don't understand the package. In addition to covering the basics of the Maya interface, this chapter also includes tips that will help you keep your rigs organized and clear.

Chapter Contents
Working with the Maya interface
Using editors
Getting to know the hotkeys and the hotbox
Deconstructing for learning and fixing
Organizing your rig

Arnold

The opening image, Arnold, created by Patrick Beaulieu, is a perfect example of pushing the 3D character medium. You will find it helpful to look at characters like this and consider how you would choose to rig them. For example, how would you control the tail or eyelids?

Working with the Maya Interface

Maya is the software of choice for many studios across the globe. It has advanced features that enable you to complete rigging tasks quickly and easily but it can be difficult to figure out if you're not familiar with it. Maya also has an underlying architecture that you can tap into with Maya Embedded Language (MEL) scripts. Scripting can provide a powerful user experience and save a great deal of time on repetitive tasks. Figure 2.1 shows the Maya interface.

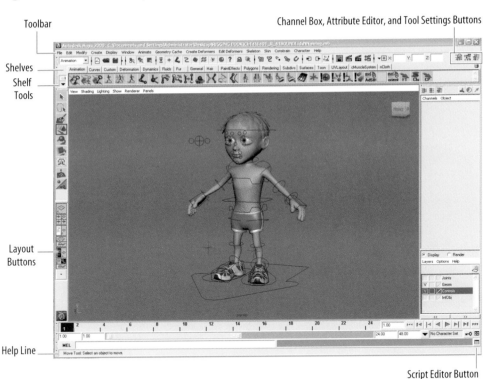

Figure 2.1 Maya interface

Knowing the Interface

The Maya interface uses floating palettes, editors, and dialog boxes. You can access commands using menus, hotkeys, and mouse shortcuts. Understanding the interface and how to quickly access commands will help you be more efficient with your rigging tasks.

The Help Line If you are new to Maya or if you just need to know what an icon means, the Help Line is very useful. It is located at the bottom of the main window user interface (UI). The Help Line displays the function for the current mouseover item. This can be a big help if you are lost in any way. The Help Line also provides tips for using different tools.

Shelves Underneath the toolbar buttons at the top of the Maya interface is a set of tabbed buttons called the *shelf*. These buttons can be customized and saved into a special grouping of buttons that can be immediately recalled. You can create a new shelf and add your favorite scripts or tool icons to it. You can also add buttons to existing shelves. When using a lot of specialized scripting commands, you can turn these into shelf buttons as well.

Making a New Shelf

To make a new shelf, simply click the Shelf Tools arrow at the left end of the shelf bar, and select the New Shelf command, as shown in Figure 2.2. This opens a dialog box that allows you to name the new shelf. The menu also includes a command for deleting shelves.

Figure 2.2
New Shelf menu command

Creating Buttons

You can populate your shelf with existing buttons, commands, and scripts. You add existing buttons to the new shelf by simply using the middle mouse button to drag and drop them on the new shelf space. You add menu commands by pressing Ctrl+Shift and clicking the command. You add scripts created in the Script Editor, again using the middle mouse button, by dragging the selected code from the Script Editor to the shelf. The script button appears with a default MEL icon.

Managing Buttons

You can delete any button from a shelf. Use the middle mouse button to drag the shelf button to the trashcan icon at the right of the shelf tabs.

The Shelf menu (at the left end of the shelf) includes a command for opening the Shelf Editor. The Shelf Editor allows you to change a shelf button's appearance and name. You can use the Shelf Editor to reorder the buttons or change the command associated with a button.

Setting User Interface Preferences

You can alter and save many aspects of the Maya interface using the window settings and the Preferences dialog box. At the left side of the interface are the interface layout buttons. You can use them to change the number of view windows and choose which editors are visible.

At the bottom of the layout buttons is a button with an arrow on it. Clicking this button opens a menu that includes options for setting the interface layout and which editors are shown in the current view, as shown in Figure 2.3. Choose an item or an editor, and it appears in the main window.

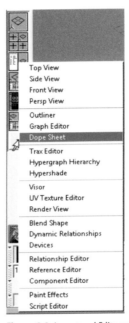

Figure 2.3 Layout and Editor menu

If you need to change the display resolution and quality of the view window, you can use the menus at the top of each view window. These are the camera attributes. You can switch to different cameras here as well as in the model view options. You will notice that most of the characters in the book are transparent. This draw style was created using the Shading > X-ray option, which lets you see through the character so you can manipulate the bones and joints.

You can also use several settings in the Preferences dialog box to customize the default layout for the Maya interface. Open this dialog box with the Window > Settings/Preferences > Preferences menu command. In the UI Elements category (shown in Figure 2.4), you'll find settings for hiding specific interface elements. Here is where you can create a default layout that appears when Maya is started.

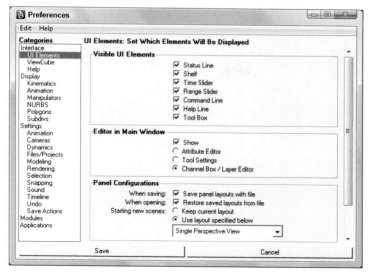

Figure 2.4 Preferences dialog box

Using Editors

One of the key benefits of Maya is its ability to customize the interface, as you've seen with the custom shelves for frequently used buttons and scripts. Maya also includes a number of editors that let you extend the functionality of the program. As well as offering other functionality, the editors let you see a scene in unique ways, such as in node view. The editors are divided into several categories and are accessed through the Window menu.

Script Editor

If you're interested in extending Maya's capabilities with scripts, then the Script Editor will be extremely helpful. Using the Script Editor, you can create custom scripts to automate specific tasks or to create a completely new task. If you are not familiar with the Script Editor, make it a goal to be. Using scripts is one of the most powerful things you can do in Maya. By creating scripts you can create very clean and efficient rigs.

To open the Script Editor, choose Window > General Editors > Script Editor from the menu bar, or click the Script Editor button ▤.

You will find the button in the bottom-right corner of the interface.

The Script Editor, shown in Figure 2.5, is divided into two panes. The top pane is the script log. It displays the commands that are executed from the main user interface or from the scripting pane in the Script Editor and their results. After entering a command, you can press the Enter key (on the numeric keypad) or choose Script > Execute in the Script Editor when you're ready to execute it. If you highlight and run your command using the Enter key on the main keyboard, the code disappears once it executes. But, if you highlight a command and then hit the Enter key on the numeric keypad, the code remains in the scripting pane. This is useful if you need to revise the code.

Script Log Panel

Script Command Panel

Figure 2.5 Script Editor

Tip: You can change the size of the font in the Script Editor by pressing and holding Ctrl+Shift and using the mouse scroll wheel.

We will get more into the Script Editor throughout the book and really look at scripting in depth in Chapter 15, "MEL Scripting: An Introduction."

At the bottom of Maya's main interface is a command line where you can enter single-line commands. Every command needs to end in a semicolon. This is the syntax for MEL. The results of the executed command are displayed in the darkened field located to the right of the command line.

All commands entered in the command line are saved in a buffer. Using the up and down arrow keys, you can move through the recent commands. Pressing the Enter key executes the selected command.

Attributes, Tool Settings, and the Channel Box

The right panel of the main interface displays the Attribute Editor, the Tool Settings panel, or the Channel Box. The buttons for selecting the display, shown in Figure 2.6, are located at the right end of the toolbar, just to the right of the X, Y, and Z fields. The editor that is displayed depends on the object or tool that is selected in the view windows.

Figure 2.6 Channel Box, Attribute Editor, and Tool Settings buttons

Attribute Editor

From the Attribute Editor (shown in Figure 2.7), you have access to all the options available for a node. The tabs show the connections that the object has. If you create a simple primitive and look through these tabs, you will see that there is a transform node, a shape node, a history node, and several surface nodes.

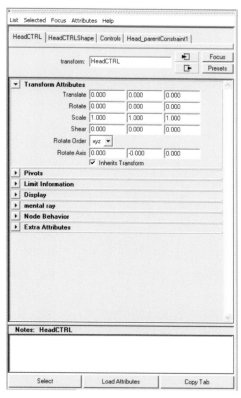

Figure 2.7 Attribute Editor

Each tab contains a number of options and settings for the node you have selected.

You can change a parameter's value in several ways. You can type a new value in the attribute field, you can select a value, and you can select a value and then modify it by dragging in the viewport with the middle mouse button. You can also modify a value by pressing and holding the Ctrl key while you use the middle mouse button to drag the value field.

Tip: Sometimes it is helpful to open the Attribute Editor in a floating window. This way you can view both the Channel Box and the Attribute Editor at the same time. To open the Attribute Editor as a floating window, open the Preferences dialog box, and in the Interface category, select the As Separate Window option for the Attribute Editor, as shown in Figure 2.8.

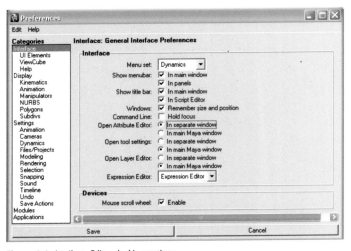

Figure 2.8 Attribute Editor docking options

Tools Settings

When a tool is selected, you can alter its parameters by accessing the Tool Settings panel. Figure 2.9 shows the Tool Settings panel for the Paint Skin Weights tool. The settings available depend on the tool that is selected. If you double-click a tool in the Toolbox, the Tool Settings panel opens automatically.

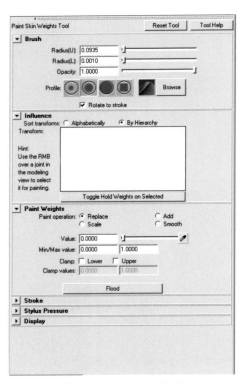

Figure 2.9 Tool settings for the Paint Skin Weights tool

Channel Box

The Channel Box, shown in Figure 2.10, displays all the attributes for the current selection. Although any given selection has a number of preset attributes, you can add custom attributes to the Channel Box by right-clicking an existing attribute and selecting the Add Attribute menu command. This opens a dialog box that allows you to name and define the custom attribute. It also allows you to key, copy, or break connections with your attribute. Make sure you are familiar with these options.

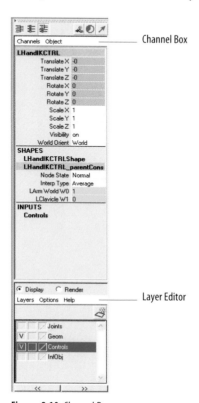

Channel Box

Layer Editor

Figure 2.10 Channel Box

At the top left of the Channel Box are three icons that allow you to see the attributes, layers, or both. With both the layers and the attributes displayed, the layer interface is located directly below the Channel Box to the right of the view windows. Layers are helpful for organizing your project. Specifically, layers can be quickly hidden, so they are great for cleaning up a project so you can focus on specific aspects such as a rig.

New layers are created by clicking the New Layer button, located at the top right of the layers panel. To add an object to a layer, select the object, right-click the layer name, and choose Add Selected Objects from the pop-up menu.

The first column of the Layer Editor indicates whether the layer is visible or hidden. The column is empty when the layer is hidden and displays a *V* when the layer is visible. The second column is used to make the layer a template. When a layer is a template, the objects in that layer are frozen so they cannot be selected or moved. Template layers have a *T* in the second column.

ATTRIBUTE COLORS

The colors of the attribute fields within the Channel Box change depending on what the controlling attribute is. These colors are common:

- Gray = locked
- Light gray = non-keyable
- Yellow = connection (direct connect)
- Pink = parent constraint
- Blue = constraint
- Purple = expression
- Orange = keyed

LOCKING AND UNLOCKING ATTRIBUTES

You can lock and unlock attributes by right-clicking the attribute and selecting either Lock Attribute or Unlock Attribute from the pop-up menu.

Outliner

The Outliner, shown in Figure 2.11, is the view of the current scene from a higher level. It displays all objects in the current scene as hierarchical nodes that are easy to access. The Outliner is helpful for selecting objects, renaming objects, and parenting objects together. You can select objects in order from the Outliner and run commands on them, such as constraints and binding.

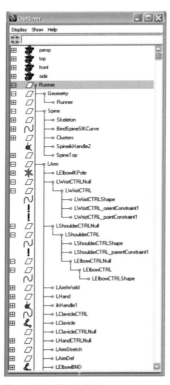

Figure 2.11 The Outliner

You can open the Outliner within the view windows by selecting it from the layout button, or you can choose the Outliner from the Window menu to open it in a separate floating window. When opened in a separate window, you can quickly select items in the scene by clicking them in the Outliner window.

PARENTING OPTIONS

The Outliner also shows which objects are parented to which objects. You can change the parenting of objects in the Outliner by dragging and dropping with the middle mouse button.

DISPLAY SETTINGS

The Outliner menu includes options that you can use to change the objects that are displayed in the Outliner. For example, selecting the Show, Objects, and Joints menu will cause only those joints to be displayed in the Outliner. This provides a way to quickly access only a skeleton's joints.

Hypergraph and Hypershade

The Hypergraph interface, shown in Figure 2.12, is great for working with the connections between different objects. It has a connection view and a hierarchy view. The Hypergraph Hierarchy window displays all scene objects as a hierarchy with children underneath their parents. The second mode is Hypergraph Input and Output Connections. In this mode, you can see how the nodes are connected with their input and output connections displayed as lines. You can open both modes from the Window menu. When you mouse over the right end of an object while the Hypergraph is in Connections mode, you can select one of its outgoing nodes and connect it to another node.

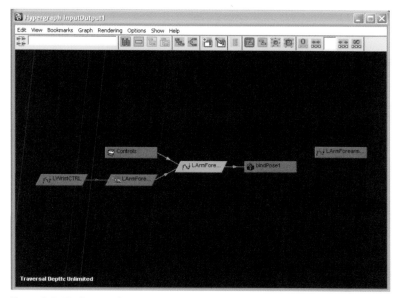

Figure 2.12 The Hypergraph

The Hypershade, shown in Figure 2.13, can be used for the same thing as the Hypergraph connections. If you select anything in your scene, you can add it to the Hypershade and show incoming and outgoing connections. The nice aspect of working in the Hypershade is that you can easily create utility nodes from the Create Maya Nodes panel on the left side of the panel. The Help Line provides explanations of what the icons mean and what each button does.

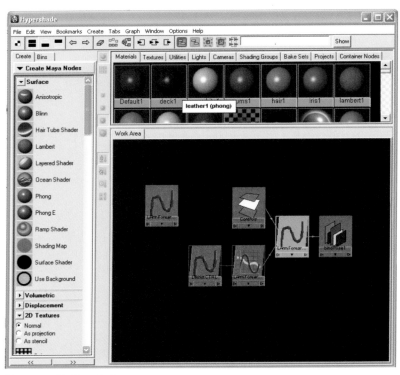

Figure 2.13 The Hypershade

In the tutorials throughout the book, we will be using the incoming and outgoing connection icons. We'll also use a command called Graph Selected, available through the Graph menu. Familiarize yourself with them. Notice the Utilities tab. When you select it, utility nodes are displayed in the top pane of the Hypershade. The work area (lower pane) will be used as we hook up a lot of our advanced rig.

The small triangle at the bottom right of each node is used for outgoing connections. You can drag connections from here onto other nodes using the middle mouse button.

Connecting with Set-Driven Keys

Another powerful feature available in the Attribute Editor is the ability to interconnect two attributes; in other words, one attribute can control the value of another attribute. This feature is called *set-driven keys*.

To create a set-driven key, you'll use the Set Driven Key > Set command on the Animate tab. You can use this editor to attach any attribute of a node to any other attribute of another node. You can also adjust the set-driven key in the Graph Editor.

This will give you even more control by allowing you to edit the key with Bezier curves. The attributes of driven keys appear orange for the driving key.

The Set Driven Key dialog box will connect two objects' attributes. You can make a sphere move vertically as you move a triangle horizontally. It sets up connections between attributes of items. The Set Driven Key dialog box is great for quickly creating relationships between nodes. When you click the Key button here, you are not setting an animation key; you are setting a value connection between the attributes. For a simple example, you can key a square's Y translation as the driver and a triangle's X translation as the driven and then move the square vertical and the triangle sideways and set another key with the same attributes selected. Now when you move the square up and down, the triangle will move horizontally.

Getting to Know Hotkeys and the Hotbox

The key to working efficiently with the Maya interface is to learn the hotkeys and the Hotbox.

Hotkeys

The hotkeys allow you to execute specific commands by simply pressing a keyboard key or key combination. Familiarize yourself with the Maya hotkeys or the hotkeys of your application of choice. Several are particularly helpful during the rigging process.

Maya also includes a Hotkey Editor. Choose Window > Settings/Preferences > Hotkey Editor to access it. You can use the Hotkey Editor to customize the hotkey for any command. You can also view a listing of all the hotkeys by clicking the List All button and then selecting the List All option. Figure 2.14 shows the Hotkey Editor.

Figure 2.14 The Hotkey Editor

Table 2.1 lists some of the important hotkeys you will be using.

▷ **Table 2.1** Important Hotkeys

Hot Key	Function	Hot Key	Function
Ctrl+A	Open Attribute Editor	B	Weight painting brush size
Ctrl+C	Copy	E	Rotate
Ctrl+D	Duplicate	F	Frame selected
Ctrl+G	Group	G	Repeat last
Ctrl+H	Hide	P	Parent
Ctrl+Shift+H	Show last hidden	R	Scale
Shift+H	Unhide	S	Set keyframe on selected
Ctrl+S	Save	W	Translate
Ctrl+V	Paste	1–8	Display options
Ctrl+Z	Undo	Arrow keys	Pickwalk in a direction
Shift+Z	Redo	X, C, V + Move tool	Snap variations

The Hotbox

Even if you don't know a specific hotkey for a command, you can still quickly access the command using the Hotbox. The Hotbox, shown in Figure 2.15, opens when you press the spacebar. It presents all the menu commands that are available for the current mouse position so you can quickly select one.

Maya also lets you customize the menus and the Hotbox. Do this by pressing spacebar in the viewport and selecting the Hotbox Controls option.

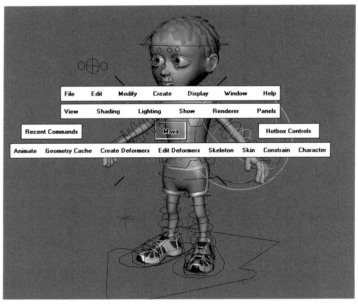

Figure 2.15 The Hotbox

Deconstructing for Learning and Fixing

If you examine the book's companion CD, you'll find a complete detailed rig. One of the best ways to learn the ins and outs of rigging is to take an existing rig and dissect it to see how it works. Feel free to take a look at our rig.

Node information One of the first places to look for information about a rig is to look at its various nodes. You can get a firsthand look at the rig nodes and their connections in the Hypergraph, Outliner or Hypershade. These nodes describe the various parts that go into the rig and show how they are connected.

Attribute Editor Once you take a close look at all the various nodes used to build the rig, you will next need to examine their attributes. Look specifically at the custom attributes, and notice their connections. By playing around with these attributes, you can get a feel for how these attributes control the character. Use the tabs to see the nodes attached to a selected object. For instance, you can select a constraint and see what that constraint is aiming at. This is a helpful tool for troubleshooting as well.

After you understand the attributes, try selecting various rig controls and moving them around in the scene. Notice how the character deforms as you move the control handles. Move them to their extreme positions, and see how the rig moves.

Deconstructing a rig In Figure 2.16, you can see how you can select a constraint and see what it is hooked to. Next, select any constraint in the rig, and look in the Channel Box to see what it's constraining. Use Show All from the Display menu to make hidden nodes visible.

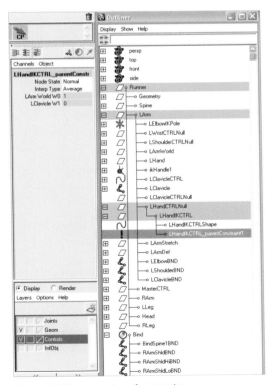

Figure 2.16 The connections of a constraint

Organizing Your Rig

Before leaving the basics, we need to present some ideas for keeping your rig organized. These are some simple concepts, but if you get too busy to do them, you'll quickly end up with a mess that will be difficult to decipher.

Grouping

The first rule of organization is to use groups effectively. It is important when using groups to remember that null groups are your friends. Null groups aren't rendered, because they are empty. They provide a quick and easy way to select an entire group of objects.

Null objects provide a way to avoid cyclical errors. Cyclical errors happen when a node is set to control another node, which in turn is linked to control another node that controls the first. This cyclical error can cause a lot of trouble by applying multiple rotations or translations to connected nodes. There is an easy way to fix this problem. A null group acts as a mediator between the two nodes. The null will be the "innocent third party" and transfer one value across to the other node without changing its attributes. It acts as a buffer between the two nodes and prevents the connections from conflicting.

An important tip to remember is to add extra nulls when in doubt. Animators can use these extra nulls to get out of rotational jams. They also help keep joints and controls separate for hiding.

You can also simply group your objects for organization. We will talk about this sporadically throughout the book. Remember to group the different body parts and then group the figure as a whole. Using groups for organization and for functionality will improve the animator's experience and allow for greater control of the rig.

Naming

The second rule of organization is to name everything. Maya by default names each new joint as "Joint" followed by a sequential number. After a while, you'll end up with a lot of joints and numbers without any idea of which joint is what.

Descriptively naming each joint, connection, attribute, and node is a simple practice, but it takes time. You can use the Outliner and Hypergraph to quickly rename new objects, but you need to remember to take the time to do it.

Maya also includes a helpful feature for quickly renaming a group of joints. Under the Modify menu there are Prefix Hierarchy Names and Search and Replace Names options. These can help you quickly rename when you need to do so. There are also great naming scripts online with even more functionality.

Having your joints named descriptively will also help you keep things straight when you're using the Outliner or Hypergraph and in selecting a joint for applying skin weights.

Adopt a naming convention that you can stick to. Consistently using a naming convention enables you to accurately type a joint's name when creating scripts, without having to select the joint to see what it is named. Good naming also will help the animator when using the Graph Editor.

There are several preferred naming conventions. It is important to use one that identifies the unique body part and side of the body that the node is on. It is good practice to use underscores instead of spaces. For example, the right shoulder could be named R_Shoulder or RShoulder.

Here's the convention that we're using throughout the book. All of the nodes for the runner character start with an R. Next, if they then need to designate left or right, they have an L or R, respectively. The body part is next and then any other descriptive words. Last, we designate the groups that need to be classified. Bindable joints have BND as a suffix, and controls have CTRL as a suffix. As an example, some of our joints will be named RHandBND and RIKShoulder.

Make sure you never duplicate a name; each name must be unique. This includes any type of node such as an inverse kinematics (IK) or a null group. Duplicate names are problematic for referencing files and make selection difficult during the rigging process.

Conclusion

In this chapter, we made our way through the Maya interface, touching on those interface elements and editors that you will use as we approach the rigging tasks. We also covered some important organizational issues, such as using groups and naming objects using a consistent convention.

In the next chapter, we'll take a close look at some important rigging concepts that will come into play over and over. By understanding these basic concepts, you'll be able to work much faster and know why certain techniques are done in certain ways.

Rigging That's Right: Rigging Concepts You Need to Know

3

Creating a rigged character is like building a house. You need a stable and secure foundation. With that in place, you can build your house and even add upgrades. Just as a sound foundation allows you to build a stable house, sound rigging practices make your rig secure and usable. You can then apply advanced attributes as needed. In this chapter, we will discuss the practices that make a stable foundation for your rig.

Chapter Contents
Working with joints
Understanding FK and IK
Using constraints
Understanding broken rigs
Working with controls
Creating attributes

Working with Joints

It is important when creating skeleton bones that you set the joint orientation consistently and appropriately rank the rotation order for each joint. Ranking the rotation order helps you avoid *gimble lock*, which occurs when two or three axes are rotated to the same direction, the gimble then cannot control the rotation of the object because of its previous rotations.

Typically, you will orient the joint so the X-axis runs locally down along the bone to the child. But check with the animator. This can change. For example, motion-capture studios often use the Y-axis to point to the next joint. Whichever axis does the pointing is called the *roll axis*. If you are using the X-axis as the roll axis, the Z-axis defines the bend angle, and the Y-axis represents the joint up (which is not world up). It is important that you stay consistent throughout your figure so that if you select multiple joints and rotate their Z-axes, they will all bend. This is easy to do with the joint orientation tools within Maya.

You want to make sure your joint rotations are zero before adding onto them. If your joint rotations are not zero, you will have rotational values in your joints at their default positions, and this is not the best practice.

Orienting Joints

1. Open the Attribute Editor or the Channel Box. You can now see the rotation values for the joint.

2. With the XYZ option selected, choose Orient Joint from the Skeleton menu, or run the script that follows to initially orient the joint:

   ```
   joint -e -oj xyz;
   ```

3. Check the orientation. If the joint does not orient how you want it to, you can adjust it manually:

   - Select the joint, and move the cursor to the desired value in the Joint Orient fields.

   - Press and hold the Ctrl key, and then drag with the middle mouse button to change the value.

   - Double check that the Rotate values are still 0.

Setting Rotation Order

If you have trouble with the rotations, rotate the joint using the manipulators, and then freeze the transformations (Modify > Freeze Transformations) of the joint.

As mentioned in the steps above, it is very important to double-check the Rotate XYZ fields to make sure there are no values in them before continuing. Your joint is now clean and ready for additional connections, as shown in Figure 3-1.

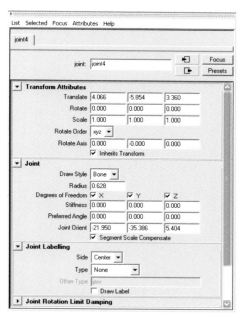

Figure 3.1 Setting up a correctly oriented joint

Understanding FK and IK

When a skeleton is first created in Maya, the individual bones, by default, are moved using *forward kinematics* (FK). This method follows the hierarchy of a skeleton in that all children bones move along with their parents. So, when the shoulder joint is rotated, the upper arm, lower arm, hand and finger bones follow.

FK works well for general, large-scale motions, but when you're trying to precisely position a child bone and you have controls only for the parent joints, it can be frustrating. Imagine trying to position a hand on a doorknob, when your figure is already moving about, and you can only do so by rotating the shoulder and elbow joints. You would have to constantly adjust—for each frame of animation and for the character's movements. Are you beginning to see the real need for inverse kinematics?

Inverse kinematics (IK) enables child bones, such as a hand or a foot, to control their parents. This makes it easy to place a hand or a foot exactly where it needs to be and have the rest of the hierarchy follow along. To accomplish this, IK adds an end effector to the chain that can be selected and moved to control the child's position.

When an IK chain is created, an IK *wire* shows the extent of the IK chain. The wire is represented by a line that connects the base joint with the end joint. At the end of the IK chain is an IK handle. If you select and move the IK handle, the final joint in the IK chain moves to follow the position of the handle, and the rest of the IK chain follows smoothly along, adapting to the position of the end joint.

FK/IK Blending

Having to work with only IK is just as bad as having to animate using only FK. The real benefit comes from being able to blend motions between FK and IK. Maya makes this possible with its FK/IK Blending feature. Using this feature, you can make a character walk a distance using FK animating methods. Then you can switch to IK and position the hand reaching for the doorknob. Maya then blends between these two modes to create a seamless motion for the character.

Using Constraints

Another way to automatically control the movement of a character is with constraints. Constraints bind the animation in certain ways. For example, you can constrain a character's foot so it will not penetrate the ground or floor. By building in such a constraint, you can ensure that the character's feet never run the risk of sinking unrealistically into the floor.

As we discuss constraints, we will refer to joints and other nodes as being either the *driver* or the *driven*. The driver controls movement, rotation, and so forth. The driven reflects the type of constraint that is used. As a way of remembering which to choose first, commit to memory, the phrase "driver, then driven." Now whenever you need to constraint anything, you can remember the order of selection is always "driver, then driven."

Point constraints Point constraints are probably the simplest and easiest type of constraint to use. They cause two objects to move together, as if they are linked. For example, a point constraint might attach a hand to a doorknob. Once constrained, the hand's translation will be driven by the knob. However, point constraints do not constrain rotation.

In a point constraint, the driver controls only the translation of the driven. The locators shown in Figure 3.2 are point-constrained to the hand control and shoulder joint. This feeds information to Maya telling the arm how to stretch. We will use this constraint later as we add functionality that makes the arms stretch beyond their original lengths. The two points that calculate distance only need to have the translation information applied to them; thus, a point constraint works perfectly in this situation.

Parent constraints A parent constraint causes a constrained object to move along with its driver as if it were parented. The difference between being parented and having a parent constraint applied is in the connections. When parenting, you will find that the secondary "child" object will follow exactly what happens to the "parent." There is a connection in the hierachy.

In a parent constraint, the driver controls both the translation and the rotation of the driven. You can always find out what is parent-constrained by looking at the translation and rotation values for an object or node. If they are displayed in blue, an incoming connection is "driving" them.

A parent constraint is different from an actual parent-child relationship. It creates a connection with attributes, as opposed to a connection in hierarchy. One of the main advantages of a parent constraint is that it allows the visibility of the objects to be controlled separately.

Also, you can parent-constrain an object to multiple drivers, as shown in Figure 3.3. You can then use an attribute switch to control the weight of the parent constraints. We will talk about this more later in the book.

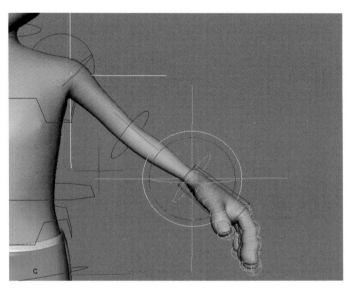

Figure 3.2 Examples of point constraints

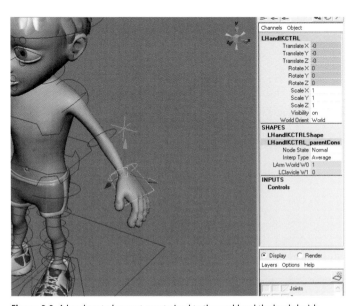

Figure 3.3 A hand control: parent-constrained to the world and the local clavicle

Orient constraints An orient constraint allows constrained objects to move independently of one another, but their orientation in world space is controlled so that each moves in the same direction. Imagine a workout class. During the workout, the students follow the instructor's movements. As the instructor turns to the left, all the students turn to the left.

In an orient constraint, the driver's rotation attributes control the rotation of the driven, as shown in Figure 3.4.

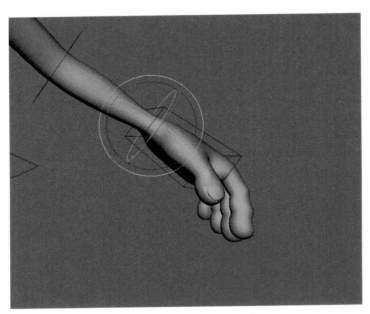

Figure 3.4 A wrist control: orient-constrained to a hand control

Aim constraints An aim constraint causes the constrained objects to point toward a designated object. This is different from the orientation constraint in that each object points toward a specific object, while the orientation constraint causes all constrained objects to point in the same direction.

The aim constraint is useful for getting eyeballs to follow an object, such as a fly, around a scene. Although the eyes appear to rotate together, when the fly lands on the character's nose, both eyes look inward in a cross-eyed look.

An aim constraint constrains the rotation of the driven object so that it always "aims" toward the driver, as shown in Figure 3.5.

Pole vector constraints A pole vector constraint defines a vector upon which an IK can base its bending. A common use for this constraint type is to use a bone such as the forearm as the pole vector to ensure that the elbow doesn't flip inward as it is moved using IK. If you create a target object that is positioned out away from the elbow and constrain the IK handle as a pole vector, then you can control where the elbow is pointing. Figure 3.6 shows a pole vector for the knee.

When using a pole vector constraint, the vector is usually defined by a third node, such as a locator, in conjunction with the start and end of an IK chain. The vector controls the direction of the bend of joints with the IK chain.

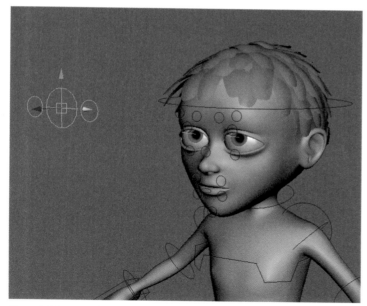

Figure 3.5 Eye controls: aim constrained to a target

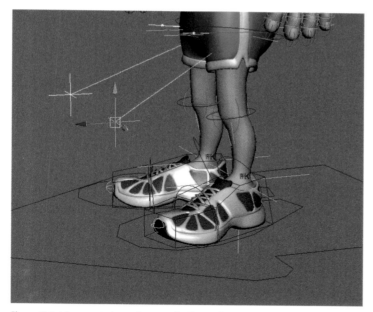

Figure 3.6 A knee control: rotation controlled by a pole vector constraint

Other constraints In addition to the constraints we've discussed, you may find several other constraints useful. The scale constraint forces a constrained object (the driven) to scale as another object (the driver) scales. Using the geometry constraint, you can make one object adhere to the surface of another object. Finally, the normal constraint keeps one object oriented to the normal of the surface of another object. The normal is perpendicular to the driving surface at any given point. Usually the value is taken from a single poly or point (vertex).

Understanding Broken Rigs

Broken rigs are detached joints and joint chains that are hooked into the main rig using constraints. You might want to break a chain if unwanted attributes are passed down through the joint chain. For instance, you don't want a spine's scale to affect the head and stretch it.

You may also want to break the joint chain for ease of use or organization. You may also want to do this for the purpose of hiding one portion and keeping another visible. Parent constraints can hook the broken parts of the rig together.

In a broken rig, each body part is its own small joint chain. Each arm, each leg, and the neck and head can become their own independent mini-rigs, all held together by point and orient constraints.

Working with Controls

Controls are probably the most important part of a rig. They are the visible representation of the functionality underneath. It is important to create controls that are easily read. You must also create a base position for each control and then zero the control to that position before hooking it up. Animators often need to zero controls many times throughout the animation process. You want to be sure that when they zero, the controls return to the base position.

The first step in the control process is to create the control.

Tip: Several good scripts are available to help you create controls. Search online for *sin rig controllers* or for *rig101 wire controllers*. Both are excellent starters for your controller library. They provide great examples of what can be done with wire controls. Here are the links: http://www.rigging101.com/ http://highend3d.com/maya/downloads/mel_scripts/character/Rig-Controllers-3818.html

Creating Controls

In this section, we'll go through the process of creating a curve or wire control for your rig. This is a process you'll use many times as you build a rig in the exercises in this book and as you animate your own characters. So, become familiar with it.

Note: If you plan to hide your joints but show your controls, you will not want to use this method. For the runner character, we are going to create null-based controls, using empty null groups.

1. Use the CV curve tool (Create > CV Curve) to create a curve. If you want to make straight lines with your curve, set the degree in the options to 1.

   You can use your top view camera and lock the CVs to the grid by pressing and holding the X key while creating them. This helps keep your control symmetrical.

However, we recommend that you use the side view to keep the controls perpendicular to the X-axis. This is the axis you will want your controls oriented against. The X-axis runs down your joints. Creating your controls in the side view will thus save you time if your control needs to be perpendicular to the X-axis.

2. You may also add a second curve to the control. This allows multiple curves that function as one. Once you parent this new curve to the first curve you created, you can have them act as a single node. Zero both controls out by freezing their transforms (Modify > Freeze Transformations).

3. Select the shape node of one curve, and then Shift-select the transform node of the other. Run this MEL script by typing it into the MEL command line:

```
parent -r -s;
```

This is also a preferred method of attaching controls to joints. With this connection however, you will not be able to hide the joints and show the controls. When the control is selected, the joint is selected.

You will need to name the control now. A good convention to use is a letter for the side, the joint and then the descriptor. You will want to add on the "CTRL" suffix for all controls. An example of this is LShoulderCTRL (the left shoulder control). Figure 3.7 shows some examples of different types of wire controls.

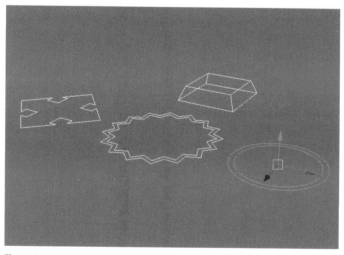

Figure 3.7 Various wire controls

Null-Based Controls

A null-based control setup places a null group between the control and the object being driven. The null group prevents cyclical errors that could propagate values exponentially through the connections and cause unwanted manipulations. We'll talk more about cyclical errors later in Chapter 5.

1. Center the pivot of your control. Choose Modify > Center Pivot.

2. Snap the control to the desired joint. Do this by moving the control and holding the V to snap to the joint.

3. Orient your control to the joint, remembering the phrase "driver, then driven." Select the joint and then the control and then Constrain > Orient. Find this same constraint in the Outliner (Windows > Outliner) and delete it. This will leave you with a control that is oriented the same direction as the joint.

   If you want your control rotated off-axis, Use Ctrl+ middle mouse drag to manipulate the curve's Rotate Axis values in the Attribute Editor.

   If you want your control to be moved off center, move your control and then use the "insert" key to move the pivot and snap it (holding Ctrl+V) back to the joint. Hit the insert key again to deselect.

   Mirror the control now, if desired.

4. Put your control in a new null group. Select your control and hit Ctrl+G. Rename the new group in the Outliner to *ControlNameNull*.

5. In the Outliner, drag the control with the middle mouse button out of the group.

6. Snap the group to the joint by holding the V key while moving. Orient-constraint the group to a joint. Select the joint and then the group, and then use Constrain > Orient. Make sure that Maintain offset is turned off in the Orient Constraint options. In the Outliner, delete this constraint.

7. In the Outliner, drag the control with the middle mouse button back into the group.

8. Freeze the transforms on the control using Modify > Freeze Transformations.

9. Parent-constrain the joint to the control. Select the control and then the joint, and choose Constrain > Parent.

10. Parent-constrain the null to the upstream joint.

Mirroring Controls

You will want to mirror controls manually to get perfect results:

1. Select and duplicate your control. Use the Ctrl+D key combination.

2. Move and Scale the X value of the duplicate control to a negative value of what its current value is. You may need to Freeze the Transformations to scale along the desired axis to make the mirrored control.

3. Freeze its transforms. Choose Modify > Freeze Transformations.

4. Now, move the control to the appropriate group on other side of the figure. You will need to rebuild the orientations and constraints.

Defining Nodes

Attributes define nodes. For example, a primitive cube requires attributes that define its size, shape, and world location. As you rig, you will create attributes for switches, morphs, and poses, so it is important to learn how to manipulate attributes to be effective. There are three common types of variables: float, integer, and enumerator.

- A *float* is a decimal number. It can hold values that are portions of whole numbers; 8.97 is a good example of a float.

- An *integer* (int) is a whole number. It is a attribute type to use if you need a switch that goes only from 1 to 0.

- An *enumerator* (enum) stores values, such as words. These values can, in turn, be used for world orients, where the targets are specific words such as *clavicle* and *world orient*.

Creating Attributes

You can easily create a custom attribute either using the Attribute Editor by choosing Add Attribute from the Attributes menu or using the Channel Box by right-clicking an existing attribute and choosing Add Attribute from the pop-up menu.

While in the Add Attribute dialog box, you create an attribute by selecting the type, the minimum and maximum default values, and the enum names, as shown in Figure 3.8. The interface changes based on the type of attribute you are creating.

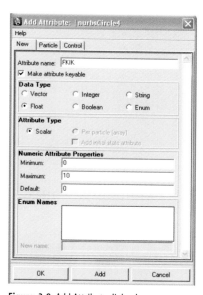

Figure 3.8 Add Attribute dialog box

Conclusion

When you understand joints, controls, attributes, and naming conventions, you will be better able to prepare your character for what is ahead. You can feel immense personal happiness when you paint weights and realize that your job is so much easier with a properly named left shoulder. You can also enjoy the sheer confidence of knowing that the control you are working with will zero out if you get into trouble while animating. These are the foundations of great character rigs.

In the next chapter, we'll dive into the actual rigging process starting with the crucial spine and torso.

Torso Rigging Techniques

The torso rig is also the foundation of the control of your animation, providing not only controls for manipulating the torso but also controls for moving the entire character. A properly rigged spine will give your character a new level of motion. Since the spine rigging is so critical, make sure you schedule and devote adequate time to torso development. Be sure to get story information and animation needs. The more you know about the motions your character will be performing, the better off you'll be.

In this chapter, we'll cover two different torso rigging approaches. Let's find out which approach is best for your character.

Chapter Contents

Planning the Spine Rig

Before diving right in and creating joints, it is always worthwhile to take some time to plan. We have done our initial character planning, so now it is time to focus our planning on the spine. Two character setup variations that we discuss in this chapter deal with how to manipulate the root and how to manipulate the spine. If you are already familiar with the rigging process, take some time to visualize what type of controls you want for the root and for the spine.

Talk with the animator or animation supervisor about the movements the story requires. Those discussions will help you plan the rigs you need. Consider the movie *Spiderman*. In scenes where he swings on a web, Spiderman's root joint needed to be at the base of the neck. With the root at the base of the neck, the animators could curl his body up from the top of the torso. Since the mass was hanging from the arms, the clear center of the rig was the collar area. If your character walks on elongated arms and the legs dangle, you would use the same approach. When Spiderman needed to walk or run, the root needed to be at the base of the hips. This traditional style of character setup allowed him to bend at the waist, which he needed for motions such as picking up objects.

Plan for the movements your character will perform. For example, if Spiderman had his root at his hips, when he needed to swing it would have been hard for the animator to move the top of the torso in relationship with the web. You can easily find yourself fighting your own rig if you don't prepare your rig specifically for the animation needs.

Consider the following checklist of items before building the hip and spine region. Use it to be sure your rig meets the animation requirements for your character. Remember, in a good rig planning the animation directs the rigger and determines how the rig is set up.

- As you visualize the torso, forget the head, arms, and legs; think only about the hips and spine.
- Consider the types of articulation your character requires. It is often helpful to act out the motion in front of a mirror to see the specific movements needed from each joint.
- Spend time thinking about the types of controls the rig will need in order to provide all the motions required by the story.

- Visualize the controls. What does each look like? What does each need to do?

- Plan controls that animators can easily use and understand, especially if you need to hand the rig off to others in the pipeline.

- Think about the rotation centers and how those will affect the spine. Think about the deformation areas as well.

- Make a written or mental checklist of the rigging that's needed in all areas of the figure, and then you can start identifying specifics for implementing each part.

Now that you have a checklist of the controls and special considerations you need, we'll talk about the parts of the torso and determine how they will be built.

Specifying the Root Joint

The root joint, shown in Figure 4.1, is the top joint in the hierarchy for a character; all other joints are connected to it. The root is usually connected to a marker or control that can be transformed to move the entire character. Manipulating this control moves the foundation of your rig. As you think about your animation needs, keep this control in mind. It is helpful to make this control rather large and easy to grab. If you set up the character control in a way that is not intuitive and lock the rig down, you'll be setting yourself up for a headache. You'll create your own unnecessary challenges in getting things to work properly as you rig the rest of the character, since so much derives from the spine. The animators will have trouble animating the character, too, if they cannot easily find the controls they need.

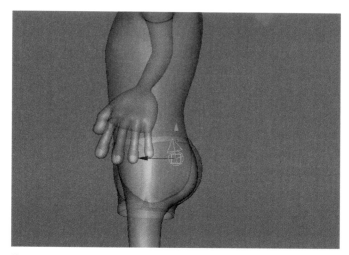

Figure 4.1 The root represents the top of the rig hierarchy.

Establishing Controls

Controls are fairly simple to create, as you learned in Chapter 3, "Rigging That's Right: Rigging Concepts You Need to Know," and although you might not think of them right after the root, they are very important. The controls are what the animator uses to produce the character's actions. Each control needs to communicate what it does without a lot of explanation. Creating a UI that makes the controls accessible provides an excellent way to work with a rig. When efficiently created, controls are valuable aids in giving the animator a user-friendly experience.

It is fairly simple to create controls for a torso. Typically, a torso consists of one main joint chain with intuitive joint rotations and limits. Remember to use limits sparingly, because the animator may want the freedom of an unconstrained joint. Sometimes, in advanced spines, multiple joint chains are used. Curve-type controls, like those shown in Figure 4.2, usually do the trick in this portion of the rig. For ease of use, you may want to consider creating a separate user interface for the spine controls. We will talk about this more in Chapter 15, "MEL Scripting: An Introduction."

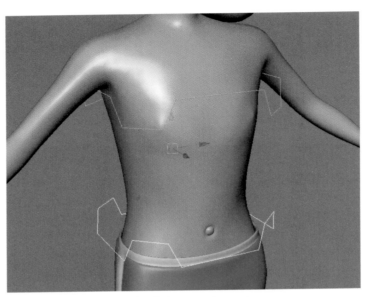

Figure 4.2 Well-designed controls make it easy to animate a rig.

Considering the Root Control

The root control is a single control that enables an animator to move the entire character. It should be highly visible, and should be easily recognizable, and usually is located on the ground, as shown in Figure 4.3. This control can also be located in areas that act as the root, as in the base of the neck or middle of the torso. Be sure the root control looks different from the rest of the controls, such as the large arrow shown in Figure 4.3, because it really serves a different function. Remember, the root control moves the entire figure rather than manipulating just a portion of the character.

There are two main types of controls for the spine and root. For the spine, curve-type controls that surround the torso work well. For a root control that is located on the ground, a directional symbol, such as an arrow or a snowshoe, is a good choice. The arrow-shaped control serves another purpose in that it shows the orientation of the character. Typically, for root controls positioned in the middle of the character, a standard box or a unique curve shape is used, but it should be large enough to be easily detected and grabbed. Experiment with different shapes and the efficiency of those shapes. Directional symbols have the benefit of intuitively showing the direction, as well as conveying ground motion to the animator. We are going to use a root control that is centered at the hip. This root control will control the rest of the figure. We are also going to use a ground master control that will be the parent of our root control.

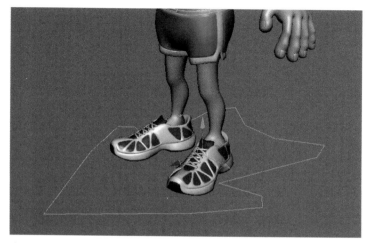

Figure 4.3 The root control should be easy to select.

Placing Centers of Rotation

When placing each control, you need to think carefully about where the center of rotation is. Keep in mind that the control's center of rotation doesn't need to be located in the center of the control. Pivots can be located independently from the control.

One option you have in creating controls is to place the control in an area away from the joint for easy selection. A collar control, for instance, often is located at the shoulder, which keeps it away from the spine controls. Another example is the head control. While being easily selected on the head, it actually controls the rotation of the neck.

Another method is to place the control right on top of the joint. Here it is easily read by the animators. You should always zero out any control so the animator can get back to the default position of the control. And, using a line of MEL script, you can make it so the selectable part of the joint is actually the control.

> **Tip:** We provided the MEL script that allows you to use the selectable part of the joint as a control in Chapter 3.

You can apply the same principle to the spine. Curve controls set in the middle of the spine, as shown in Figure 4.4, imitate the actual center of rotation. Since the vertebral column is long and moves somewhat gradually, you might find that the best place for the center of rotation is outside the actual control, a few joints away.

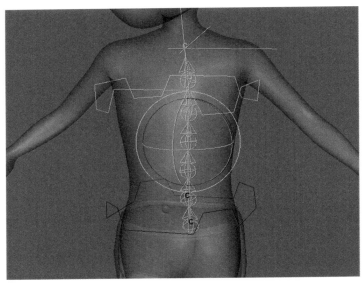

Figure 4.4 Sometimes, you will want to place the control away from the driven nodes.

Planning Deformations in the Torso

It is now important to consider the way the character's torso needs to bend. Are you going for realism, with a defined skeletal structure that needs to remain ridged? Are you rigging a cartoony figure that can bend and stretch? Realistic figures will require some of the same setups that cartoony figures do, but in a more localized area and with more accuracy in the joint locations. You also will need to think about how the geometry will need to deform. Most unwanted deformations can be cleaned up easily, if you've spent time getting to know the weight painting system. When you get to this stage of development, the replace and smooth brushes become your best friends, along with the opacity setting. Normal weight painting should be your first line of defense. You can also use influence objects to correct unwanted deformation from skinning.

Tip: Another way to deal with deformation issues is with a set of external scripted tools. The Pose Space Deformers toolset, which is a free download from http://comet-cartoons.com/melscript.php, is a great set of tools. In fact, the tools were used extensively on the Human Torch character in the *Fantastic Four* movies to get accurate body deformations.

Using Body Root vs. Free Root

There are two methods for establishing the character's root node—the classic body root and the free root. Each method has advantages and disadvantages. The "right" one depends on the type of motion the character requires.

You will need to provide a way of swiveling the hips independent of the main control. The classic body root is not an advanced concept. You will need to be familiar with its purpose, if you are not already. The free root method is preferred by most studios for main characters, but the classic root is occasionally used for background characters. As you have seen, the main character that we rig in this book uses a classic body root setup, but allows for hip movement with the aid of the cluster splineIK based spine.

Building a Classic Body Root

The traditional root joint of a simple character is located at the hip joint. This is the simplest and easiest way to create a skeleton. For this method, the root joint has three children—the spine and a joint for each leg. Table 4.1 lists the strengths and weaknesses you encounter when using a classic body root.

▶ **Table 4.1** Strengths and Weakness of a Classic Body Root

Strengths	Weaknesses
Simple to create	Less functional for independent control of hip
Easier to do simple animations	Cannot easily mimic realism
Great for acrobatics, tumbling, and flying	
Well-known technique; easy to hand off to others	
Very stable and reliable	

In Figure 4.5, you can see the single joint chain creating the spine, as well as each of the legs emanating from our root joint. If your character is going to be tumbling, flying, or doing anything other than walking or running, hip control may not be as important to you, and this is the rig to choose. Simple rigs get just as much done in these circumstances as heavily tricked out ones. There is an art to simplicity, so if you know what you need, do not be afraid of building only for that purpose.

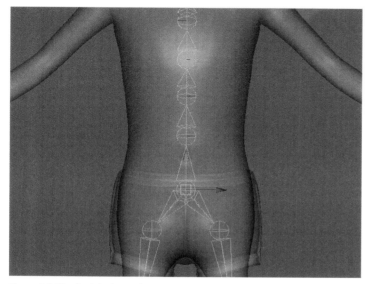

Figure 4.5 The classic body root rig

Building a Free Root

The free root is the preferred method of torso rigging. You can create it using any of several methods. No matter which method you choose, all free roots are based in one main premise: the character's hip can freely rotate. This gives your character the ability to shake its hips. The hip can freely rotate independently from the main portion of the hierarchy. Table 4.2 lists the strengths and weaknesses of this method.

▶ **Table 4.2** Strengths and Weakness of a Free Root

Strengths	Weaknesses
Expanded functionality (more freedom to rotate the hips)	Setup is just a little more involved than the classic root but is well worth it
Ease of animation	
Great for walking, running	
Intuitive to animators	
Follows Isner ideology	

Two methods are commonly used to create a free root. First you can simply build the root joint one joint higher than the hip joint. In Figure 4.6, you can see that the hip is actually downstream from the root. This allows the hip to be moved independently of the root. With this setup, you run into a problem where the root joint cannot bend. Thus the area of the root joint is static. To fix this, you can create two more joints that are right next to the root joint that will allow for more spine control.

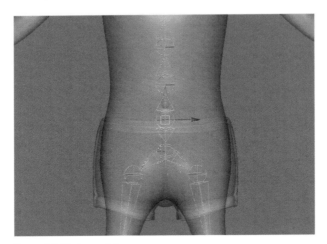

Figure 4.6 The free root rig

The other common way to create this effect is to drive the hip portion of the skeleton around the same lower back point we used in the previous example. You can use a deformer, such as a control or cluster, to rotate the hip area. The joints need to be tied to a control or cluster, thus in effect making the lower back the root of the figure, as opposed to the hip.

Remember, you can create a free root using variations on these methods, and there are other great spine setups out there. We will talk about some of the variations later, as we discuss the different components of each rig type.

Learning the Isner Spine

You now can begin to consider the various methods for rigging the spine. Generally, there are two different types of spine rigs:

- A flexible under-the-hood system, which figures spine movement for you
- The simpler approach using mainly the FK control

Both of these methods are presented in the coming sections.

Many techniques are good for particular types of movement, but one, the Isner spine method, is good for all the movements you could want. It has an overall cartoony feel if it is used for the entire spine, however it can also be used for the lower part of a realistic spine for the deformation between the rib cage and the hip.

What Do You Really Want?

So now, ask yourself, "What do I really want this spine to do?" You may be saying that you want an animated spine to act as a real spine would—a tall order, if you think about how complex the spine actually is. You also want to make sure the controls are functional above all and not cumbersome for the animator. You want to make the controls super easy to use and very intuitive. After you have done this, you can add the ability to stretch the spine. And finally, if you wish, you can add two different controls for compressing the spine.

To facilitate these needs, we have split the spine rigging tutorial into several smaller, logical sections. You may choose to use only certain sections to add functionality to your rigs, but we recommend you go through each section at least once. You will learn about Maya's functionality and create a really sweet spine rig!

The spine rigging method we'll introduce to you loosely follows the Isner spine idea. You can look up the Isner spine on the Internet to find out more, but the basic Isner spine has two controls, has stretchy attributes, and uses lattices for linear compression. In the tutorials, we will show you how to use utility nodes to create two types of compression that move along the spline IK that forms the basis for our spine control. This idea mimics a compression wave with different frequency falloffs for each of the two compression options. This is somewhat like a sine wave, so naturally, in homage to the sine function, it is dubbed the Spine Wave method.

Who Is Isner?

The Isner spine rig is named for its creator, Michael Isner, chief technology guru and genius at Softimage.

The following is an overview of the Spine Wave components:

Independent controls Our Spine Wave spine needs controls on each end. Each control requires an offset rotation center point, so it rotates from an intuitive location. For example, we'll place the rib cage area control just under the armpits and the rotation center for the area under the rib cage on the spine joint. That way, the upper part of the torso rotates from the middle of the back but is grabbed near the center of the rib cage.

Falloff between controls We want to make sure there is a gradual falloff between the controls around the chest and the hip in our Spine Wave spine. This permits smoother deformations for cartoony characters. We use a spline IK to accomplish the gradual falloff. For a realistic character, this deformation could be isolated to the abdomen area.

Stretchable spine Having a stretchable spine in a character is a no-brainer. We all want stretchy spines, don't we? This ability gives the character an amazing way to squash and stretch. Think of Mr. Fantastic from the *Fantastic Four*. How he was able to stretch his arm out and still bend his wrist and elbow? Animators will use the stretchiness you build in ever so slightly for good animation follow-through as well as for exaggerations. If you are not convinced, play around with the finished rig on the CD, and you will be sold on the idea. We will tap into the length of the spline to determine the scale on the joints to make the stretchiness happen.

Fluctuating falloff Fluctuating falloff is an add-on that we will introduce at the end of the tutorial. It allows a stretched spine to be adjusted according to the needs of the animator. To accomplish this, we will add two compression options that play nicely with the stretchy attribute of the spine. To understand how this works, think of a slinky that is stretched and held at the ends. The first compression/expansion is a Singlewave, similar to what happens when a person grabs the center of the slinky and moves it toward one end. The slinky compresses on one side and expands on the other. Figure 4.7 shows how this works.

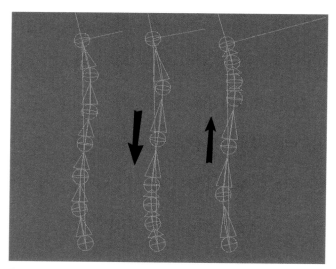

Figure 4.7 Compression and expansion in a Singlewave

The second compression option is a Doublewave. This is what occurs when a person grabs the slinky in two locations, at ¼ and ¾ of the length. They then could push these points together, so the slinky compresses in the middle. Alternately, if they pull the points away from each other, the slinky expands in the middle and compresses near the ends, as shown in Figure 4.8.

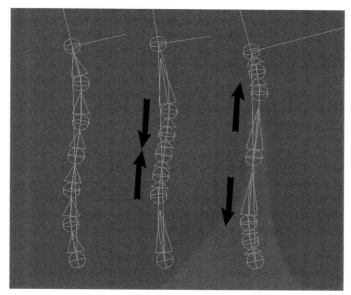

Figure 4.8 Compression and expansion in a Doublewave

The Ribbon Spine

There is a really great new option for spines that has to do with attaching the spine joints to a NURBS curve. You get all the benefits of the properties of a curve. One of these is that the orientation of the joint that is following that section of the curve stays correct. This is the byproduct of orienting against a follicle on the NURBS surface. This process was developed by Aaron Holly at Fahrenheit Digital LLC. For the Maya Complete user, there is a modification to this spine setup created by Geordie Martinez that attaches to a pointOnSurface node. The results are almost identical. These spines can stretch and twist. They are great for adding to the lower portion of a realistic torso or the full spine of a cartoony character. You can find it at www.negative13.com.

Creating a Basic Spine

The classic or simplest way to create a spine can be the foundation for more advanced types of rigs as well. This is the spine you'll want to create for use with a Spine Wave setup. It is built by creating a joint chain emanating from the hip or from a point slightly higher than the hip. If you place the root joint slightly higher than the hip, in the small of the back, then your hip and legs can rotate freely from the root. For most advanced spine setups, including the one we'll walk you through in this book, you will want to use a directional joint chain that starts from the hip. If you do not, you'll find that the spline IK will not work with a bi-directional chain.

Once the spine is built, you can create ribs that are either connected to the spine or floating and constrained to the spine, as shown in Figure 4.9. This type of setup serves two purposes. First, it helps you with your skinning and weight painting because the geometry closest to each rib joint will be affected most as the character moves. Second, it gives your character a torso volume that helps you better visualize the character as it moves. The ribs don't need to be complex, just one or two joints to fill the volume.

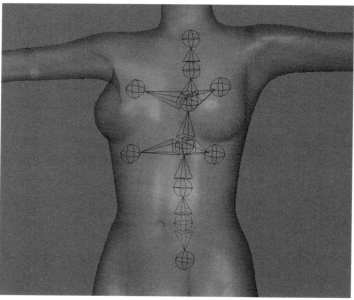

Figure 4.9 Including a set of ribs makes the character easier to skin.

When using the classic spine rigging technique, consider joint placement. A centralized joint placement produces more tube-like deformations, which is good for more cartoony characters but lacks the realism for a motion such as bending at the waist. Conversely, you can create your spine in the anatomical location for more realistic bending, but this results in more work for yourself during the skinning phase to minimize pinching. A combination of the two is usually the most beneficial.

Creating a Classic Spine

The classic spine is simple to create, and it provides a framework that we can add to as part of the Spine Wave rig. To create a classic spine, follow these steps:

1. Create an initial spine in Maya by selecting Skeleton > Joint Tool, and in the orthographic side view, build your joint chain. Create your joints starting from the hip and ending at the shoulders. If you plan to use this rig to build an advanced spine, create a chain that has seven joints, as shown in Figure 4.10.

2. Name the joints descriptively. Remember that after you create any joints in a rig, you want to rename the joints to avoid problems with other joint sets and naming. We recommend using the Modify > Search and Replace Names feature. To use this feature, select your joint chain, and replace the word *joint* with **Bind_Spine**. This renames the joints leaving the joint numbers in place. There are a number of renaming scripts at http://highend3d.com.

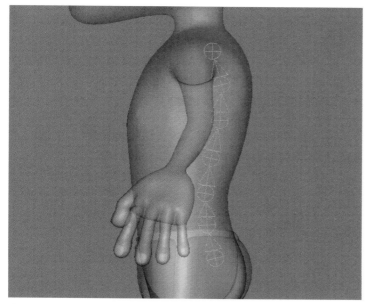

Figure 4.10 Create a spine with seven joints.

Note: If you are already familiar with free root setups, you can skip ahead to "Stretching Along a Spline IK Curve (Used in Spine Wave Setup)" and get started on the next tasks you'll need to perform to create the Spine Wave rig.

Creating a Spine for a Free Root Rig

A variation of the classic spine is the free root rig. It basically moves the root of the rig away from the hip to allow for free movement of the hip. This rig is a great alternative to the more advanced Spine Wave setup. A lot of the features found in the Spine Wave are present with this spine rig. You will be able to easily parent controls to the skeleton, without having to worry about maintaining the bells and whistles of a more complex rig such as stretchy bones and compression. Be aware that you cannot add the curve-based advanced rigging we'll show you later in this chapter to a joint chain that emanates both up and down from the middle of the back. Using a spine with a free root limits the features you can add to it later. Now that you have been warned, let's get started.

When building this type of spine, remember you can use joints to simulate ribs (either attached to the main spine or just constrained to it). You can add rib joints after the spine is complete. Some prefer to use a spine like this for its clear benefits for skinning; however, you can still get a great rig from a straightforward simple joint chain up the back. Time is needed, however, for good skinning and painting weights. Greats rigs can be simple, but most of all, a great rig is user-friendly and functional. To create a spline for a free root rig, follow these steps:

1. Create your initial spine. Choose Skeleton > Joint Tool, and in orthographic side view create the joint chain. Create your joints starting from the small of the back, ending at the shoulders.

2. Now, select the root joint with your joint tool by clicking it.

3. Once you have identified the root joint, create one final joint for the hip that extends down toward the ground. You may want to add a joint just above the root and just below the root for more flexibility. Remember that joints that emanate from the root are controlled by the root. You may want to bend in the general area of the root. Adding these joints will help you do that.

4. Name the joints descriptively. Remember that after you create these joints, you want to rename each joint to prevent problems later and avoid confusion with other joint sets. We recommend using the Modify > Search and Replace Names menu selection. First, select your joint chain, and then replace *joint* with **Bind-Spine**. This renames the joints and leaves the sequential numbering in place.

Stretching Along a Spline IK Curve (Used in Spine Wave Setup)

Starting with the classic joint chain we previously built, we'll show how to add overall stretchiness to our spine. To do this, we will do the following:

1. Create a spline IK curve.

2. Add stretch to the chain.

3. Scale the joints.

4. Add a stretchiness switch.

After stretchiness is added to the spine rig, you need to be aware that the joints are fine as they follow the curve length. If the control is moved in such a way that the spine becomes longer than the constraining curve, the end joint will maintain the last tangent of the curve. Since this happens only in extreme stretch and the spine maintains its scale and direction of travel, unwanted results are usually negligible.

Creating a Spline IK Curve

The Spline IK curve provides a smooth path for the spine to follow. It allows you to move controls located along the spine and have the rest of the spine joints follow the movement naturally.

Tip: Before creating the Spline IK, double-check the orientation of the joints (select the spine joints, select Skeleton, and then select the Orient Joint option box). Select XYZ Orientation. Figure 4.11 shows the correct joint orientation with the X-axis running parallel to each spine joint's bone. We will cover this important topic of orientation in this chapter, but if you need to, orient the joints with the methods described in Chapter 3.

Pajama Gladiator

Here are a couple of the rigs used for the short film *Pajama Gladiator* done at BYU. Both of these characters were built using MEL. As you can readily see, the cow character required an interesting setup. For each arm, there is the ability to stretch with a spline-based system, or you can switch to an FK setup. The joints also scale smaller as the limb extends. This creates a very cartoony feeling in the character. You can see, too, that the facial setups are constrained to the character. The cow has facial controls that are viewed through another camera that is constrained to look directly at the facial joysticks. The Eli character has a similar squash and stretch setup, as well as having general scaling that can be applied to the whole rig while animating.

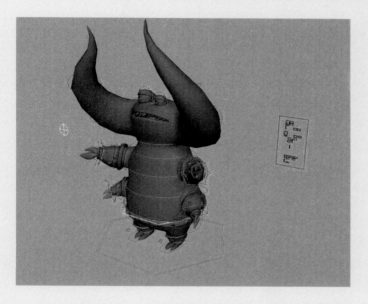

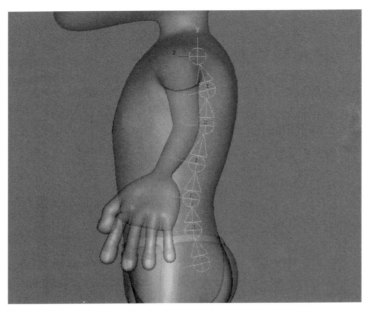

Figure 4.11 Check the joint orientation before applying spline IK.

To create a Spline IK curve, follow these steps:

1. Let's create a spline IK chain with the main spine joint chain (already named Bind_Spine). Use the Skeleton > IK Spline Handle Tool > (options). Deselect the Auto Parent Curve check box, and then select two spans and the options shown in Figure 4.12. Be aware that with the Auto Simplify Curve option enabled, the shape of the spine will change a little.

You can lessen the effect on your oriented joints by simplifying the curves of your joint chain (by straightening it out) before applying the IK spline. Likewise, you can compensate for the correction by creating your spine a little more curvy so that when the IK is added, it straightens to the right curvature. We will correct for the orientation problems later in this chapter.

Figure 4.12 Disable the Auto Parent Curve option when creating a spline IK chain.

2. Now use the IK Spline Handle tool options to define your Spline IK. Select the root (hip) joint and then the last joint up by the shoulders. This creates a curve running the length of your spine. The curve now controls the joint positions.

3. Switch to Component Type, and move the curve's CVs to test the result, as shown in Figure 4.13. Choose Undo to back out of the testing.

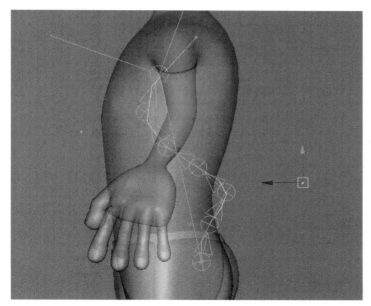

Figure 4.13 Test the spine joints after spline IK is applied.

4. Use the Outliner to rename the curve, effector, and handle. Rename the curve to
    BindSpineSIKCurve. Double-click the curve, and then rename it. Remember to
    press Enter after changing the name to set it. Next, rename the effector that is
    parented to the end of your joint chain to **BindSpineSIKEff**. Lastly, rename the
    IK handle to **BindSpineSIKHandle**. Renaming at this point, while the spline IK is
    clean, is important to prevent possible naming conflicts.

Adding Stretch to the Chain

As you moved the CVs in step 4 of the previous exercise, you saw that as the
curve lengthened, the joint chain snapped and pulled the curve down to compensate.
The chain did not stretch. So, to get this chain to stretch, you need to get the curve
information node. To add the stretching ability to the spline IK curve, follow
these steps:

1. Open Window > Rendering Editors > Hypershade to prepare for this node.

2. Type the following on the MEL command line:

        arclen -ch on BindSpineSIKCurve;

3. Select BindSpineSIKCurve, and from within the Hypershade select Graph > Add
    Selected to Graph. Now that you have the curve node in the lower panel of the
    Hypershade, you can create the curve info node.

    To view your newly created node, within the Hypershade, select Graph, Input,
    and Output Connections, and your info node will appear along with the spline
    IK node and the curve shape node.

4. Select your curve info node, and right-click to rename it to **BindSpineCurveInfo**.
    To see the length of your curve, select the info node you just renamed, look at its
    attribute information (Ctrl+A), or just double-click the node.

Scaling the Joints

The next step is to scale each joint so they are proportional to the difference in curve length so that when the curve length increases, each of the joints scales by a proportional amount to simulate a spine stretching. Thus, if the curve is scaled to 120 percent of its original length, you want each joint to be scaled to 120 percent of its original length. To scale the joints, follow these steps:

1. Create a multiply divide node by clicking the node type listed in the Create Maya Nodes tab on the left side of the Hypershade window. The multiply divide node is located under General Utilities. Once you have created the multiply divide node, right-click, and rename it **BSSIKMultiplyDivide**.

2. Click and hold the arrow on the bottom right of the Curve Info icon. This displays your outgoing parameters. Select the arcLength output, and then connect it to the multiply divide node by clicking the node and selecting Input 1, Input1X.

3. Now look at the Attribute Editor for the multiply divide node. Verify that the Input1X field now is connected to the length of the curve.

4. Copy the Input1X value, and paste it in the Input2X field, as shown in Figure 4.14. (Your curve length most likely will be a different value from the value shown in the figure.)

5. Change the operation from multiply to divide. Now Input1X will be divided against Input2X and will give you the difference in scale of the current curve length divided by the original curve length. We can now use this information to scale each joint.

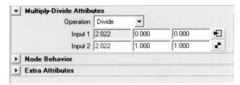

Figure 4.14 Connect the Input1X field to the length of the curve.

6. Add all the joints to the Hypershade by selecting the joints and using Graph > Add Selected to Graph. This connects the outgoing divided value to the scale of the length of each joint.

Tip: You can do this quickly by going into the Script Editor and using History > Echo All Commands. Use the Add Selected to Graph command, select the commands, and then drag them with the middle mouse button into your animation shelf to create a new MEL icon. Now, pickwalk (with the down arrow), executing your MEL script for each joint, except the last.

Adding a Stretchiness Switch

The final step of adding stretchiness to your spine is to add a switch for stretchiness. This gives you a way to easily enable and disable the stretchiness of the spine. To add a stretchiness switch, follow these steps:

1. On the Create Maya Nodes tab on the left side of the Hypershade window, locate and add a condition node (found near the multiply divide node).

2. Attach the OutputX of the BSSIKMultiplyDivide multiply divide node to the ColorIfTrue, ColorIfTrueR input.

3. Right-click the new node, and name this conditional node **StretchCond**. Change its operation to "Not Equal".

4. Now hook up the OutColorR of the condition node to the ScaleX nodes of the joints except the last. The last joint will not need to scale because it influences no other joints downstream. Set the Second Term option to 1.

Now we have the First Term option to hook to anything we want, such as a Boolean attribute or the movement of a switch. We talked about setting up these attributes in Chapter 3. Once you have the switch in place you will need to hook up the switch to the condition node with a set driven key. If you are not familiar with this, we will talk about this type of connection later in the chapter. Most animators will want the functionality of being able to turn off stretch. However, you may want to have stretch on permanently. If you don't want to include a switch, follow these steps:

1. Connect the multiply divide node OutputX value to the ScaleX value of all the joints in the spline IK joint chain, except the last. The last joint in the chain does not need to scale. Figure 4.15 shows what the stretchy spine switch looks like the Hypershade.

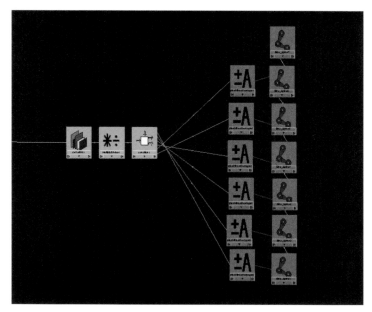

Figure 4.15 The stretchy spine switch in the Hypershade

2. Test by translating some of the CVs of the curve around. Your spine will now stretch with the length of the curve, as shown in Figure 4.16.

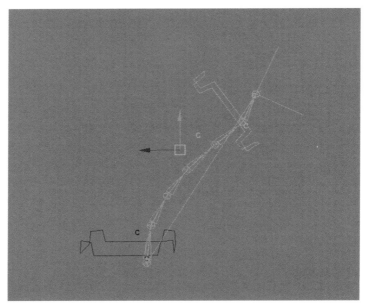

Figure 4.16 Stretchy spine testing

Controlling Overshoot

With the stretchiness feature enabled, the spine joints scale as the curve scales, but if the control is moved in an extreme manner, the joints can overshoot the curve, as shown in Figure 4.17.

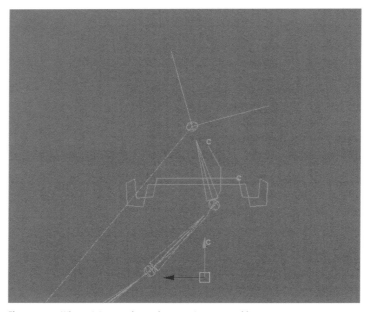

Figure 4.17 When a joint overshoots the curve, it causes problems.

This overshooting problem is not really a big concern because your figure will follow the skeleton and because the skeleton will behave appropriately as if the spline extended along its end vector. If you think you must have the spine exactly on the end of the spline all of the time, you may add another multiplicative node that allows you to add a value to manually stretch the spine back down to the curve. This workaround is usually not needed, since the spine will behave properly. Test the spine to make sure it suits your needs.

Adding Spine Controls and Enabling Compression

So far the spine rig is coming along nicely. We've already added spine IK and stretchiness to the spine rig, and in the next section dealing with the Spine Wave rig, we'll add some controls along with the ability to compress the spine. Since an Isner-type spine is our goal, we need to create the two spine controls and place them in a position that is easily read. In this next section, we'll hook up the controls to the spine curve.

Cluster Method (Spine Wave Setup)

We are now going to attach controls to our curve. The cluster method is the recommended method to use with the Spine Wave rig because you have multiple CVs on the curve that you need to easily control. To add cluster controls, follow these steps:

1. Attach clusters to the CVs of the curve by selecting the curve, Ctrl+right-clicking, and then selecting Cluster from the pop-up menu.

2. Use the Outliner to pick each cluster, and uncheck the Relative option in the Attribute Editor. While you have the Attribute Editor open, rename your clusters so there are no future naming conflict issues.

3. Create the control curves that you want for controlling the spine. For ideas about unique control creation, refer to the "Working with Controls" section in Chapter 3.

4. Place the controls at the top and bottom of the torso. For our stylized character, the controls will be at about armpit level and at hip level, and they will be fairly tight to the body, as shown in Figure 4.18, so as not to be confused with the other future controls. These are great rotation positions for the two ends of the spine.

5. Rename the controls to **TorsoCTRLHi** and **TorsoCTRLLow**, respectively.

6. Clean up their history by selecting Modify > Freeze Transformations and Modify > Center Pivot.

7. Move the top pivot to the center joint in the spine by hitting Insert. Then hold the V key to snap it to the correct joint.

8. Move the lower controls pivot to the third joint from the bottom.

9. Parent the top three clusters under TorsoCTRLHi by dragging them with the middle mouse button under that curve in the Outliner.

10. Parent the bottom two clusters under TorsoCTRLLow by dragging them with the middle mouse button under the curve in the Outliner. Check the clusters attributes again to make sure the relative boxes are not checked.

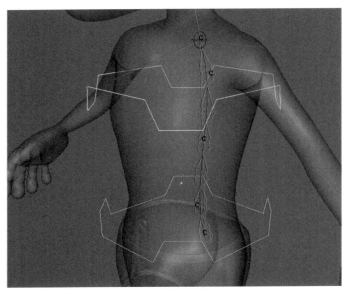

Figure 4.18 Place the curve type controls close to the torso.

You now can test the controls and watch the spine stretch and bend, as shown in Figure 4.19.

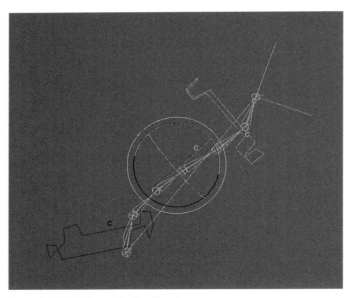

Figure 4.19 Stretching and bending the spine

Solving the Rotation Dilemma (Spine Wave Setup)

Try selecting the top control and rotating it on the Y-axis. If you look at the joints closely, you will notice that they are not rotating but remain aligned along their X- and Z-axes. When you first encounter this, it may seem odd, but it is caused by the way the joints are automatically constrained to the curve.

From our earlier tests, we know that translation is affecting the curve and the spine, but how do we get rotation to affect the spine as well? There are a few ways to resolve this. One of the easier methods of overcoming this problem involves a useful function that Maya prebuilt into each spline IK. To add Y-axis rotation to your spine, follow these steps:

1. Select BindSpineIKHandle, and look in its IKSolver attributes. Expand Advanced Twist Controls, and check the Enable Twist Controls option.

2. Change World Up Type to Object Rotation Up.

3. Change the Up vectors for the X attribute to 1.0 and the Y attribute to 0.0, as shown in Figure 4.20.

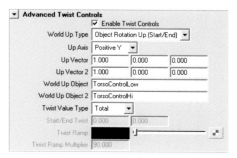

Figure 4.20 Change the Up vectors to X.

4. Assign World Up Object to the TorsoCTRLLow control and the World Up Object2 to TorsoCTRLHi.

5. Freeze Transformations on the root joint to align all of your joints. Also, to keep scaling from not being perpetuated into the limbs and head you can create a new joint, and snap it to the joint at the top of the spine. Parent-constrain the floating joint to the top of the spine, and use this joint for hooking the arms and head onto.

Rotation now affects your spine, and when you scale it, the change will be isolated only to the spine.

The Compressible Spine Wave Add-On

The reason for adding these two types of controls comes from the Isner spine idea. The Isner spine idea deals with falloffs that are near the ends of the spine. The Isner spine uses directional lattices to achieve its compression result. The Spine Wave setup is similar in its general concept but is different in that, as the joints compress, they compress along the shape of the spines' spline curve. To create a spine wave effect for six joints, we will add to our spine:

- A Singlewave attribute for the TorsoCTRLHi control
- A plus minus average node
- A multiply divide node

The first step is to enable the TorsoCTRLHi control with the ability to propagate a Singlewave up and down the spine joints. To enable Singlewave compression in the spine, follow these steps:

1. Add an attribute called "Singlewave" to the TorsoCTRLHi control. Set the attribute to be of type float with a minimum value of -1, a maximum value of 1, and a default of 0. Hit the "OK" button to make the attribute.

2. In the Hypershade, create a PlusMinusAverage node for each of the six scalable joints in the chain.

3. Replace the connections of the outputs from the StretchCond condition node to the joints by hooking them into the first value (input1D[0]) of the AddMinusAverage node of each of the six joints. For each PlusMinusAverage node, connect its Output1D value to the scaleX of its respective joint.

4. Add the TorsoCTRLHi control to the graph, and add a new Multiply Divide node. Name the new node **SinglewaveMD**.

5. Connect the Singlewave attribute of TorsoCTRLHi to the input1X of the SinglewaveMD multiply divide node. Set the Input2x value to −1. This will swap the values of the Singlewave slider and allow you to assign the original value to the top three joints and the inverse value to the lower three joints.

6. Attach the Singlewave attribute to the second value (input1D[1]) of each of the add nodes for each of the top three joints.

7. Attach the outputX of the SinglewaveMD node to the second value (input1D[1]) of the add nodes for the lower three joints, as shown in Figure 4.21.

8. Test your attribute by moving the TorsoCTRLHi control up and down. The more curve that your spline has, the more that this setup will make the joints stretch slightly past the top of the curve. This is expected.

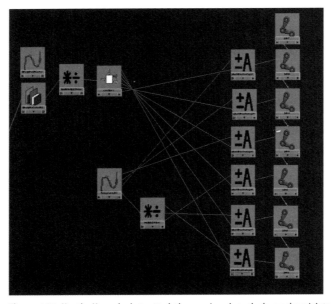

Figure 4.21 Use the Hypershade to attach the wave's node to the lower three joints.

The Doublewave Compressible Spine Wave Add-On

The Doublewave compression ability adds to the Singlewave by allowing a wave to move up and down the spine at the same time. This effect stretches the middle and compresses the ends or, inversely, compresses the middle and stretches both ends. Since this is a complex operation, let's work on only three joints now to avoid confusion. These three joints represent half of the spine (the top three joints of the spine from the middle on up).

Now let's think about how this is going to work. When the Doublewave slider moves to the positive, we want the first joint in the chain to grow by a given size, while the other two joints scale to the negative by half that size, thus keeping the spine the same length. Likewise, moving the slider in the negative should grow the third joint and shrink the first two by half the size.

Now that we have our problem, let's get figuring. Consider only an end joint for now. We want it to scale up by an amount equal to the slider movement in the positive, and the other joints each need to scale down by half the slider's value. Thus, the three joints will still be the same original length, but when the slider goes the other direction, we want the other end joint to scale up relative to the slider and the other two to scale down by half each.

Consider the middle joint. The middle joint needs to scale down by half the value of the slider no matter which way the slider moves. Its value must always be negative unless, of course, it is zero.

Now let's think about the two values that we have to deal with. We always want the joint that is stretching positively to be stretching at the same value as the slider. This first value needs to be passed into our condition node and, depending on the direction of the slider, must be passed to the appropriate joint. Inversely, we have a second value that must be half the value of the slider multiplied by −1 so that it always remains a negative number, with a maximum value of 0. This second value can be hooked directly into our center joint. The values for the end joints will have to be controlled by a main condition node that switches when the slider goes from a positive value to a negative one.

Now we have considered half the spine. The other half of the spine uses the same values only in reverse. So, we have six joints to scale. Either the middle two will be scaled large or the outer two will be scaled large (depending on slider location/value), and the other joints will compensate for the remainder of the distance.

To create a Doublewave effect for the spine joints, we will add the following to our spine:

- A Doublewave attribute for the TorsoControlHi control
- A main Doublewave conditional node
- Two "slider value" conditional nodes (positive and negative)
- Two "color if" conditional nodes (true and false)
- Two multiply/divide nodes (positive and negative)

The Divine Spine

The divine spine is another great spine setup that is available. It uses three chains connected together to produce a very precise method of control and bend. It can be found in the book *Inside Maya 5* by Mark Adams, Erick Miller, and Max Sims. Despite it having been written for an older version of the software, the book is a great resource for learning how to set up this very articulate spine and setting up dynamic IK chains. Everything regarding the connections with these rigging setups works with the current version of Maya.

Creating the Main Conditional Node

Let's get started. To create the main conditional node, follow these steps:

1. Add a Doublewave attribute to the TorsoCTRLHi control. Set the attribute type to float with a minimum value of -5, a maximum value of 5, and a default of 0. Hit the "OK" button to make the attribute.

2. Connect the Doublewave attribute from the TorsoCTRLHi output to the first term of a new condition node, and assign the Operation to "greater than." Leave the second term as zero. Name this node MainDoublewaveCond. This is the main node that sends expansion and compression values out to the end joints.

Creating the Positive Stretching Number

Now we need to create the positive and negative values to feed into the MainDoublewaveCond node. To create the positive stretching number, follow these steps:

1. Create a new condition node. Hook up the Doublewave value to the first term of the new node. Name this node **PositiveValueCond**. Leave the second term at 0, and set the operation to Less Than.

2. Hook the Doublewave attribute from the TorsoCTRLHi value to the input1X to a new multiply Divide node. Name this node **PositiveValueMD**. You need the number coming out of this node to be positive even when the slider goes negative, so set the node to take the Doublewave value, and multiply it by -1 by putting -1 into the input2X value. You will use this value for times when the slider goes negative to bring the number back to the positive.

3. Now hook the OutputX of the PositiveValueMD multiply divide node to the ColorIfTrueR value of the PositiveValueCond condition node. Hook the Doublewave value from the TorsoCTRLHi control into the ColorIfFalseR value of the PositiveValueCond condition node.

Creating the Negative Stretching Number

Now let's work on the negative stretching number. We could repeat the same process that we used with the positive stretching value, but let's create this one a little. To create the negative stretching number, follow these steps:

1. Create a conditional node, and name it **NegativeValueCond**. It needs to output a value that is half of the Doublewave value and that is always negative except when at zero.

2. Hook up the Doublewave value from the TorsoCTRLHi control to the first term of the NegativeValueCond condition node. Set this node's Operation to Greater Than. Type -2 in the Color If True X field. Enter 2 for the Color If False X field. You will pass these values into a multiply divide node to make the number always stay negative and to divide it by 2.

3. Create a new multiply divide node, and name it **NegativeValueMD**. Set the operation to Divide.

4. Hook the Doublewave value from the TorsoCTRLHi node to input1X of the NegativeValueMD node.

5. Hook the NegativeValueCond OutcolorR value into the input2x of the NegativeValueMD node.

Connecting the Stretching Values

Now that you have both our negative and positive value stretching values, you are ready to hook them into the main condition node. To connect the stretching values to the main condition node we need to create connections that:

1. Hook the positive stretching value into your MainDoublewaveCond condition node.

2. Set up a switch now that, when the Doublewave attribute is positive, gives the first value the positive scale and the second value the negative scale. Alternately, when the Doublewave slider is negative, set the switch to give the first value a negative scale and the second a positive scale.

To create these two processes, follow the steps below.

Hooking Up the Outer Joints

Once this is complete, you can cleanly hook up your outer joints. To hook up the outer joints, follow these steps:

1. Connect OutcolorR from the PositiveValueCond condition node to the ColorIfTrueG and ColorIfFalseR nodes of the MainDoublewaveCond condition node.

2. Connect OutputX from the NegativeValueMD node to the ColorIfFalseG and ColorIfTrueR nodes of the MainDoublewaveCond condition node.

3. Since your spine has seven joints and only six need to be scaled, you are not going to connect the last joint. Both the root joint, since it is the first joint in the chain, and the sixth joint, the end joint, must be connected to the OutColorR output of the MainDoublewaveCond node. Do this by hooking OutColorR from the MainDoublewaveCond node to the Input1D[2] values in the addition nodes for the first and sixth joints.

4. Alternately, connect the MainDoublewaveCond OutColorG node to the Input1D[2] on the third and fourth joint addition nodes.

5. The second and fifth joints are middle joints. These joints need to have a negative value applied to them, since they need to scale in the negative whether the Doublewave slider goes in a negative or positive direction. Connect them by attaching the OutputX of the NegativeValueMD to the Input1D[2] addition list in the second and fifth joint.

That is it! Test your Doublewave with the slider, and feel the power. Your Hypershade should look something like Figure 4.22. The four nodes at the top control the automatic stretch. The two in the middle are the Singlewave, and the five at the bottom control the Doublewave. Set the minimum and maximum values of each attribute high so that when your spine stretches many times past its original length, you will still have control. You can modify attribute minimum and maximum limits using the Attribute Editor under Attributes > Edit Attributes and set the limits to your liking.

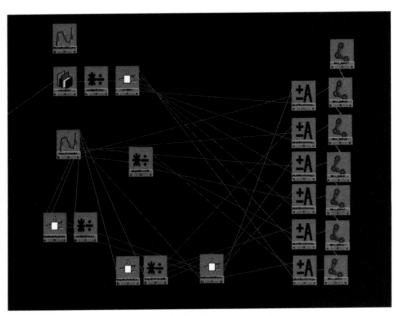

Figure 4.22 Use these connections to enable Doublewave compression.

Conclusion

Having effectively rigged the spine, you now have a solid foundation for the remaining rigging tasks. This chapter presented a couple of different spine rigging techniques, each with its advantages.

In the next chapter, we'll move downward from the spine and cover the rigging of the pelvis. The pelvis rig is a key component for enabling how the character's main controls will work.

Creating Contrapposto: Perfecting Pelvis Rigging

Once the spine is complete, the next step in finishing the torso rig is to work on the joints to control the pelvis and hips. There are two main techniques for rigging this region: the rigid hips technique and the free hips technique. The rigid hips follow the movements of the spine. The free hips can move independently of the spine. We are also going to discuss the master control and root control for your figure. Lastly, we will go over how to create a current center of gravity for your character. This will allow it to do flips about its center of gravity.

5

Chapter Contents
Rigging a pelvis
Setting up world-relative controls

Pelvis Rigging

In this section, we will be working with a hip-based root. If you have already built a hip-based root that works with the Spine Wave setup from the previous chapter, you can skip this control. If you have a separate spine setup, you will want to add a free hip control to your rig.

The pelvis and ground-based root portion of your rig is simple but important. The animator selects the control for these parts for general movement throughout the world. This section also determines the control you will use for rotating your figure in place. It is your master control for the major movement.

If this section of your rig is not well thought out, you could have unwanted values passing into your animation. For instance, if your root is not set up properly, you could move your character to the side and then, while he is not above his master control, set a keyframe. This unwanted value could then accidentally be perpetuated to the future animation. You want to be able to zero your figure's controls back to their figure's relative positions. You can zero out controls you create using the Freeze Transformations tool. This will allow animators to return to the default position when they get unwanted rotation values during the animation process. If you do not zero out your controls when placing them, the controls will return to their point of creation when zeroed.

Let's begin with the hip setup of your rig. Put simply, the hip connects the spine to the legs. When you make this connection, you want to consider several issues. You want to watch for deformations coming downstream from the spine, such as scaling. You want to stop these from perpetuating into the legs because the legs need to be controlled individually and not be controlled by the spine. You also want individual control over your joints and any downstream joints. Consider the hip. Will you need a control for the hip itself? In the classic setup, we will need a control for this, and with the advanced setup, the hip will be a child to the lower spine.

There are several major issues with the hip rig and world controls:

- The hip joint can be rotated by only rotating the entire figure and then adjusting the spine and legs.

- The legs need to be prevented from scaling as the spine is stretched.

- Avoid cyclical dependencies within the rig in situations where a child joint drives its parent.

The first two issues have to do with the two main types of hip rigging. We'll look at those next. The last one can be avoided using a null group. This is covered later in the chapter.

You can take two main approaches, and each of them addresses these issues in different ways. The first approach is to rig the hip in a rigid fashion where the hips are the center of your rig, meaning that the spine and legs both emanate from the hip joint. In the second approach, you can create the hip with a free hip rig. This is where the center of the skeleton is in the small of the back. Both of these techniques have their advantages and disadvantages, as you'll see in the sections that follow.

Using the Rigid Hips Technique

For this technique, you can rig the hip in a rigid fashion. Using this method, the hips are located at the center between the spine and the legs, meaning the spine and legs both emanate from the hip joint. This hip joint can be the root, but we'll deal with the root and its world controls later in the chapter.

Generally, you will not want to use this hip rig for a character. Even minor rigs that you build often need free hips. We use and control the rig in the Spine Wave setup. This setup mimics the control of a free hip and gives the animator some slick spine deformation options.

For most of us, the rigid hips setup is the first way we learned to rig a character. You will want to take the spine and leg joints and attach them at the hip. This rig is simple to make and very intuitive, but it doesn't have the ability to rotate the hips easily. Table 5.1 lists the benefits and drawbacks of this technique.

▶ **Table 5.1** Rigid Hips Technique Strengths and Weaknesses

Strengths	Weaknesses
Simple setup	Cannot rotate hips easily
Simple to use	Less realistic
Great for simple animation	

This technique creates a root that is very easy to keep track of, as shown in Figure 5.1, but will make it harder to animate realistic objects.

It is more difficult in the sense that the hip cannot rotate from the mid-spine. This is frustrating when you want to raise one side of the hip or make a contrapposto stance, shown in Figure 5.2. The contrapposto pose is a common model pose for artists. For this pose, the figure has shifted weight onto one leg, the hip is relaxed, the other leg is slackened, and the spine is curved. This pose is possible only when the hips can swivel. To achieve this pose using a classic body root, you must first rotate the figure from the hip and then pose and adjust accordingly. Using other setups, your character can attain this position with fewer modifications and less posing.

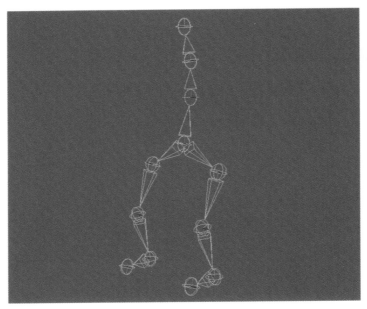

Figure 5.1 A simple rigid hip setup

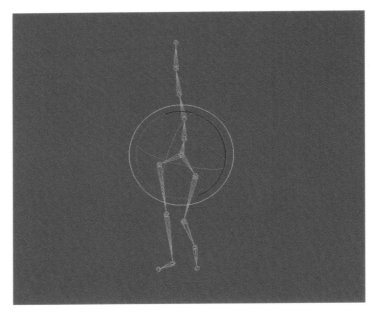

Figure 5.2 Simple rigid hip contrapposto

Consider a wooden drawing mannequin, like the one shown in Figure 5.3. It is fairly realistic in the ability to pose but, alas, is tied to the earth with a base connected to its hip. To offset the rotation of the hip, you must rotate the base and the entire figure. This same problem exists when you rig using the rigid hip method. To rotate the hip on the character, you must rotate the entire figure and then adjust the legs and spine.

Figure 5.3 A wooden drawing mannequin

Now, there are some benefits of having this type of rig. It is easy to set up and follow in the animation process. The basic control is easy to follow if you are beginning your animation studies. Also, you will find that this setup can be reliable, even with the problem of rotating the figure to rotate the hip.

You can easily direct the movement of the character from the most central portion of the body. You can also easily follow the movement of the hip while animating.

We are actually going to use a rigid hip for the Spine Wave rig that we started in the previous chapter because that hip is already free, coming from the curve-driven spine. This joint system mimics a traditional rigid hip in that it originates from the hip, but the hip we create will have the capabilities of a free hip. Figure 5.4 shows a simple rigid hip setup.

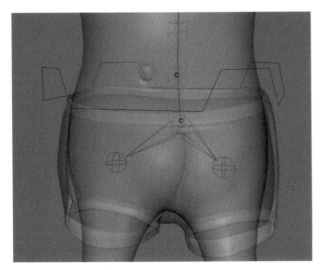

Figure 5.4 A simple rigid hip setup

Adding the Hip to the Spine Wave Rig

You're ready to begin creating the final piece of the torso for your character. Notice as you work through the tutorials that our joint hierarchy follows exactly the root joint of our spine. Since the hip is already freely controlled by the curve, when we're finished, we will be able to shift the hips, as needed. So, we do not need a free hip setup. Notice, too, that we take care so the joints from the hip down do not take on the scaling attributes of the spine. Now, let's get to it. To add a rigid hip to the spine wave rig, follow these steps:

1. Open the Spine Wave skeleton you created using the tutorials in Chapter 4, "Torso Rigging Techniques."

2. Create a double joint chain close to the hip using Skeleton > Joint Tool.

3. Press and hold the V key while you snap the first joint to the hip. This snaps the first joint to the hip joint specifically, as shown in Figure 5.5.

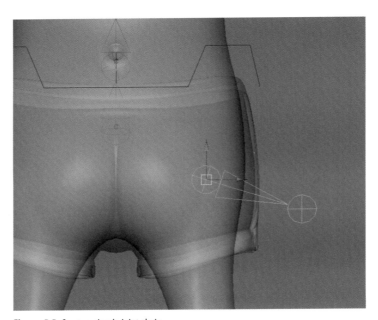

Figure 5.5 Create a simple joint chain.

4. Move the joint into the place where the femur connects to the pelvis. Make sure your placement is accurate in relationship to where the figure's actual hip would be in both the front and side views.

5. Mirror the downstream thigh joint using Skeleton > Mirror Joint, as shown in Figure 5.6. Name the hip joint **Root** and the thighs **RThigh** and **LThigh**.

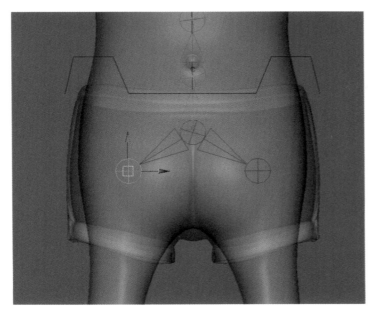

Figure 5.6 The mirrored hip

6. Select the root joint of the spine (driver) and then the root joint of your new hip (driven), and point-constrain them using Constrain > Parent.

7. Test your system using the lower control of your spine. This now has created a hip that is not influenced by the stretching of the spine.

You now have a secondary joint system that is driven by the first but without the scale influence.

In the example figure (included on the CD), we use a broken rig. Refer to the figure to see how this is done. Look specifically at the constraints that are placed and how they relate to the hip itself. We will talk more about how to build a broken rig in Chapter 7, "Getting a Leg (or Two) Up: Understanding Legs and Feet," specifically, in "The Advanced Leg" section. A broken rig allows translational as well as rotational movement, which gives the animator a little more freedom.

Using the Free Hips Technique

Now, everyone wants hips that can animate easily, right? Creating a free hip is the most basic way to accomplish independent hip control that is easily animated from the joint chain. You can think of this type of control as a way to get the contrapposto stance, like Michelangelo's *David*, or to re-create Elvis' flashy hip movement. Both of these hip articulations can be hard to duplicate with basic hip root rigging. The most basic hip roots will not be able to rotate independently from the spine. Therefore, if this animation is to be achieved, the rest of the body has to compensate for the rotation and translation of the hip. The free root is the answer to our problems. It gives us a root based at the small of the back that allows the hip to move independently. Table 5.2 lists the strengths and weaknesses of this method.

▶ **Table 5.2** Free Hips Technique Strengths and Weaknesses

Strengths	Weaknesses
More realistic	None
More functional	
Very intuitive	
Simple setup	

Consider a wooden mannequin used for figure drawing. Some include a few sections in the spine. If you attach the base to the section above the hip, the hip can freely move without moving the base or the chest. A free hip rig works the same way.

It is a simple setup, and because the hip is free from the rest of the body, it is easy to animate and thus creates more realistic movement. You can easily have a swinging hip while in a walk cycle or pose a contrapposto figure. We recommend this style of hip as a good, all-around hip setup. Movement can be really exaggerated with the hips, and it will be very easy to add weight shifting to your character's movement.

Creating a free hip joint is relatively easy. If you created a simple spine joint chain positioned at the small of the back and up, then you simply create another joint below the joint in the small of the back. You can now create your thigh joints from this new joint as well as create a control.

Once the free hip joint is created, you need to remember to create a control for the animators to use. In fact, animators should never have to touch a joint. The controls should allow the joint to move. To create a free hip rig, follow these steps:

1. Start by rigging a spine and creating an opposing hip joint, like the one shown in Figure 5.7, or open one of the spine rigs created in Chapter 4.

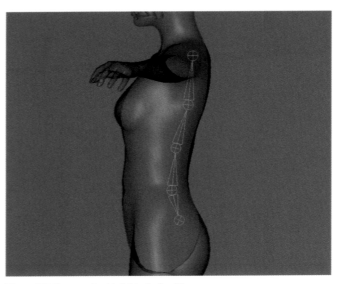

Figure 5.7 The opposing hip joint of a free hip

2. Now, create the secondary (thigh) joint.

3. Mirror the joint across using Skeleton > Mirror Joint.

4. Name the hip joint **Hip** and the thighs **RThigh** and **LThigh**.

5. Name your other joints **Root, Abdomen,** and **Chest.**

Figure 5.8 shows the completed free hip rig.

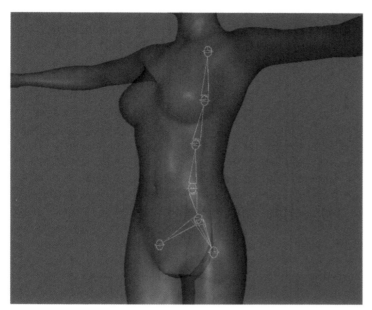

Figure 5.8 A complete free hip rig

Setting Up World-Relative Controls

Now that the joints are created, you can turn your attention to building the controls that allow the animators to move the hip joints. The controls that move your character must be organized and clean, because if the animators can't make sense of the controls, they won't be able to use them effectively.

There are two basic types of world-relative controls: ground-relative and figure-relative. In this book, we will discuss ground-relative controls in terms of "rigging for ambulation" or movement across the ground. If your character mainly walks and runs, this is the type of setup you need.

However, if your character flies, swings, flips, or performs other acrobatic movements around the center of mass or gravity, you need figure-relative controls. We'll discuss these in terms of "rigging for flight." By positioning the hip control at the hip's center, the character can be easily animated flipping or bending about this point. It is the location of the hip center that is key to this control.

Table 5.3 lists the differences between rigging for ambulation and flight.

Rigging for Ambulation	Rigging for Flight
Mainly for walking, running, and dancing	Better for flying and acrobatics
Movements based on ground	For flipping, falling, and flying
Jumping works as well	
Great for most animations	
Based on center of gravity	

When choosing world-relative controls for your rig, keep in mind the types of motion the story requires of the character. In this book, we may not present rigs that exactly meet the needs of your characters. We hope the ideas we present will inspire you to further your studies and progress in different directions. Our rigs are created in sections with options that add functionality, so feel free to pick and choose, mix and match, and use what best suits your needs.

Tip: One of the best ways to learn rigging is to play around and deconstruct an existing rig to see how it works. There are many free professional rigs for download at http://highend3d.com. You can improve your rigging skills by picking apart these rigs.

Rigging for Ambulation

Ambulation is, by definition, walking or moving about. This section focuses on one way to hook the figure to the ground using a control that can easily be identified. This makes animation easier by separating movement through the world from the movement of the figure.

Using this method, we can isolate the translate and rotation controls and make them available to the animator from the ground control or the root of the figure. If we make the hip relative to the master (ground) control, our character should be able to move where, when, and how we need it to move. A character can run up a wall by rotating the master ground control. We also have the option, if the character will be on the wall for only a short time, of leaving the ground control on the ground and moving the character onto the wall with the root control. With the setup we'll show you, all this movement is relative to the ground control.

Using this technique, the character is driven first by the master control. The master control can move and rotate in all directions. The root (hip area) also can move independently from, but always in relation to, the ground master control. This can be used on both biped (two-legged, upright walker) and quadruped (four-legged) characters.

To be useful then, the animators need to know that the master control was designed to move the body. They will know this if it is in the correct place and easily read. For example, with our figure we used a ground arrow to define the character's movement in relationship to the ground. The animators also need to easily be able to figure out which control is the root control and that the ground is always relative to the character. In our figure, we have made the root control a little wider than the torso controls in an effort to define its relationship over the torso controls. For example, if the figure is going to jump in a circle, the root control can be used to control the jump, while the master control is animated to move the figure in a circle. Easily read and intuitive controls are what make good riggers so valuable.

To get the maximum amount of movement out of your rigging, you'll need to create a separate control for the torso and parent the hip to that new control. The controls work together and enable the movements shown in Figure 5.9. You will want to make sure that your models face down the Z-axis, because this is the generally accepted standard.

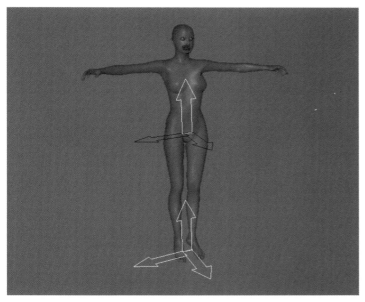

Figure 5.9 You may want to limit the translation of the master control. Remember, however, that it is good to keep these options open for animators.

Leave as much control for the animators as possible. You may, however, limit the translation and rotation of your controls. In the setup shown in Figure 5.9 and Figure 5.10, the master control can rotate freely. Y-axis rotation is reserved for the master because the master control determines the direction the character is traveling through the scene. Basically the ground control we'll create for the character moves the character in relationship to the world. The torso control moves the character in relation to the spot where he is standing in his current location. Figure 5.10 shows the enabled rotations of this type of setup. Again, remember that the figure is facing down the Z-axis.

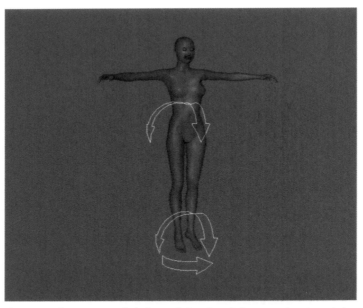

Figure 5.10 You may want to limit the translations through the torso and master controls. Remember that it is good to keep all options open for the animators. Only restrict movement if you have to.

Creating Torso and Master Controls

Creating the torso and master controls for ambulation is fairly easy. The only trick is to get the parenting correct.

To create torso and master controls, follow these steps:

1. Create a control that represents the ground master by snapping a curve to the grid (as described in the "Creating Controls" section of Chapter 3, "Rigging that's Right: Concepts You Need to Know"), move the control into place (usually this is under the figure, like a shadow), and freeze its transformations using Modify > Freeze Transformations. Name this control **MasterCTRL**. Remember that with each control you make, you will also have a null. Name the null with the name of the control and then add "Null" as a suffix. In this instance, the name is **MasterCTRLNull**.

2. Now create your torso control (see the descriptions in the "Creating Controls" section of Chapter 3).

3. Snap the control to the root. Press and hold the V key while you move the control to snap it to the root joint. Now, offset it by hitting Insert, and while holding V, snap the manipulator center to the root joint. Freeze the root control

transformations in Modify > Freeze Transformations. Name this control **RootC-TRL**. Figure 5.11 shows the controls on two very different characters. For our runner character we have a choice. We can parent both of the torso controls, as shown in the figure, or use a separate torso root control to drive the upper and lower torso controls.

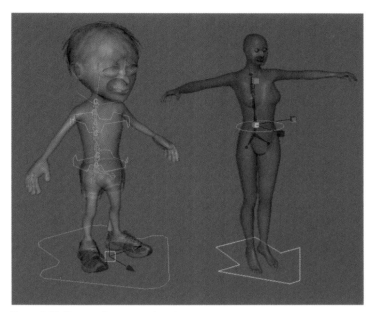

Figure 5.11 Master and torso controls variants

4. Now it's time to parent your root joint to your root control. In the Outliner, drag your root joint with the middle mouse button into RootCTRL. Then drag your RootCTRL with the middle mouse button under your MasterCTRL.

5. Lock any of the translation or rotation values your character doesn't need in the Channel Box or Attribute Editor for each control. For example, if you want your master control to stay on flat ground, you may want to lock the Y-axis translation. In the Channel Box, select the value, and right-click. Then select Lock Selected from the pop-up menu. In the Attribute Editor, right-click the value, and select Lock Attribute. Be careful what you lock down at this time. Animators usually want as much control as they can get. We can go through the rig later, when it's more finished, and lock down everything that the animators do not need.

Now, whenever you want to move your character through space, simply grab the ground master control. This, in turn, moves the torso controls, which are parented to the root control.

Creating a Ground-Based Master Control for the Spine Wave

For our Spine Wave rig, the next step is to add a ground-based master control to the rig. This control will let you animate the character moving through the scene. To add a ground-based master control to the Spine Wave rig, follow these steps:

1. Open the Spine Wave rig created in Chapter 4.

2. Create a control that represents the ground master by snapping to the grid (as described in Chapter 3).

3. Move the control into place beneath the character, and freeze its transformations using Modify > Freeze Transformations. Name the control **MasterCTRL**.

4. Create a root control and move it to either a position between the torso controls or around the hip. If you move it around the hip, your figure's main control will pivot from the hip. If the control is placed between the torso controls, your figure will rotate from mid chest. Where you place your root control is entirely up to your preferrence. Freeze its transformations using Modify > Freeze Transformations.

5. In the Outliner, use the middle mouse button to drag the two spine controls (TorsoCTRLHi and TorsoCTRLLow) under the root control. Then drag the Root control with the middle mouse button under the MasterControl curve you just created. Figure 5.11 shows the ground control for the spine wave rig.

Now you can test your controls. In the 3D viewport you will see that any of your locked attributes are now grayed out and cannot be manipulated. You can also test the hierarchy of the controls by making sure the master control moves the root control.

Rigging for Flight

Flight rigging is best for characters that are swinging or flying through the air. A setup like this is beneficial for any character whose primary animation is not on the ground. A great example of this is a rag doll. If the character flies, swings, is held by the middle, or will be thrown, this is the master control technique to use. This setup is very cumbersome for walking or running because it is not relative to the ground.

So, what type of control do you need to create this rig? You need to be able to move the character from a central location on the rig. A ground control would be of little use on a character like this because the character isn't always standing up straight and walking. So, for the master control on this character, let's create a center of gravity and use that to place the rotational center of the character. This allows you to animate the character around its center of gravity and achieve fluid tumbling animations. The center of gravity will also be used to translate the character.

In this tutorial, we will focus on building the center of gravity control. The translation manipulators will be centered at this control. The center of gravity position will be determined using an average of the positions of the joints that make up the majority of the mass. For instance, in this example we will use the hands, feet, head, shoulders, and thigh joints to define our center of gravity. This will give you a good approximation of the character's center of mass. For this tutorial, you will want to make sure all the joints you are using to calculate the center of gravity are final. You will want to create your skeleton and revisit this chapter to set up the center of gravity.

Creating a Center of Gravity Control

To enable a rig for various types of acrobatic motion, a control at the center of gravity is the best solution. This control can be added to the spine wave rig or to any other type of rig that includes spine controls. To create a center of gravity control, follow these steps:

1. Open the Spine Wave rig you created in Chapter 4.

2. Create a control (as described in Chapter 3) that represents the center of gravity. The control in Figure 5.12 was created by snapping a one-degree curve to a simple poly sphere and then deleting the sphere.

3. Now center the pivot by using Modify > Center Pivot.

4. Snap the control to the origin, and freeze its transformations by using Modify > Freeze Transformations.

5. Rename the control to **COG** for center of gravity.

6. In the Outliner, select the two spine controls (TorsoCTRLHi and TorsoCTRLLow), and use the Ctrl+G key combination to group them. This creates an invisible null group, which you can use to rotate your entire figure.

7. Rename the null group to **MasterCTRLNull**.

8. Use Modify > Center Pivot to center the pivot between the controls.

9. Select the feet, wrists, thighs, shoulders, and head joints, and then select the COG control, shown in Figure 5.12. Use Constrain > Point Options, and make sure Maintain offset is turned off. Apply the point constraint.

10. Test your COG by manipulating the torso controls.

You can add many of these types of master control nodes to your figure if you need multiple master controls. Do this by parent constraining the parts of your figure that are constrained to the world or master control to these other controls as well. Then make a Boolean attribute that switches the parent constraints.

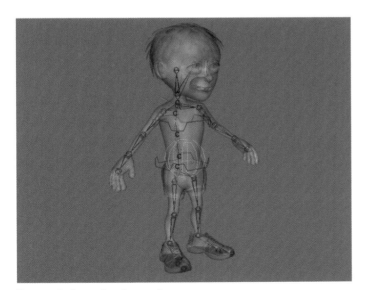

Figure 5.12 Center of gravity control

Creating a Script Node

We are going to create a scriptJob (which is the same as an expression) to get around an error created by the center of gravity. A scriptJob is a piece of code that is evaluated as you move the skeleton, and they can be processor-intensive because they are constantly evaluating.

The scriptJob we are creating here will help solve a cyclical error that was created with the center of gravity control we just created. Since the center of gravity is driven by the joint location and the joint root is driven by the center of gravity, we created a cyclical problem. Thus, as the center of gravity is rotated, the joints rotate and drive the center of gravity in an exponential fashion. This scriptJob gets around the problem by simply moving the master control's pivots to the location of the center of gravity.

Now, in order to get around the cyclical problem that was created by having the joints control the COG and then having the COG control the master group of the joints, we are going to add a script node. (You'll learn more about scripting in Chapter 15, "MEL Scripting: An Introduction.") To create a script to resolve the cyclical problem, follow these steps:

1. Open the rig you created in the COG control tutorial.

2. Choose Animation Editors > Expression Editor from the Window menu, and then choose Select Filter > By Script Node Name.

3. Name the new script **COGScriptNode**, and drop this code into the script field:

```
scriptJob -e "SelectionChanged" "string $sel[] = `ls -sl`;

 if($sel[0] == \"COG\")
{select -d COG;

 select MasterCTRLNull;

float $attr[] = `getAttr \"COG.t\"`;

move $attr[0] $attr[1] $attr[2] MasterCTRLNull.scalePivot
MasterCTRLNull.rotatePivot ;}"
```

The first line of this code gathers the selected items into a list. The if statement then creates an ongoing connection between the location of the COG and the pivot attributes of the MasterCTRLNull.

4. Now, hit the Create button, and then enable the option to execute on open/close.

5. Now choose Test Script in the Expression Editor, and then select the COG on your character.

Figure 5.13 shows one type of motion made possible by moving the COG control. Notice how the limbs seem to fall behind the rest of the body.

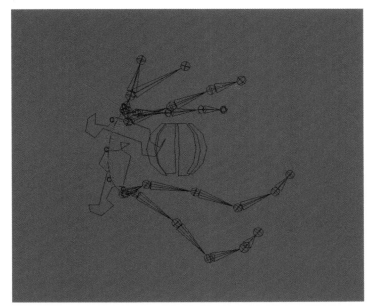

Figure 5.13 Skeleton with center of gravity

Now you have a working center of gravity that updates as your character moves around and your characters master controls are shown on the selection of the center of gravity. Also, as your center of gravity updates, the manipulators for your master group follow the center of gravity and are always positioned there. When you animate, you will need to set keyframes on both torso control movements since they are downstream from the master control null. You may want to make a MEL script that selects both controls and sets a key for them. With a control that accurately reflects the center of gravity, flips and aerials have never been easier to animate!

Conclusion

The pelvis and master controls of the rig, coupled with the spine, completes the backbone of the character and gives the character the ability to move around the scene. Whether you've selected to use the rigid hips technique or the free hips technique, your character is ready to move on to rigging the limbs. This chapter also covered the important control for moving the character in world space since the pelvis acts as the skeleton's root.

In the next chapter, we move on to the arms and shoulders. The arms include the forearm and shoulder blades.

Arms of Mass Deformation: Real and Unreal Arm Creation

6

The arms are rather difficult—not because of the elbow joint but because of the clavicle and the forearm. The clavicle is capable of many varied motions that are hard to duplicate effectively. The forearm will need additional rigging to be rotated correctly. In this chapter, we'll show you several methods for handling these involved body parts.

Chapter Contents
Shoulder and arm planning
Rigging the shoulder
Scapula deformation
Arm rigging
Handing forearm twist
Adding an FK/IK switch

Approaching the Shoulder and Arm

The shoulder and arm need a bit of forethought before jumping in. You need to decide on the level of detail you want to include in this area of your character. At this point, you should have a fairly good idea of the animator's needs and the movements required of the character.

When starting on the arm rigging, you should consider how the setup for your clavicle must be created in order to get the type of motion you want. You also need to consider how to handle the forearm rotation. Even if your character has a snakelike arm without any clavicle movement, it will most likely need to have forearm rotation so that you can turn the character's hands over. Another key decision is whether your character needs scapular (shoulder blade) deformation. Finally, decide on what you want constrained to your controllers and what you want left free to be controlled independently. All these determinations must be made during the planning phase.

In addition to covering the basics of arm and shoulder rigging, we will show you some tricks that can be added to the arm rig to increase its functionality. These include being able to switch from FK to IK and between IK and a spline-based rig. Figure 6.1 shows the completed shoulder and arm rig we want in this chapter.

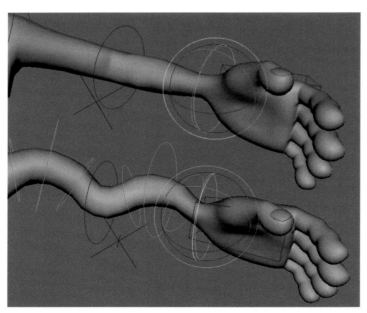

Figure 6.1 Finished shoulder with deformer and forearm twist

Once you've decided on the type of movement required, you'll need to focus on the approach you want to use and the associated controls that the animator will need.

The arm and the shoulder are going to need separate controls. The shoulder and clavicle will be controlled from the clavicle control. The hands will need separate controls because they will be at the end of the IK chain. The hands will also need to be able to constrain to the rest of the arm for movement. We will also show how to create an option for FK animation. This will require controls for the whole chain from the shoulder to the hand. We'll cover the hand setup in detail in Chapter 8, "Hands That Grab Your Attention: Hand Rigging Techniques." We'll show you how to build a wrist with two joints to avoid gimbal lock. Some riggers like to do this with the shoulder and knee joints as well. This can allow for a better bend but is really required only for joints like the wrist that require all three axes of movement.

Now, thinking of the arm as a whole, you can take care of the shoulder rotation and elbow hinging with IK and FK. You can select these joints when they need to be edited in FK, but you will also need controls for IK. In addition, you will want a control for the rotation of the clavicle for shrugging the shoulders. To accomplish this, we'll show how to place individual controls on each side, since shoulders need to be controlled independently. You'll also want a wrist control for the end of the IK chain (called the *IK handle*). In addition, you'll want another control at the wrist for rotation. Keep these controls simple so that the animator does not confuse the IK controls with the FK set. In this chapter, we'll keep them simple by creating clavicle, shoulder, elbow, and wrist IK joint controls that are similar in shape.

In summary, in this chapter you'll be adding the following controls to the shoulder and arm segments:

- FK arm control (including controls for the shoulder, elbow, and wrist)

- IK arm control at the wrist

- Clavicle rotation control for shrugging

- Switches for world and local movement

In Chapter 14, "Deforming, Organizing, and Bomb-Proofing Your Rig," we will talk about ways to deform your limb bones with secondary joint systems. We will also show how to create a stretch attribute for the limbs. In this chapter, we will focus on good rig building techniques. These will serve as a great foundation for the later, more advanced chapters.

In this chapter, we will show you several different options for shoulder, clavicle, and scapula setups. We will also show some elbow and forearm setups, and introduce some advanced tricks, such as an FK/IK switch. In each section, we present multiple ways to rig the arm and shoulder. Choose what you need, what your time constraints will allow, and have fun.

To keep things nice and clean, you will want to create groups dedicated to the separate parts of the figure. For the left arm, we are going to create an empty null group called LArm. You will want to take some time now to organize the spine and

95

■

APPROACHING THE SHOULDER AND ARM

master controls with separate null groups. As you group and organize, make sure you can hide joints without hiding their controls. One of your goals is to make a rig where the joints are not even visible and the animator worries only about animating the controls.

You will also want to mirror your arm, leg, and so forth, as you work through the tutorials. Mirroring basic rigs works with a little help, but basically, you will need to mirror from scratch. This is one of the more monotonous parts of rigging, but you will be glad you spent the time in the end.

Rigging the Shoulder

Before you begin rigging the shoulder, you need to make a decision: do you need clavicle and/or scapula deformations? Furry and cartoony characters often can get away without scapula deformation, but a human figure or most any CG character will need scapular deformation to be believable. If you don't need clavicle and scapula deformation, then you can save time on the rigging and skinning procedures. The simple shoulder setup we describe in the next section is an example of just such a rig.

Creating a Simple Shoulder Setup

In the simple shoulder setup, you create your shoulder straight from the root. You might want to do this if your character is going to be used as a background character or for a simple, no-frills rig. Table 6.1 shows the benefits and drawbacks to this setup.

▶ **Table 6.1** Simple Shoulder Setup Strengths and Weaknesses

Strengths	Weaknesses
Simple	No clavicle movement
Quick to set up	Less realistic
Great for background characters	

This setup does not allow clavicle or scapula rotation. It gives you a shoulder that has a defined, relative position to the upper spine. Now, this shoulder joint can move in a fairly realistic manner, but your character will not be able to shrug or droop his shoulders. It is used for simplistic, background characters that just don't need that type of functionality. Take a look at Figure 6.2, and then try creating one yourself. You will need to make a control for the shoulder. Make sure your control can be understood by all. The control that is built in the next section is a good example of the type of control you should use.

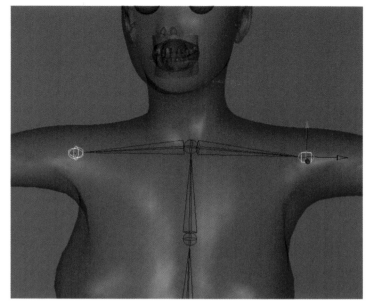

Figure 6.2 A simple shoulder setup

Creating a Clavicle-Shoulder Setup

The clavicle-shoulder setup lends itself to realism and allows drooping and shrugging shoulders. It also allows you to rotate bones upstream, which is needed for scapular rotation. Table 6.2 lists the strengths and weaknesses of this setup.

▷ **Table 6.2** Clavicle-Based Setup Strengths and Weaknesses

Strengths	Weaknesses
More realistic	More complex in setup
Allows for shrug and droop	
Used with scapular deformation	

One of the best ways to understand how this setup works is to pay careful attention to your own shoulder as you move it. Move your shoulder around, and notice its pivot point. The shoulder rotates around the point where the clavicle meets the sternum. Thus, the shoulder blades move a bit when the shoulders are pulled back because their pivot point is so far away. In Figure 6.3 you can see the clavicles and that they rotate from a position close to the midline.

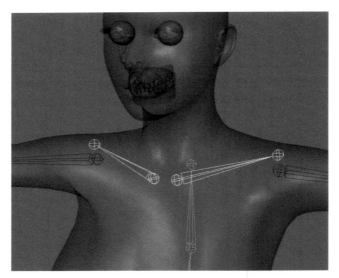

Figure 6.3 Temporary bone placement to show the pivot points

You need to carefully place the controls for this area. The clavicle, for instance, actually rotates from near the sternum. One control will be used for rotation for each clavicle. You want to be as clear as you can with your joint controls and communicate exactly what the animator can do with each. The rig we'll teach you next can be added to any figure. To create a clavicle-shoulder rig, follow these steps:

1. Create a clavicle joint. Make sure it is placed where the clavicle meets the upper sternum. This will be the rotation point for your clavicle and, later, for your scapula deformations.

2. Create a shoulder joint. Place it where the socket of the shoulder would be, as shown in Figure 6.4. Be cognizant of how the armpit will deform with bending. This might influence you to extend the shoulder joint a little farther than the actual shoulder's position for the sake of a better joint.

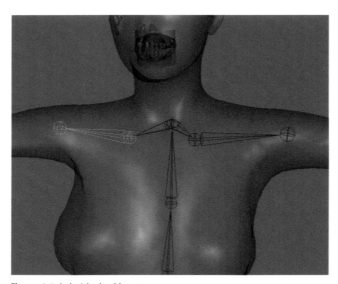

Figure 6.4 A clavicle shoulder setup

3. Orient your joints as described in Chapter 3, "Rigging That's Right: Rigging Concepts You Need to Know."

4. Rename the joints LClavicle and LShoulder. You can also mirror the new joints now, as shown in Figure 6.4.

Now, you'll need to create a control for the clavicle. You'll put this control on the shoulder so that it can be easily grabbed. You won't parent the control to the collar, since the collar's rotation will be driven from the control. If you did parent the control to the collar, it would cause a cyclical error, which happens whenever a parent's child becomes the driver of the parent. We talked about this issue in previous chapters. Be sure you understand this problem. By understanding why this occurs, you will be able to plan ahead and prevent cyclical errors from arising.

You will use this node-based control setup a lot during the creation of your character. Having a node-based control allows you to escape compounding rotations (cyclical errors) that are created with less carefully thought out controls. As you complete each step, consider the details and how you can customize the process for other parts of the body. As you use this control setup more and more, you will be able to quickly duplicate it, using only what you need. This setup is crucial for the final steps of the process because it makes controls that can still be visible after the skeleton is hidden.

Now, think about the best way to represent your shoulder controls. One control will be used to rotate each clavicle. You want to be clear when you create these joint controls and communicate exactly what the animator can do with each. Figure 6.5 shows some examples of descriptive controls. You can create an upstream joint control for the clavicle using the tutorial in Chapter 3. As an alternative, you can use groups to bypass the possible cyclical error problem. Either setup will work well here.

Figure 6.6 shows the finished setup.

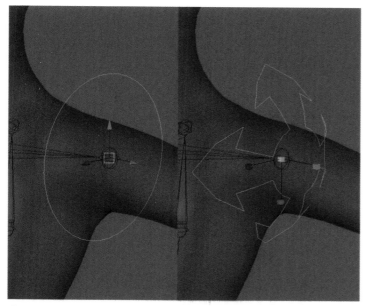

Figure 6.5 A clavicle control

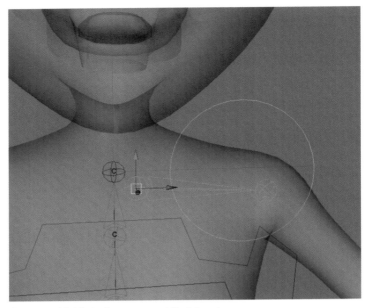

Figure 6.6 A finished collar setup on a stylized character

Handling Scapular Deformation

You can create scapular deformation in many ways. Most riggers have a favorite way of creating specific scapular deformations. Your favorite way will likely depend on the types of controls that drive the deformation.

You can create scapular deformations by just painting adequate skin weights. You need to be careful, however, in using some of these jointing methods, because they can create relationships where joints affect geometry that is not next to its parent. For example, if the character shrugs their shoulders, you wouldn't want the mesh lower than the scapula to necessarily move up with the shoulders. Another potential problem is that you might get unwanted pinching; if the mesh folds over itself, you'll get a bad seam.

In the tutorials that follow, we present two ways of overcoming the problems that exist in creating realistic scapular deformation. The two solutions we present here move the geometry and, basically, are an aid for creating the influence with painted weighting. The first solution is a bone setup, where the weights are adjusted for the scapula. The second solution is a cluster setup, where the affected geometry is driven by a cluster constrained to the clavicle itself.

Creating a Jointed Scapula

In real life, the scapula floats above the rib cage. In the jointed scapula solution, we will mimic the movement of the scapula under the skin and actually pull the skin in the direction of the clavicle rotation. The rig we'll teach you next can be added to any figure. To add a jointed scapula to the rig, follow these steps:

1. Create a joint that emanates from the origin of the clavicle and goes back to the top section of the scapula.

2. Next, create another joint that extends to the lower portion of the scapula. These bones will aid in the painting weights later in the book. Keep the skin weight of these joints at low values; you want there to be minimal deformation. Major deformation may cause bunching and artifacts in rendering. Remember that these joints do not have a parent-child relationship with neighboring joints of the spine.

3. Name the joints LScapulaUpper and LScapulaLower. You can also mirror here and create the right-upper and right-lower scapula joints.

You might want to lock all the translation and rotation attributes of the scapula joints, since they will not need to move. These joints will be driven by the clavicle in a realistic setup. So, to lock your joints, go into the attributes of each joint, right-click, and then select Lock Attribute from the pop-up menu. Figure 6.7 shows the completed jointed scapula setup.

Tip: To achieve even more realism, you might want to rotate the scapula joints around a defined point and mimic the floatation of the bone over the rib cage. If you choose to provide this functionality, don't lock the joints.

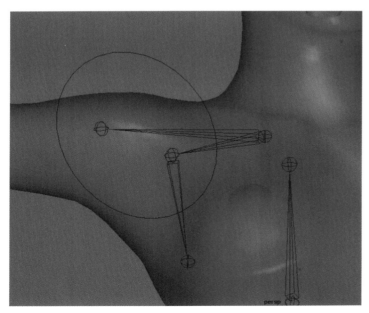

Figure 6.7 A jointed scapula setup

Creating a Cluster Scapula

Here is another setup that can help you in weighting the scapula. The cluster approach is easy to set up. It uses a different system to control the deformations. Clusters are nodes that drive groups of vertices. You can weight a cluster like a joint. The rig we'll teach you next can be added to any figure. To create a cluster-based scapula rig, follow these steps:

1.   Select the area you want to be affected by the scapula cluster. Select a generous area since you want a falloff that spreads away from the scapula.

2.   Create your cluster by using the cluster tool (Create Deformers > Cluster).

3.   Parent the new cluster handle under the collar joint by dragging the cluster with the middle mouse under the collar object in the Outliner.

4.   Name the cluster descriptively, such as LScapulaCluster.

   Figure 6.8 shows the finished cluster scapula setup.

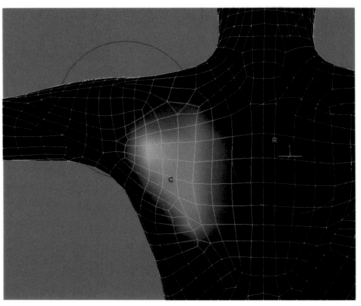

Figure 6.8 A cluster scapula weighting

Adapting Scapular Setups for the Spine Wave

When using a scapular setup in a character with a deformable spine, make sure that none of the spine deformation echoes down through the arms. Be sure to connect to the highest joint in the BindSpine, and build your clavicles and shoulders from there. No scaling will be perpetuated.

Creating the Arm

When creating an arm, you need to know where you are going before you start creating. You need to identify what type of forearm rotation will be needed by your character and decide whether to include deformers and/or stretchiness. There are a few popular techniques for creating forearm rotation, including the forearm joint, the cluster, and the advanced setup with a point on the surface node. Each of these methods, although different in their setup, will produce similar results. If you choose a cluster-driven forearm rotation, you will not need an extra joint. The cluster acts as an additional joint. If you elect to go with a jointed forearm rotation, you will need an extra joint. The extra joint will make for easy initial painting weights of the forearm. We'll show you an advanced setup that uses a point on the surface node. Look at the options for rotations, and compare them to the type of forearm motion your character needs.

Dealing with Forearm Rotation

Forearm rotation is one of the standard problems in rigging. If you look at your own forearm, you will notice that when you bend your wrist, the movement of the skin is localized around the wrist. This is also the case if you rotate your wrist down and then up. However, when you roll (or twist) your wrist, the skin falloff from the hand carries all the way up the forearm, causing the muscles that run up your forearm to wrap around the arm. We want to create an automated process for achieving a similar forearm in 3D. Even if your character is cartoony, you will want to plan for forearm rotation. If you don't add the ability to handle a forearm twist, then the skin at the forearm stretches at the wrist, causing unsightly artifacts.

A single-joint wrist makes different falloff control for various rotations difficult, unless you create some way to give the animators that control. A single wrist joint causes the skin to be pulled together in an unrealistic and undesired way. You can see this effect when any long cylindrical geometry is twisted, but it is most noticeable in the forearm. It is also called the *candy wrapper effect* or *collapsing geometry*. Several solutions are available to deal with this problem.

The first solution actually places an additional bone in the forearm and then limits its rotation abilities. The limits allow this extra joint to rotate only on its X-axis, which faces down the chain.

The second solution is a cluster-driven forearm. Think of it as a controlling entity, a grouping of all the vertices that allows the animator to manipulate them from a specific point or control. If you create a cluster that rotates half as much as the wrist, the forearm can be driven by this joint, so when the wrist twists, the forearm gradually twists along with the wrist. This is an elegant solution that doesn't require an extra joint. You can use this solution for additional control after the skinning is done.

A third option, which we will cover later in this chapter, includes an advanced setup using FK/IK switching. It creates a floating joint that works similarly to the inline joint method, but you gain individual control over the joint's position. You do not have to add anything to the forearm at this time. Table 6.3 compares the various forearm rotation techniques.

Forearm Bone Setup	Cluster Forearm Setup	Advanced Setup
Easy to create	Easy to create	More complex
Requires limits with IK setup	Doesn't interfere with bone structure	Requires FK/IK switch
Defined with weight mapping	Defined with weight mapping	Forearm rotation will be handled automatically later, with advanced deformations
	Doesn't need special IK system	

Creating a Double-Joint Forearm Roll

The double-joint forearm roll is the more commonly used setup. You can even use another joint in the upper arm (upper arm area), if you want, to help distribute weights in the shoulder deformations. This is usually easier to use as compared to the setup that uses a cluster. It is easier to set up because it will weight itself fairly accurately when binding. It still requires regular joint cleanup, which we will talk about in Chapter 18, "The Skinny on Skinning: Effective Surface Attachment." You'll use a modified version of the double-joint forearm later in this chapter in the advanced setup of the arm. The modified version will actually have a floating joint in place of an in-line joint.

CREATING THE JOINTS

The first step in creating a double-joint forearm rig is to build the joints. To build the joints for the double-joint forearm rig, follow these steps:

1. Create a humerus (upper arm) and forearm. The humerus needs to be only one joint; the forearm needs to be two.

2. You can easily set up equal joints here by placing an isolated joint where you want your wrist to be. Check its position in perspective view. Now, create a locator, as shown in Figure 6.9.

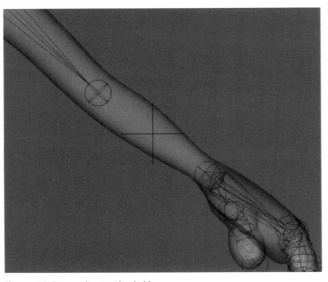

Figure 6.9 Forearm locator placeholder

3. Point-constrain the locator to both the wrist joint and the elbow joint. First select the two joints, then select the locator, and finally choose Constrain > Point.

4. Create the forearm middle joint. Use the joint tool, select the elbow joint, and then create a new joint, as shown in Figure 6.10.

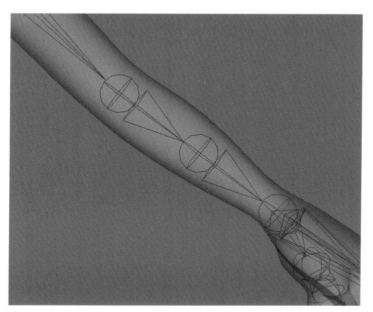

Figure 6.10 Forearm joint for rotation

5. Snap the new joint to the locator by pressing and holding the V key while moving the joint. Using this approach, the middle forearm joint is always centered between the wrist and elbow.

6. Move the wrist under the new middle forearm joint by middle mouse dragging in the Outliner.

7. Delete the locator, and then mirror the joints to create the right arm.

8. Name and orient all the joints. Make sure you name the joints something easily understood, such as LForearm and LWrist. Be sure to orient the joints so the X-axis runs parallel to the joints and the Z-axis is the major axis for bending. Orient according to the tutorials in Chapter 3.

Tip: You can orient the joint quickly and properly by using an aim constraint. Have the center joint aim at the wrist joint. Aim down the X-axis, and have the shoulder joint be the Up vector object. This places it perfectly in line. When you're finished, delete all the constraints, and it will be ready to be placed into the hierarchy.

ADDING SCRIPTED CONSTRAINTS

The next step in creating a double-joint forearm rig is to add some constraints using MEL scripting. Usually, you would now orient-constrain the joint to the control, but since you are controlling it partially, you need an expression for this one.

To add the scripted constraints to the double-joint forearm rig, follow these steps:

1. Make a new expression by selecting LWrist and then opening the Expression Editor. Choose Window > Animation Editors > Expression Editor.

2. Create an expression called LForearmRot.

3. Add this code:

```
LForearm.rotateX = .5 * LWristRotationCTRL.rotateX;
LWrist.rotateX = .5 * LWristRotationCTRL.rotateX;
LWrist.rotateY = LWristRotationCTRL.rotateY;
LWrist.rotateZ = LWristRotationCTRL.rotateZ;
```

4. Now test the rotation of the wrist to see whether it rotates the forearm joint and wrist, as shown in Figure 6.11.

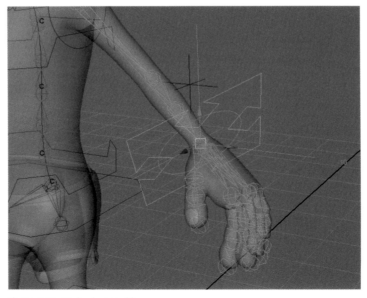

Figure 6.11 Finalized setup of forearm

ADDING IK

The final step in creating a double-joint forearm rig is to add IK. The IK we create here will be a little different from a typical IK chain. The middle forearm joint will need some special attention. The pole vector for the IK must be created correctly with the right orientation. We'll show you how in the tutorial that follows.

To add IK for the double-joint forearm rig, follow these steps:

1. Choose Skeleton > IK Handle Tool, and use the tool to select the shoulder and then the forearm joint.

2. In the Hypergraph, choose the Input and Output Connections button, and select the effector.

3. Press the Ins key, and snap the effector to the wrist.

4. Lock the Y and Z rotation values of the forearm joint.

5. Create a locator, and parent-constrain it to LClavicle. Now, snap it to the elbow using the Move tool while holding the V key and then Freeze Transformations. Select the IK handle, and look in the Channel Box. Move the locator by placing the pole vector X, Y, and Z values into the Translate box of the locator. We recommend you double or triple each value to get a good distance from the back of the elbow. You want the locator to be far enough away from the arm that it is not be easily passed with regular arm movement. Use Freeze Transformations again to zero out the locator.

Tip: Some scripts are available that will orient pole vectors for you. Some good scripts for orienting pole vectors are ggmLegPoleVector.mel by Geordie Martinez and djBuildPoleVector by David Johnson. Both of these solutions create a pole vector without reorienting the rotations of the chain.

---

6. Pole vector–constrain the IK handle to the locator by selecting the locator and then the IK handle. Then choose Constrain > Pole Vector.

7. To set up the wrist translation control, create a curve control, and snap the control to the wrist joint. Orient the control so that its X-axis is in line with the joint. Parent-constrain this control's null to LClavicle. Use Freeze Transformations on the control.

8. Select the control's null and then the IK handle, and perform a point constraint. You might want to lock the Translate values for the IK handle so it isn't accidentally moved from this position.

9. Aim-constrain the control's null to the forearm. For correct rotation, be sure to use Object Rotation Up with the shoulder joint as the object. Make sure that the correct axis of the joint is identified as up. In this case, identify the Z-axis.

In Chapter 14, we'll show you how to add stretching ability to the arms. Once you get to that chapter, you can revisit the arm rig and add this feature. Remember that you have an extra joint and you will need to account for the stretching in that joint too. The final scaling that will come from the setup will need to be applied to the forearm joint, as well as the shoulder and elbow joints, to drive the stretching.

Creating a Cluster-Driven Forearm Roll

Although the double-joint forearm rig is more common, you can use the cluster-driven forearm technique if you need to improve results after the joint weight painting is finished. It is generally applied after the skin cluster is calculated, so it won't interfere with the skinCluster node. The cluster will influence the surface after it is bound. It will need to have painted weights just like the joints.

To create a cluster-driven forearm rig, follow these steps:

1. Create a humerus and forearm. For this setup, you'll need only the elbow and wrist joints. Name the joints LElbow, LForearm, and LWrist. You can mirror now to create the right elbow, forearm, and wrist.

2. Now, select the vertices between the wrist and the elbow, as shown in Figure 6.12.

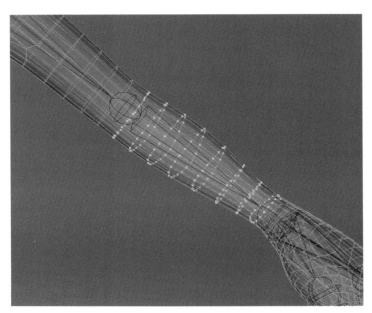

Figure 6.12 Selection for cluster forearm. Final weighting will happen after skin eights are painted

3. Create a cluster using Create Deformers > Cluster. Name the cluster LForearmCluster.

4. Orient the cluster using the orientation principles in Chapter 3. Select the cluster, and orient its X-axis down the arm.

5. Hook the wrist rotation to the wrist rotation control named LWristCTRL. Refer to the control process in Chapter 3 for details on how to create this type of control.

6. Use the Expression Editor to make a new expression. Select the LWristControl, and choose Window > Animation Editors > Expression Editor. Create an expression called LForearmRot, and use this code:

```
LForearmCluster.rotateX = .5 * LWristRotationControl.rotateX;
```

7. Now test the wrist rotation to see whether it rotates the cluster and the wrist.

8. Remember to parent the cluster under the elbow so that the elbow rotation moves the cluster. Select the cluster and then the elbow joint, as shown in Figure 6.13, and then press the P key (child-parent-P) or drag the cluster under the elbow joint. This creates a null group. Name the group LForeArmClusterNull.

Figure 6.13 Selection for cluster forearm

Once the cluster is created, you can add IK controls to this setup. For a step-by-step refresher, see the "Adding IK" section in the double-joint forearm roll tutorial earlier in this chapter. The process works the same for the cluster-driven forearm rig. Figure 6.14 shows the completed forearm setup.

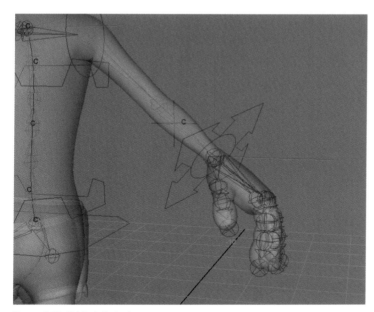

Figure 6.14 Finished cluster forearm

Using an Advanced Skeleton Setup and an FK/IK Switch

To prepare for the advanced setup you'll create later in the book, you need to create sections of the arm that can distort and break without breaking your rig. When you're finished, the rig simulates a forearm turned to rubber; you'll be able to stretch and bend it into a U shape.

You will also tackle an FK/IK switch. Animators usually want, and regularly need, the ability to switch from IK to FK on the fly. Animators then have the option to switch to FK joint animation when they need to do so. It is always best to give the animators the option, if you can. Maya includes a built-in FK/IK blending that allows animators to switch control after they have set up an IK chain. Some animators and studios might want this functionality built from scratch rather than use Maya's prebuilt setup. Here is a way to build your own FK/IK switching system.

To add an FK/IK switch to the arm rig, follow these steps:

1. If you haven't already, create a humerus and forearm. For this setup, you need only one elbow and one wrist joint. Name the joints LElbow and LWrist. This is the setup we will use for the advanced setup.

2. Orient your joints using the methods described in Chapter 3. Make sure your joints orient appropriately. You will be using the orientation to hook up handles and such. If the joints don't orient appropriately, you can manually edit the joints, as we explained in Chapter 3.

3. Duplicate your arm from the shoulder down. Select the shoulder, elbow, and wrist joints. Duplicate the arm twice, naming one chain LShoulderIK, LelbowIK, and LWristIK. Name the other chain LShoulderFK, LelbowFK, and LWristFK. Parent-constrain LShoulder to the IK and the FK joints. Repeat the process with the elbow joints and the wrist joints. Parent-constrain them to their FK and IK counterparts.

4. Now that you have your joints named, you can add IK to the IK joint chain, as we described earlier in this chapter in the "Creating the Joints" section.

5. Parent-constrain the elbow locator to LClavicle. Make sure there is a parent constraint on the clavicle to its handle and from its null group to the top of the spine.

6. Create a floating secondary wrist joint downstream from LWrist. Name it LHandBND, and snap it to LWrist. We will use the floating joint for orienting the hand. You can add quick fingers here, if you want, downstream from LHandBND.

7. Make sure all your joints are oriented, and make sure all your nulls and joints are named descriptively, consistently, and uniquely. There should be no "group1" or "joint4" elements listed in the Outliner.

 Tip: Remember, it is good habit to orient and rename when creating joints, null groups, and controls in Maya so that organization and functionality does not become a problem.

Adding Hand Controls

In the next procedure, you'll create hand controls. These controls are fairly simple. They allow the animator to grab one and control the hand IK. This handle will be able to move, and the arm will follow. It will also be able to stretch automatically (after you add the advanced rigging from Chapter 14).

To add hand controls, follow these steps:

1. Create a left hand control. We used one that looks like a cowbell and positioned it around the palm. Move the control into place, near the joint it is controlling, and freeze its orientations. Name this control LHandIKCTRL.

2. Create and orient its null group. Name the null group LHandIKCTRLNull. Use the control creation process we showed you in Chapter 3. Remember that the control should be zeroed and free from values or constraints. The Null group is used for these values and connections while the control needs to be animated.

3. Offset the center of rotation for both the null and control so that they are on the wrist joint. Point-constrain the IK handle to the hand control.

4. For the world orientation switch, parent-constrain LHandIKCTRLNull to the LClavicle. Parent-constrain the LHandIKCTRLNull to an empty group named LArm. We will use this group for organization a little later in the chapter. Remember to select by "driver then driven."

5. Create an enum attribute (as described in Chapter 3) for LHandIKCTRL. Name the attribute World Orient. Name the options World and Figure. Have a set-driven key drive the parent Figure and World attributes you just created.

6. Create a wrist control, give it a null group, and make sure the null group and the control are oriented to the joint. Name this joint LWristCTRL. Use Freeze Transformations on this control.

7. Select the LWristCTRL joint and the LHandBND joint, and create a parent constraint between the two using the Constrain > Parent command.

8. Select the LWrist joint and then the LWristCTRLNull. Then create a point and an orient constraint between the two using the Constraint > Point command and the Constraint > Orient command.

9. Select LHandIKCTRL and then LWristCTRLNull 0, and create a parent constraint between the two using the Constraint > Orient command.

Creating an FK/IK Switch

The next step is to actually create the FK/IK switch. This switch allows the animator the flexibility to animate IK as well as FK. The IK and the FK setups each have their own controls for manipulation. The switch is an attribute of the LWristCTRL, which will follow the arm whether in IK or FK.

To create an FK/IK switch, follow these steps:

1. Select LWristCTRL, and add a float attribute FK/IK. Set a minimum of 0 and a maximum of 10 with a default of 0.

2. Select the LShoulder, and in the Channel Box, change LWristIKWO to 0. Do the same with the LElbow and the LWrist.

3. Create a set driven key by assigning FK/IK as the driver and each joint in turn as the driven. If you want to use FK as the default control, choose FK/IK = 0 for a weight of 1 on the IK system, and then make the FK/IK = 10 for the FK system. For an IK default, choose FK/IK = 10 on the IK system and FK/IK = 0 on the FK system.

4. Select LWristCTRL and then the LHandBND joint, and create a parent constraint between the two using the Constrain > Parent command.

5. Point-constrain the IK handle to the hand control by selecting the LHandIKCTRL (driver), selecting the LArmIKHandle (driven), and then choosing the Constrain > Point command. You can lock the translate values of the IK handle now by right-clicking the values in the Attribute Editor.

6. Orient LWristCTRLNull to the LHandIKCTRL by selecting the LHandIKCTRL (driver), selecting the LWristCTRLNull (driven), and then choosing the Constrain > Point command.

Orienting the Wrist

Now, let's work on wrist orientation. The wrist must follow the forearm system that you chose. You need that same type of setup in the FK/IK switch to orient the wrist control.

To orient the wrist joint, follow these steps:

1. First, point-constrain the position of your wrist control to the LWrist joint. To do this, select LWrist and then LWristCTRLNull, and use Constrain > Point.

2. Now orient-constrain the wrist control null group. Orient LWristCTRLNull to LHandIKCTRL and then to LWrist. Remember to select "driver then driven." Now your wrist control should be oriented to the wrist joint and the hand control.

3. Open the Channel Box for LWristCTRLNull. You will see two weights, LWrist and LHandIKCTRL. In the Set Driven Key window, start to hook this up. Of course, when the FK\IK switch is on IK, the weighting for LHandIKCTRL will be 1, and the LWrist will be 0. For the FK, the values will be switched. When you save your scene, it will save whether the switch is set for FK or IK. Since you call the switch FKIK, you make it so 0 equals FK and 10 equals IK. This is because of the order of their names. This process sets up the world orientation for the IK control. Figure 6.15 shows the final switching FK/IK setup.

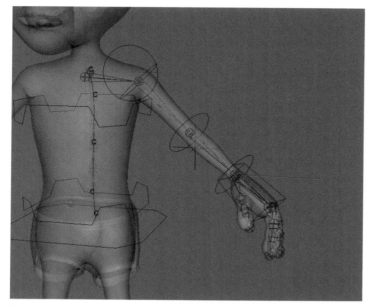

Figure 6.15 FK/IK and world switches in an FK/IK arm

Figure 6.16 shows the final advanced rig, and Figure 6.17 provides a diagram of the constraints you used. Remember that the controls need to have rotation and translation values of zero. Its null has all of its rotation values and connections.

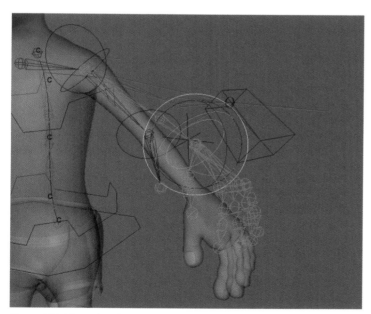

Figure 6.16 Advanced rig showing FK/IK switching

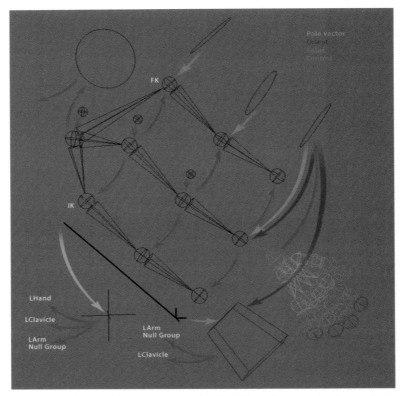

Figure 6.17 A diagram of the constraints needed on the FK/IK arm. Remember that the control nulls have the constraints.

Grouping the Arm

When grouping and organizing the figure, you will want to have the figure under the main group that we talked about in Chapter 3. You will also want to separate your figure into its parts. Each part has its own null group. Each of these groups also acts as the world-relative control for the specific part of the figure. For instance, the pole vector for the wrist and the IK control for the hand both need a world-relative control. They can be parented to the LArm null group, which holds all the left arm parts.

You want to clean your rig's hierarchy in the Outliner as you create it. You also need to make sure your controls and joints are in separate hierarchies so you can hide the joints later.

Mirroring the Arm

When you create the right arm, you will want to mirror the basic joint chain and then reorient it because it will, most likely, have taken on some of the orientation from the left arm. You will also want to duplicate and mirror your controls. You can do this by duplicating the curve and scaling it across the X-axis numerically upon creation. Build the rest of the right arm from scratch. Current mirroring tools will not take over all the controls and orientations correctly. There is really no easy way to mirror advanced controls across the midline.

Conclusion

This chapter introduced you to rigging limbs, beginning with the arms. We tackled the arms first because they can be tricky with the twist in the forearm and the specialized handling required for the clavicle and the shoulder blades. Then, we went over how to build an FK/IK switch from scratch and add it to the rig. After all that work, the final arm and shoulder rig looks great and moves realistically. In Chapter 14, we will add independent deformers that will allow the bones to bend and to stretch. So, now that you have tried a variety of ways to articulate your arm, you are ready to continue.

In the next chapter, "Getting a Leg (or Two) Up on the Competition: Understanding Legs and Feet," you'll move on to the next major limbs, the legs, and we'll cover feet, too!

Getting a Leg Up on the Competition: Understanding Legs and Feet

7

Like the arm, the leg has a main ball-in-socket joint with a hinge joint immediately downstream. But, when you are working on an arm, your focus is on the rotation of the forearm, where the shin, with its similar bone structure, does not rotate to the degree of the forearm. Also, with the leg you have the ankle and foot joints to deal with. This chapter will go over some ways to tackle the leg and foot rig, and each has unique benefits.

Chapter Contents
Planning the legs and feet
Creating the classic legs
Creating the classic reverse foot setup
Creating an advanced leg

Planning the Legs and Feet

One fact that will help when rigging the legs and feet is that they are limited in their freedom of rotation. The hip joint is a universal or ball-in-socket joint type that can rotate around all three axes, but the knee joint is a hinge joint with only a single axis of rotation. Because the knee joint is a simple hinge joint, you will need to include a pole vector constraint to ensure that the knee bends only in the right direction. The heel joint is flexible but fairly restricted with only a limited ability to twist to the right and left. The ball of the foot joint is also a simple hinge-type joint with a single axis of rotation.

Figure 7.1 shows a completed leg and foot rig.

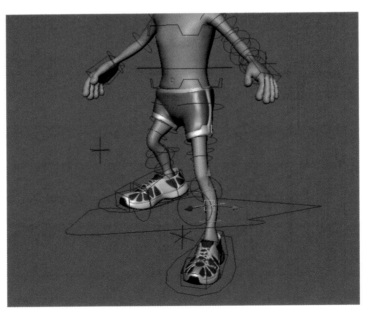

Figure 7.1 Completed leg rig

General Planning

With multiple rotating joints, the leg rig requires several IK chains in order to enable the joints to rotate. One IK chain runs between the hip joint and ankle joint and will bend at the knee. A second IK chain runs from the ankle to the ball of the foot, which enables the ball of the foot to rotate. A third IK chain runs from the ball of the foot to the toe, which lets the foot rotate about the toe.

To automate the animation of the foot, we'll show how to use additional IK chains that run in reverse. These IK chains enable the foot to bend automatically as the foot control is moved backward in world space. We will show you two ways to set these controls up. First, you'll see a traditional IK leg, which includes a secondary reverse rig that allows rotation from the tip of the toe as well as from the ball of the foot. We will refer to this as the *classic reverse foot setup*. The second, which we call the *advanced foot setup*, relies on null grouping to achieve a similar animation experience.

Understanding Pivots

When it comes to feet, pivot points play an important role. Correctly placing the pivots enables the leg and foot to rotate realistically. Also, a good understanding of the types of IK solvers available helps you choose the right solution for creating a realistic foot.

The pivot for the knee typically is positioned at the front of the knee so that the joint is slightly bent. This helps the IK chain bend properly. The ankle pivot needs to be located at the heel, and the ball of the foot joint's pivot needs to be located at the ball of the foot. This is so the ankle and the ball can rotate from the correct area.

Tip: If your character absolutely has to have a straight knee, as is common for many cartoon characters, you can set the preferred angle value on the knee joint. This will tell the IK handle which way to bend.

What Are Your Goals for Movement?

One of the key factors when planning your leg rigs is to consider how your character moves. Will the character be walking with a normal stride? Will the character walk on their toes? Is the character's leg IK going to be standard IK with a human, knee-like joint, or will it bend backward like a flamingo? Take a look at the joints of your figure. Are they going to be able to sustain the bending that they will need, without becoming *faceted* (rough-looking)? You might need to make changes at this time to ensure that the model has the resolution for proper and efficient bending and articulation.

Once you verify that the model has sufficient resolution, the next planning step is to consider where you want to place the controls. What kind of movement will the controls need to facilitate? Do you want the ability to roll the foot onto its toes? If you understand how the legs need to move, you can build the leg rig with the controls needed to produce the desired movement.

When planning the leg and foot rig, think of the animator and how they intend to accomplish the animation needed. Will they make the character walk by moving the character's joints individually using forward kinematics (FK) or by rotating the entire leg to position the feet using inverse kinematics (IK)? Using FK is an easy way to move the entire leg, but it requires that you rotate the feet independently and line up their positions with the ground plane. If you need to control exactly where the feet are positioned, then IK is usually a faster solution. A rig with the ability to switch between IK and FK provides the best of both techniques.

Leg Rig Options

For leg and foot rigs, you'll look at two basic approaches. The first we will take you through is the traditional IK leg with the reverse foot setup. This approach is easy to implement and provides simple, basic movement.

The second option is an advanced IK/FK, world/local switch, reverse foot modification technique. Don't worry; it is easier than it sounds. With this type of rig, the leg and foot can switch between IK and FK and between world and local orientation, giving you the ability to control what drives the end of the appendages. This will also allow you to accurately move your character within world space. Table 7-1 lists the advantages of the leg rig, and Table 7-2 lists the advantages of the foot rig.

▶ **Table 7.1** Leg Rig Option Comparison

Classic IK Leg	Advanced Leg
Easiest to create	More complex
Simple organization	IK/FK switch, world/local foot switch
Simple to use	Offers more options to animators

▶ **Table 7.2** Foot Rig Setup Comparison

Classic Reverse Foot	Reverse Foot Modification
Traditional setup	Simpler setup
Uses reverse bones	Uses constraints and controls for reverse foot functionality

Creating the Classic Legs

The classic leg consists of bones for the upper leg, the lower leg, the foot, and the toes. The upper leg attaches to the hip joint. The joints for the leg and foot rig are located at the knee, the ankle, and the ball of the foot.

Classic Leg and Foot with IK

The difficult part of the leg and foot rig is setting up the IK chains. The rig actually has three separate IK chains that work together and a separate IK chain set that runs backward. You will create a main chain, an FK chain, and an IK chain. The main chain can be driven by either the IK or FK chain, depending on how you set up the switch. You will also create a series of IK chains to control the foot rotation. This part usually is referred to as the *reverse foot* setup.

The first IK chain runs between the hip and the ankle to enable the hinge joint at the knee. For this IK chain, you'll want to set up a pole vector constraint to define the direction that the knee will bend.

Creating IK for Legs

To create the IK for the legs, follow these steps:

1. Display your leg in the side view. Select the left hip joint. Then, using the Skeleton > Joint tool, create all of the joints down to the toe, including the thigh, knee, ankle, ball, and toe joints. If you need to tweak their position, press and hold the Ins key, and with the middle mouse button drag the joint into place. Tweaking will not affect the downstream joints. Use the Skeleton > Orient Joints comment on them, and follow up by finishing their rotations using the concepts introduced in Chapter 3, "Rigging That's Right: Concepts You Need to Know." Now, rename the joints LThigh, LKnee, LAnkle, Lball, and Ltoe, respectively. Figure 7.2 shows the correct position of the leg and foot bones for this rig.

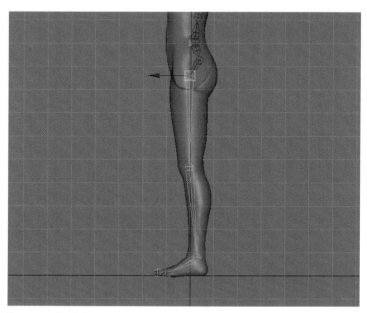

Figure 7.2 Simple leg setup

2. Using the Skeleton > IK Handle Tool command, select the thigh joint and then the ankle joint. This creates an RPSolver IK, which means its motion is controlled by a rotate plane. Name this IK handle LLegIK.

3. Create a locator, and snap it to the knee by pressing and holding the V key and then using the Move tool to reposition the locator. Use Freeze Transformations on this locator. Name the locator LKneePole.

4. Select the LLegIK IK handle, and check the Channel Box for the vector values. Move the locator by placing the pole vector values into the Translate box of the locator. We recommend you double or triple each value to get a desired distance, as we talked about in Chapter 6, "Arms of Mass Deformation: Real and Unreal Arm Creation," with the elbow joint. This positions the locator a distance from the knee so it is easy to select and manipulate. You can also use the tools that we discussed in Chapter 6 to get a correct pole placement. Use Freeze Transformations on the locater now. This will be its new default position. By freezing transformations again, you can easily get back to the bind pose by entering values of 0, 0, 0.

Tip: You can find scripts at sites such as HighEnd3D.com that automate the process of setting up a pole vector constraint. Also, you'll need to make sure your thigh and knee are not rotated after constraining to the pole vector. This erroneous rotation might cause bad rotation values later.

5. Select the LKneePole locator and then the LLegIK IK handle. Choose Constrain > Pole Vector.

Once the pole vector is in place, the IK for the leg is complete, as shown in Figure 7.3. You will set up the LKneePole locator's parents later. The locator will be able to be driven by the foot, hip, or world.

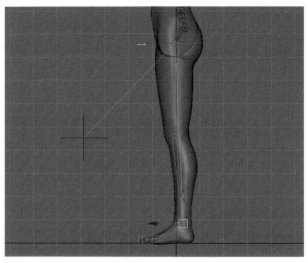

Figure 7.3 Leg IK setup

The Classic Reverse Foot Setup

The leg setup is straightforward and easy, but the foot requires a little more attention. Foot rigging begins with the IK chains we talked about earlier in the chapter. The first foot IK chain runs from the ankle joint to the ball of the foot joint, and a second chain runs between the ball of the foot and the end of the toes. These IK chains let the foot tap up and down and allow the toes to flex and point.

The final foot IK chain set runs in reverse to automatically bend the foot and toes when the foot is pulled backward. Three more IK chains run from the heel to the toes, from the toe to the ball of the foot, and then from the ball to the ankle. Figure 7.4 shows the various IK chains for the foot. Remember that each control on the diagram actually has a null that holds the control values and is constrained.

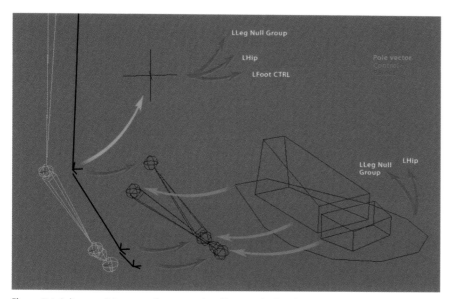

Figure 7.4 A diagram of the reverse foot connections. The control nulls will have the incoming constraints.

To control IK for the foot, you'll want to add controls at the heel, the ball of the foot, and the toes. With these controls, you can rotate and position the feet exactly where you need them to be.

Creating a Reverse Foot

To create a reverse foot, follow these steps:

1. Create the left foot and toe joints. Set up two SCSolvers. You can find these using the Skeleton > IK Handle command option box. Specifically, you can find the option under Current Solver. Create one that runs from the ankle to the ball and another from the ball to the toe, as shown in Figure 7.5. Name these LHeelIK and LBallIK.

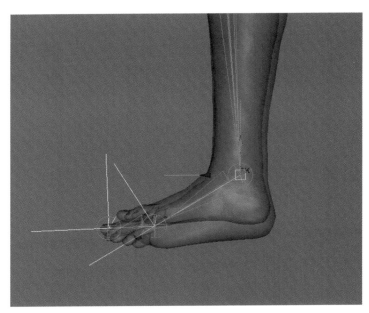

Figure 7.5 RPSolver and SCSolvers preparing for a reverse foot

2. Create a new reverse joint chain that starts at the heel. The next joint is snapped to the toe, then next to the ball, and then next to the ankle, as shown in Figure 7.6. Use Skeleton > Orient on the joints, and rename them to LRvHeel, LRvToe, and so on.

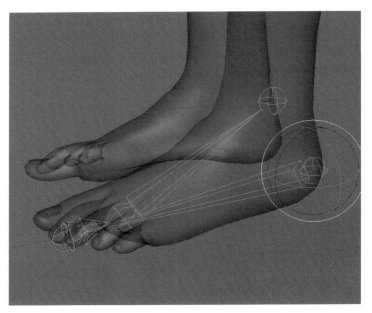

Figure 7.6 Reverse foot joint chain

3. Next, parent-constrain each of the IK handles of the main skeleton to the corresponding reverse foot joints. For instance, the LLegIK handle needs to be parent-constrained to the LRvHeel joint. Remember to select "driver then driven." The drivers are the joints.

4. Create a foot control, a toe control, and a ball control. Use the control creation techniques we introduced in Chapter 3 to create and align these controls. Figure 7.7 shows a sample control.

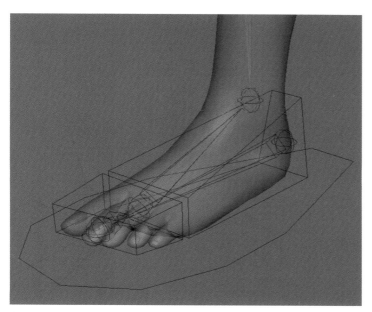

Figure 7.7 Example control design

5. During this process, name the foot control LRvHeel. You can leave the pivot for the foot at the heel. The foot box will control the ball rotation, and the toe box will control the toe rotation. Figure 7.8 shows the resulting rigged foot.

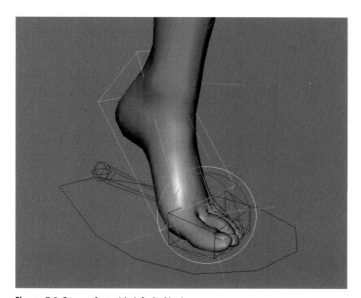

Figure 7.8 Reverse foot with default skinning

Creating the Advanced Leg

The classic leg rig works for simple characters, but as a character's animation needs become more complex, the rig needs to be more advanced. The limits of the classic leg rig become apparent during animation, particularly when compared to a stretchy FK and IK leg setup. The ability to switch between FK and IK greatly speeds up the animation process. The world and local parenting also adds to the value of the rig. Many of the advanced options you can create in a leg are addressed with an advanced leg rig that allows switching between FK/IK, stretchy joints, and world/local orientation. All of these little things add up to some great legs and easy animation.

You can use Maya's stock FK/IK switch as well. When you create an SCsolver IK or an RPSolver IK, the IK Blend attribute controls whether you manipulate the joints by IK or FK. The stock switch also is color-coded so you know which joint type you are on. The choice of which IK set will show up as the default will probably be made by the Character Setup Lead. This can be set upon the final state of these switches at final save.

Creating Legs and Feet with an FK/IK Switch and a World/Local Switch

Animators usually prefer to animate with IK, but sometimes a character's movement requires the precise control of FK. Establishing a rig that can easily switch between IK and FK is a huge help to animators. To accomplish this, we'll show how to create three joint chains for the main part of the leg. The first will be a main chain that will be parent-constrained to the other two. Then we'll show how to create an IK chain and an FK chain. Finally, we will show how to set up a switch to control the parent constraint weight.

Once you've set those up, you'll add the ability to switch between local and world space. With this ability, the feet can be positioned using world coordinates, which makes it easy to keep a character on a path or sidewalk, while still maintaining the ability to offset the character using local coordinates. Figure 7.9 is a diagram showing the connections. Remember that you want the controls free from incoming connections. Each control here has a null that takes these connections, so that the actual control can be used for animation.

To create an advanced leg and foot with duplicate chains for IK, follow these steps:

1. Create an individual floating joint, and name it LHip. In the Outliner, parent the new floating joint to the lower torso control. Middle mouse drag LHip under TorsoControlLow.

2. Create the rest of the leg and foot joint chain starting with the thigh joint. Orient the joints, and name them LThigh, LKnee, LAnkle, LBall, and LToe. Label these joints in the Outliner or in each individual joint's attribute label field. Figure 7.10 shows the joints needed for this rig.

3. Duplicate this joint chain twice, and rename it with Modify > Search and Replace Names. Give one of the chain names the prefix of LIK and the other LFK.

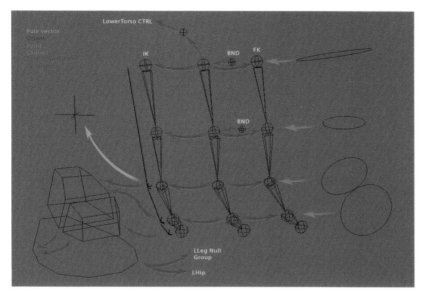

Figure 7.9 A diagram of the FK and IK leg . The controls should remain free of constraints for animation. Their nulls hold these connections.

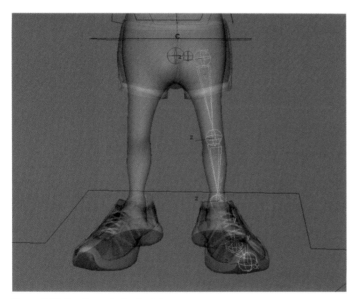

Figure 7.10 Creating and orienting joints

4. Set up the IK on the LIK chain:

   a. Make an RPSolver IK that runs from the thigh joint to the ankle.

   b. Make a locator, and snap it to the knee.

   c. Freeze the locator's transforms.

   d. Get the pole vector values from the IK. Then double or triple them, and add those new numbers to the locator's XYZ translation.

Tip: Remember that you can get scripts for orienting your pole vector constraints. Then, once the constraints are oriented, freeze them in this new position to define their new default location. Select the IK handle and then the locator, and use Constrain > Pole Vector. There are several ways to orient a pole vector constraint. If you are unfamiliar with them, refer to Chapter 3. Now, set up the SCSolver IK for the ankle and ball of the foot using the process outlined earlier in this chapter.

5. Create the controls for the FK chain. Orient the controls so that the X-axis runs down the joint, the Z-axis is bending, and the Y-axis is side-to-side rotation. Also, group each FK control individually, from the thigh to the toe, and label the group as a null. For example, use the Ctrl+G hotkey while selecting LThighCTRL to create a group. Name the new group LThighCTRLNull. Repeat the process for all the FK controls down to the toe.

6. Make sure you use the process we introduced in Chapter 3 to align your nulls and controls. Remember that the controls need to have zeroed values and the null groups will have the values and constraint connections.

7. Now select each control in turn, along with its associated joint, and parent-constrain each of the FK joints.

8. Create the toe, ball, and foot controls. Use the general control process to create and orient the nulls and controls. Snap the center of rotation of the toe control to the ball. Snap the center of rotation of the Ball control to the ball. Snap the center of rotation of the Foot control to the Ankle, as shown in Figure 7.11.

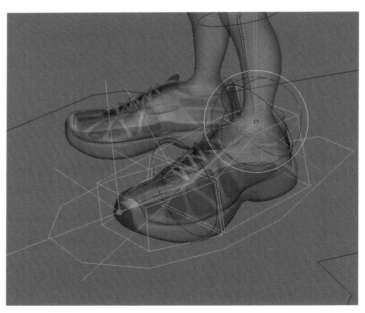

Figure 7.11 The controls for the foot

9. Parent the toe and the ball controls under the foot control. From the Outliner, middle mouse drag the toe and ball controls under the foot control, or select the child and then the parent and hit the P key.

10. Select the Ball control and LLegIK, and choose Constrain > Parent.

11. Now you need to parent the main joint chain to both the IK and FK chains. Parent the main joint chain by selecting both LIKThigh and LFKThigh and then selecting LThigh, and then use Constrain > Parent. Use this process for each of the joint sets (such as the knee, ankle, and so on) that are downstream.

12. Now you'll create an IK/FK switch. Go into each of the joint's parent constraint in your main chain, and in the Channel Box, set LFKThighW0 to 0, and make sure the other, LIKThighW1, is set to 1.

13. Select the foot control, and give it a new attribute. Name the attribute FKIK, and make it a float attribute. Set the minimum to 0, the maximum to 10, and the default to 0. Use the Animate > Set Driven Key > Set command, and load in the foot control as the driver. Select its FKIK attribute. Now load the thigh parent constraint as the driven. Select both LFKThighW0 and LIKThighW1, and press Key.

14. Now, set the IKFK attribute of the foot control to 10, and switch the values on each joint's parent constraint so that LFKThighW0 equals 1 and LIKThighW1 is 0. Run some tests by manually changing the FK chain and manipulating the constraints. After running through your constraints, assign the set-driven key.

15. For the pelvis hookup, select LHip and then FKThighCTRLNull, and choose Constrain > Parent. Now, select the LHip and then LIKThigh, and select Constrain > Parent. Select HipCTRL and then LHip, and then select Constrain > Parent.

World Switch Setup

Now for the world switch setup on the foot. Remember that we're creating this switch so that you can switch between moving the foot relative to the world and relative to the figure. For instance, if the foot is relative to the world, it will stay in place when you grab the torso of the figure and move it. This makes the character's feet stationary, while the body moves.

1. Check to be sure that nothing is selected, and create a group using the Ctrl+G hotkey. Name the group LLeg. Select the master control, MasterCTRL, and then LLeg. Choose Constrain > Parent. Select LLeg and then LFootCTRLNull, and select Constrain > Parent. Select the LHip, then LFootCTRLNull, and then Constrain > Parent.

2. Create a world switch on the foot control:

   a. Select the foot control, and make a new attribute.

   b. Go to the foot control's Attribute Editor, and choose Attributes > New Attribute.

   c. Make the attribute an enumerator, and name it World Orient.

   d. Give the attribute two enum names, World and Figure.

3. Set the LFootCTRLNull parent constraint to weigh 1 for the world and 0 for the hip. With World selected in the switch, open the Set-Driven Key window (Animate > Set Driven Key > Set). Set that attribute of the LFootCTRLNull as the driver, and set the parent constraints LLegW0 and LHipW1 as the driven. Now choose Key.

4. For the figure setting, set the LFootCTRLNull parent constraint to weigh 0 for the world and 1 for the hip. With Figure selected in the switch, now choose Set.

5. Let's make the world switch for the IK pole vector: Create a null group for each of the KneePoles if they don't have them already.

   a. Select LFootCTRL and then LKneePoleNull , and choose Constrain > Parent.

   b. Select LHip and then LKneePoleNull, and choose Constrain > Parent.

   c. Select LLeg and then LKneePoleNull, and choose Constrain > Parent.

6. Now make an enum attribute for LKneePole called World Orient. Give it three values: Hip, Foot, and World. Set up set-driven keys with the LKneePole as the driver and the parent constraint as the driven. Set keys for each of the attribute options that drive the constraints orientation. A completed leg rig is shown in Figure 7.12. Remember that none of these controls have values and are actually zeroed. Their null groups hold their rotational values and their constraints so that the controls are free to be animated.

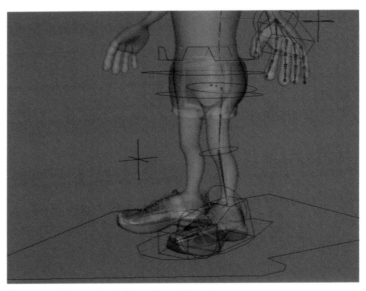

Figure 7.12 The completed advanced leg and foot rig

Grouping the Leg

When grouping and organizing the figure, you will want to have the figure under the main group that we talked about in Chapter 3. You also want to separate your figure into its parts. Each part has its own null group. Each of these groups also acts as the world-relative control for the specific part of the figure. For instance, the pole vector for the knee and the IK controls for the foot and toe all need a world-relative control. They can be parented to the LLeg null group you created earlier.

Just as with the arm, you will want to clean your rig's hierarchy in the Outliner as you make it. You need to make sure your controls and joints are on separate hierarchies so that you can hide the joints later.

Mirroring the Leg

To mirror the leg, you want to mirror the basic joint chain and then reorient it. The right leg created with the mirroring process will most likely take some of the orientation from the left leg, and you need to correct that. We did this same process with the arms. You will also want to duplicate and mirror your controls across. You can do this by duplicating the curve and scaling it across the X-axis numerically upon creation. Build the rest of the right leg from scratch. There is really no easy way to mirror advanced controls across the midline. Current mirroring tools will not bring all the controls and orientations over correctly. If you want to do it right, you have to do it from scratch.

Conclusion

In this chapter, you created a single completed limb and mirrored the leg and foot to create its opposite. Before you leave the limbs entirely, you'll need to revisit the hands, which are more complex than feet because of the movement and number of joints you need to deal with. Hands are presented in the next chapter.

Hands That Grab Your Attention: Hand Rigging Techniques

One of the first giveaways of an incomplete character rig is when the character does all their actions with an unrealistic hand. Hand animation is one of the main ways to communicate expressively. Slight, realistic movements of the hand will add belief in your character. The hands can be incredibly expressive, but if left in the same position through the animation, the character can look fake and unfinished.

8

With the correct controls, you can rig a hand to open and close, to spread and contract the fingers, to bend and flex the palm, and to make the thumb work independently of the fingers.

Chapter Contents

Lune

The opening image, *Lune*, created by Xavier Marquis, is an example of what can be done with great character design. Hands can really make or break a figure. Spend time on the overall shape. If you are going to model them, spend time making nails, making sure to get them correctly shaped and placed. There are lots of hands out there that are mediocre. Usually, the same applies for the rig. The bend of the joints can be either right or wrong. If they are wrong, you will know it. The knuckles will have a rubbery look and will bend unrealistically.

Planning the Hand Rig

As always, the correct way to start is with planning. The time you spend planning the rig will save you time in the long run. It is an important exercise to know what types of hand motions you're going to need and how visible the hands will be in the final animation sequence. Figure 8.1 shows some fully rigged hands.

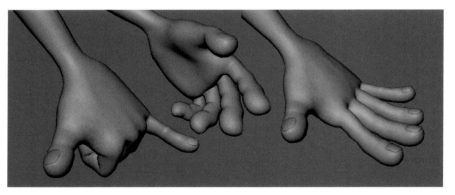

Figure 8.1 Final fingers

How Will They Be Used?

The first step of the planning phase is to determine how the hands are going to be used. Will the character be fighting with other characters? Will it hold objects, such as a gun, and need to pull a trigger? What do your animators require? Is the character close to the camera with the hands clearly visible? Is it a film where the hands need to be realistic? Will the hand movement be figure-relative and world-relative? Is the character a minor background character that simply walks around with their hands by their sides?

Characters require all sorts of motion. You need to determine how an individual character's hands will be used throughout the scenes before you begin the rig.

What Type of Movement Do You Need?

Once you know how the hands will be used, you can determine the types of movements the hands need. If your character fights in the animation, you'll want hands that can make a fist or a karate half-fist. If your character is going to be doing handstands, the fingers need to bend backward and spread out, as though they are bearing the weight of the body.

Hand movements are directly tied to how the hands will be used, but even a simple hand motion could require multiple movements. For instance, grabbing a small object requires a palm curve, as well as separately animated fingers. Be sure to keep a detailed list of what you need so that you can map these movements to controls.

Where Are the Controls Going to Be?

You need to provide a way to control hand and finger movements. Some popular methods include buttons in a UI window or buttons on a customized interface shelf. These are commonly used to pose a hand using MEL scripts. The method that we will use in this chapter drives the hand positions with set-driven keys. By using set-driven keys, you can move the hand only partway by dragging a slider that is linked to the hand's motion. For instance, a fist control can give the fingers a relaxed look at 50 percent and then bring all the fingers into a fist at 100 percent. Set-driven keys are a great way to set up definite hand shapes at varying values of the controlling attribute. We will explain this further later in the chapter.

In addition, you can place the controls for the hands in many ways. You can make separate controls for each knuckle or a single control for the whole hand. Some animators prefer to have hand controls separate from the hands, in the form of sliders and switches, because the controls bunch up when all placed together. Other animators like the controls parented to the hands so they are easy to locate when the hands are in full view. For either system, it is helpful to have a switch that can turn the hand controls on and off so they aren't in the way when working with the full-character motions.

If the controls are planned and placed effectively, they can be intuitive for the animator and easy to use. In our character, we are placing all the controls for the hand and finger movement on the wrist control. These controls will follow the hand as it switches between FK and IK. Remember to keep things simple by placing the controls out of the way and make your controls effective by giving the animator lots of movement options.

Secondary Control

When using set-driven keys, you will notice that if you manipulate any of the joints individually while they are driven by the set-driven key connections, they will snap back into place when the set-driven key is applied. To get around this, you can set up the structure to include null groups above your joints in the hierarchy and then drive the null groups with set-driven keys. Using this approach on the base level of the skeleton, you can still control the joints. Now, your character can still make a fist if he has a broken finger or two.

Set-Driven Is the Key!

One way to avoid the complexity of hand controls is to automate common hand motions using set-driven keys. With set-driven keys, all fingers can act together under the control of a single slider motion. This is an easy way to simplify the hand controls while still providing a complete set of controls. Remember, always include a switch to disable the set-driven feature so you can work with individual fingers as well.

Set-driven keys provide the means for one or more of the joints to react based on the value of any attribute. They set up a connection between the two values. A joint can move a joint, an attribute can move a joint, and so on. Let's go over some common uses for set-driven keys in hands:

Curl/lift When the fingers on a hand curl over the palm, like when you're holding something small in the hand, they typically all curl together. You can set it so that the middle, ring, and pinky fingers curl and lift along with the index finger using set-driven keys.

Palm curl Another subtle hand motion is the palm curl, which happens when the thumb and the pinky come close together. This motion is used when a hand grips a ball and the fingers wrap around it.

Fist The fist is a specialized version of the finger curl. For a fist, the finger joints curl underneath each other to form a dense weapon. To handle this common motion, you can set a control using set-driven keys to clench and unclench a fist using a slider control and a check box.

Spread When a hand reaches for an object, the fingers typically spread to form a wider grasp, but all the fingers spread roughly equally (unless you're dealing with a Spock-like character). Using set-driven keys, you can easily create a control that equally spreads the fingers. This motion can include the thumb spreading as well. We'll show you how to create a spread across the four fingers on each hand. With that knowledge, you can go to the next level and create side-to-side controllers for each finger.

Gradual fist A toggle switch is good if you need your character to quickly assume a fighting pose, but if the character slowly grows angry and gradually forms a fist, then a slider is required to give time for the fist to form. If you use a set-driven key that is driven by an attribute with a 0–10 range, you can set keys along the path of creating the fist. For instance, you can move the pinky before the index finger, making the whole motion seem more fluid and real.

Thumb The thumb is a special case that likely will need its own controls, separate from the fingers. Its motion is unique. When making a fist or grabbing an object, the thumb usually wraps over the curled fingers, and when stretching the fingers, the thumb is extended in a different direction. Set-driven keys are way sweet, because they allow you to set specific values of rotation at specific values of the attribute. So, if you want your thumb to wait for the fist to be made and your slider/attribute ranges from 0–10, you can bring all the fingers into the fist with the thumb still out. Then you can set a key at the value of 7 and bring your thumb in at a value of 10. The thumb waits for the fingers and then moves into place for a fist.

Orienting a Hand to a World Object

Another common task for a hand is picking up and holding objects in the world. The hand needs to be able to orient itself easily to world objects. When gripping a smaller object, such as a weapon, the object needs to move with the character, being locked to its hand.

But, when the character is holding onto a world object that doesn't move with the character, the motion is completely different. For example, when a character grabs the handle of a moving train, the character's hand must be parented to the train and move along with it. The train is moving in world space so the hand needs to be oriented to the train in world space.

Jointing the Fingers

When jointing hands, you will create several joints that span the palm and run from the wrist to the first knuckle of each finger and thumb. Each finger and thumb then has three joints added, including a separate joint for the fingertip. These joints allow the fingers to bend at each knuckle.

With all the hand joints you'll create, it is important to name them correctly using a consistent labeling method. This will help you keep the various joints in order and is especially important as you build set-driven keys. It is better to have something named appropriately so you can select the correct node from the Outliner later. Descriptive and consistent naming will be a big help with general organization and selection, but it will be most important when you are looking at node lists, like with the Outliner. In some editors, you will need to identify and appropriately select items from a list of names. You will find lists like this in the Set Driven Key Editor and the Paint Skin Weights tool.

Meet Stephen Candell

Stephen Candell is a lead facial rigger at Sony Pictures Animation (SPA). He worked on *Polar Express*, *Monster House*, *Surf's Up*, *Hotel Transylvania* (yet to be released), and *Cloudy with a Chance of Meatball*s (2009). We asked him to give us some insight into the world of studio rigging.

What software do you use? What software do you prefer and why?

Maya, because it's easy to use, easy to modify, and has a huge user base.

Can you tell us anything about your role on your current project?

Currently, I am working as the lead facial rigger on the SPA feature *Cloudy with a Chance of Meatballs*. The style of the film is unique and echoes the strongly silhouetted designs of the 1950s cartoon studio, United Productions of America (UPA). I design the 3D interpretations of the character's facial expressions. Also, I am in charge of designing the facial animation control layouts. Throughout the production, I work closely with all the animators, and I help then achieve their character performances by teaching them the philosophies and the limitations of the facial rigs.

Continues

Meet Stephen Candell (*Continued*)

What do you consider best practices for rigging?

1. Always know that animators are your clients.

All of your work, your entire profession as a rigger, is to assist animators in achieving their desired character performances. Keeping that in mind, it is a good idea to have them be involved with the rig development and construction. Many riggers tend to bury themselves in their work, closing themselves off from the animators, and blindly release rig updates that end up not being what the animators had in mind. I recommend sitting down with the animators and making a priority list. Be sure to estimate the time required to achieve each element on the list and discuss the technical limitations your production is up against.

2. Budget your time wisely.

It is very easy to overdevelop a rig. I have seen many riggers who get too focused on inconsequential aspects of a rig, only to find out later that the entire rig is slow, poorly designed, and unusable. If your budget or schedule allows it, pencil in a few weeks or months for rig development. Also, keep in mind that no rig is perfect.

3. The coolest solution is rarely the best.

Without going into detail, let me say this—I am constantly surprised to find that the most low-tech of solutions often yields the best results. For example, having an advanced muscle system that automatically detects collisions and prevents volume loss sounds absolutely fantastic. But in reality, these high-tech systems tend to require a lot of development and constant supervision—not to mention the patience that they demand from animators and riggers alike.

What are some typical problems that cause animators to send a rig back for rework?

I have seen many reasons why an animator would or could be discontented with a rig. The usual issues that come up are poor core rig design, ugly deformations, or rig speed. The first two should be easily preventable. If you involve animators in the design of the rig, they are unlikely to complain about the design later, either because they are content with the rig or perhaps too proud to admit its faults.

What are the main staples for a film character rig: stretchy IK, type of facial setups, and so forth?

At Sony Imageworks, we tend to use a skin-cluster-based facial system. Our system prevents volume loss, provides excellent motion arcs, and provides us with extreme deformation limits.

What percent of your time is spent coding versus using prebuilt tools?

30 percent coding, 70 percent prebuilt tools.

Hand Rigging Techniques

You can employ a couple of different hand rig techniques. The one to choose depends on the type of motion needed for the hand. The simplest setup is the classic single boneset palm. More advanced setups use palm bones. The big difference between these two techniques is the ability to cup the hand, a subtle yet critical motion for realistic hands.

Comparing a Single Boneset with a Palm Bones Setup

Using the single boneset palm technique, a single bone spans the entire hand for each finger connecting it to the wrist. This is an easy setup, but it loses the ability to bend the palm around objects that are being held. Table 8.1 lists the strengths and weaknesses of this technique.

▶ **Table 8.1** Classic Single Boneset Palm Strengths and Weaknesses

Strengths	Weaknesses
Simple setup	Lack of a functional palm
Easier to animate	

The palm bones technique includes some additional bones between the wrist and the first finger knuckle. By moving these bones relative to one another, you can cause the palm to bend. The additional palm bones make the rig a little more complex, but it also gives better control over the thumb's movement. Table 8.2 lists the benefits of this technique.

▶ **Table 8.2** Palm Bones Strengths and Weaknesses

Strengths	Weaknesses
More realistic movement	Somewhat more difficult to set up with the correct rotation angles
Controllable palm shaping	

Classic Single Boneset Palm

To create a class single boneset palm, follow these steps:

1. Start creating your fingers by looking at the hand in an orthographic view and creating a single chain down one finger starting from the knuckle to the tip, as shown in Figure 8.2.

2. Change to a perspective view, modify the joint placement, and then orient them (Skeleton > Orient Joint).

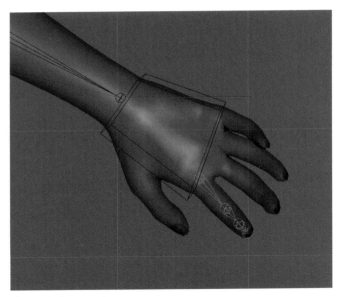

Figure 8.2 Finger creation

3. Create the rest of the fingers and the thumb by duplicating the chain. Use the hotkey Ctrl+D. Move the fingers and thumb into position, and freeze their transforms (Modify > Freeze Transformations) to remove any rotations you may have applied, and orient (Skeleton, Orient Joint) them as well. Also create the thumb joints now. Rename your joints LThumb3, LThumb2, LThumb1, LIndex3, LIndex2, LIndex1 and so on.

4. Orient the joints as described in Chapter 3. Make sure the joints are oriented as shown in Figure 8.3. The X-axis should run down the length of the bone while the Y-axis should denote the bend vector.

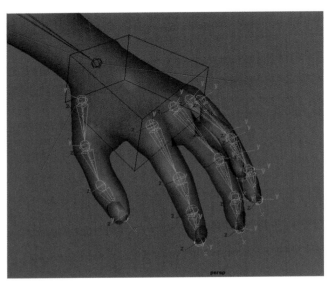

Figure 8.3 Finger orientation

5. Now, in the Outliner, drag the finger joints with the middle mouse button to under the wrist or hand joint (depending on the skeletal setup you used for the forearm). Parent it to the wrist joint in the Advanced Setup.

Now you are ready to skip ahead to the controls and set-driven keys setup. Figure 8.4 shows the completed classic palm setup. The next tutorial will teach how to add the palm joints.

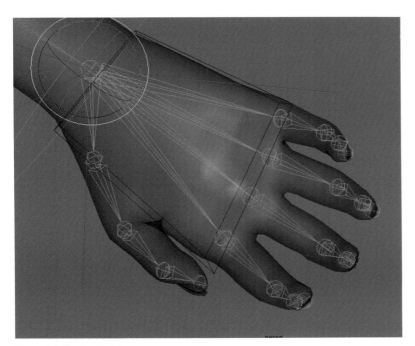

Figure 8.4 Classic palm joints

Palm Bones with an Opposable Thumb

To create palm bones with an opposable thumb, follow these steps:

1. Create your finger and thumb joints by following steps 1–4 of the previous tutorial.

2. Now that you've created the finger and thumb joints, you'll make two extra joints in the palm for bending. Make sure your setup looks like Figure 8.4.

3. Orient the new joints so they are oriented down the length of the palm. Name the joints LPalmIndMid and LPalmPinkyRing. We recommend they be oriented so that the X-axis is mostly oriented toward the middle or ring finger, respectively, but just slightly toward the other joint.

4. In the Outliner, use the middle mouse button to drag the fingers under the corresponding palm joint, as shown in Figure 8.5. Then, use the middle mouse button to drag the thumb under the wrist.

Now you are ready to set up the controls and set-driven keys. Figure 8.6 shows the palm bones setup applied to a character with stubbier fingers.

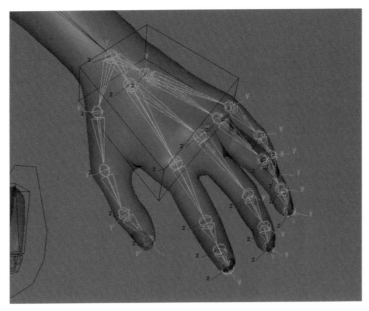

Figure 8.5 Palm bend joints

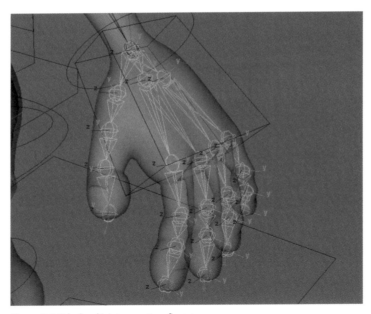

Figure 8.6 Palm bend joints on cartoon fingers

Adding Finger Animation Controls

Once the joints are created and in place, you can begin to build the set-driven controls for the various finger motions. As you build these controls, remember to keep the control placement positioned where they'll make sense to the animator. In our character, we'll show how to attach the controls to the wrist controls. These controls will follow the bound joints whether they are on the FK or IK, thus the controls for finger manipulation will be easily accessed.

Variants in Location

With the large number of controls positioned all over the hand, consider using finger joint controls like the ones shown in Figure 8.7. Finger joint controls are nice because the bend control can be animated by grabbing multiple controls. For instance, if you have all your finger joints correctly oriented along the same axis and you select all the controls, you can then use the rotation tool to rotate all of them at the same time.

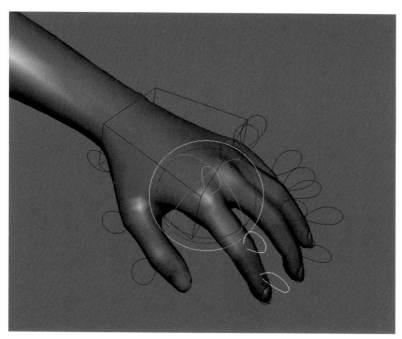

Figure 8.7 Finger joints control option

Instead of creating controls for each joint (you learned to set up individual joint controls in Chapter 3), you could create an individual control for each knuckle to operate the bend set-driven key for that finger. As an alternative, we'll show you how to create individual bend controls at the wrist control. This way, you cut down on the number of controls that the fingers require.

In the realistic figure, we will show how to add the bend controls to the hand control since we do not have a wrist control or FK chain on that simpler arm. On our advanced rig, since we have both FK and IK functionality, we need to add the bend controls to a control that will be available for both IK and FK animation. The hand control is used only for IK, so we use the wrist, as shown in Figure 8.8, to control the hand. Since the wrist control is constrained to the wrist joint, it will always be available and handy.

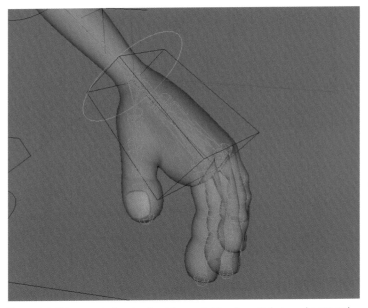

Figure 8.8 Wrist control where hand and finger set-driven keys attribute can be accessed

Set-Driven Keys

As we said earlier, the trick to making the hand and fingers easy to animate is to use set-driven keys. With these controls in place, the fingers move in concert with each other. This takes some time to set up, but once the keys are completed, the task of animating multiple fingers is so much easier.

General Setup

Before beginning the set-driven keys, there are some general setup tasks to complete. First, each new attribute must be defined with a name and a default value. The default or neutral value is the initial value of the attribute. Set it within the range of the movement, not at either extreme.

Next, you need to define the range for the attribute's maximum and minimum values. For example, if you are building an attribute for finger bending, then the range can be set from –10 to 10, with a neutral value of 0. For a directional function, such as a cupping hand, where 0 is neutral and 10 is a bent palm, there is no reason to go into the negative values.

Bidirectional Control

The most common method of defining set-driven keys is to simply have the driven keys mirror the joints that drive the motion. So if an index finger is the driving key, the other fingers simply follow along as the driving finger is bent.

Bidirectional set-driven keys control motion in the positive and the negative. A fist and a finger stretch are good examples of the motions controlled with this type of setup. At the value of 0, the fingers are in their default positions. At –5 they are stretched outward, and at 10 they are curled into a fist. This allows for much more realistic movement, especially when compared to setups that use poses.

Staggered Control

Another type of set-driven key staggers the motion of the fingers using a delay. With this setup, the pinky finger begins to bend followed, at a small delay, by the adjacent finger. The pattern continues to the last finger in the group. Staggering the set-driven keys causes the character's hand to slowly form a fist by moving the fingers independently. We will go over how this is done.

Enabling Bend/Lift, Spread, and Palm Bend Controls

The following tutorials use the bidirectional and staggered control methods to create the set-driven keys for spread, fist, lift, and palm curl controls.

Finger Spread Set-Driven Key

Create the set driven key hookups to control your fingers. Follow these steps:

1. Select LWristCTRL, and in the Attribute Editor, add an attribute (Attributes > Add Attribute).

2. Make this a float attribute called Spread. Give it a minimum value of –10 and a maximum value of 10 with a default of 0.

3. Now, go to the Set Driven Key Editor (Animate > Set Driven Key > Set), load the wrist control into the Driver box, and select Spread from the right side of that box.

4. Select all of the knuckle joints. (They are the only joints that bend on the spread.) Go to the Outliner (Window > Outliner), double-check your selections, and then load the knuckle joints into the Driven box of the Set Driven Key Editor. Select these joints, and then select the rotation x, y, z values on the right. This selects the rotation values for all your joints. Make sure all the joints in the driven part of the panel are highlighted.

5. Now, in 3d view, select LWristCTRL, and look in the Channel Box. Make sure that Spread is set to 0 and your hand is in the default shape. Click the Key button in the Set Driven Key Editor.

6. Let's set the value for the more precise position first. In the Channel Box of your wrist control, type the value **–10** in the value for the Spread Attribute.

7. Rotate your joints so that the fingers are next to each other, in the opposite of a spread. Move the middle finger just slightly out (away from the thumb), and then bring the other fingers in next to it. With the Spread attribute as the driver and the rotation values of the joints as the driven in the Set Driven Key Editor, click Key to set the position.

8. Now, set the Spread attribute in the Channel Box to 10, and move all the fingers out to a spread position, as shown in Figure 8.9. Remember to use your own hand as a reference. Press Key to set this final value.

9. Now test your set-driven key functionality. You should have some sweet finger-spreading action.

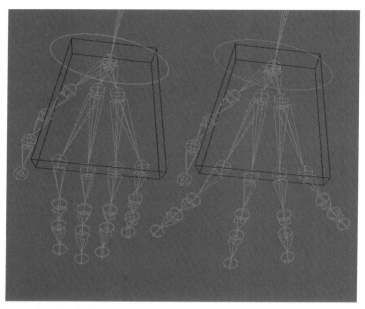

Figure 8.9 Spread attribute extremes

Finger Bend Fist/Up Set-Driven Key

The finger bend fist/up setup uses in-between tweaks (tweening) while bending fingers. Follow these steps:

1. Select LWristCTRL, and in the Attribute Editor, and add an attribute (Attributes > Add Attribute).

2. Create a float attribute called Fist. Give it a minimum value of –10, a maximum value of 10, and a default of 0.

3. Go to the Set Driven Key Editor (Animate > Set Driven Key > Set), load LWristCTRL into the Driver box, and select Fist on the right side of that box.

4. Now, select all the finger and thumb joints affected in the bend, from the knuckle down. Exclude the tips, because they are not affected in the bend. Go to the Outliner (Window > Outliner), double-check your selections, and load the joints into the Driven box. Select the joints and the rotation x, y, z values on the right. This selects the rotation values for all of the joints. Make sure all the joints in the driven part of the panel are highlighted.

5. Now in the 3D view, select LWristCTRL, and look in the Channel Box. Make sure the Fist attribute is set to 0 and your hand is in default shape. Hit the Key button in the Set Driven Key Editor.

6. In the Channel Box for LWristCTRL, enter the value −10 in the Fist Attribute text box.

7. Rotate the finger joints so that the fingers are stretched outward, opposite from a fist. Most of this bending happens at the knuckles. With the Fist attribute as the driver and the rotation values of the joints as the driven, in the Set Driven Key Editor, click Key to set the position.

8. Now set the Fist attribute in the Channel Box to 10, and move all the fingers and thumb to a fist position. Remember to use your hand as a reference. Press Key to set this final value.

9. Now you'll add a tween (in-between) that will create a realistic relaxed hand. Set the Fist attribute to 5, and pose the hand so that it is in a relaxed position. In this position, the pinky is bent to about 50 percent of the fist shape, the ring finger is bent to about 30 percent, the middle finger is bent to about 15 percent, and the thumb and index are in the 0 position. Click the Key button to set the position.

10. Now add another to fix the fist. If your fist is like this character's, the thumb and the index finger are colliding at about value 7 on the attribute. Find the value with the greatest amount of collision.

11. With the attribute set at this value of greatest collision, set all the rotations of the thumb joints to 0, and set a key there. Now, with the Fist attribute selected, use the middle mouse button to drag in the viewport. As the fist opens and clenches, you will see that the thumb now waits for the fingers to close before it comes into the fist. Figure 8.10 shows the stretched, normal, relaxed, and closed fist positions.

Figure 8.10 Fist attribute stages

Individual Finger Bending

You can also create controls that allow individual fingers to bend independently. This is a nice feature to have as well because you can select multiple attributes, use the middle mouse button to drag them into the viewport, and modify all of them at once. You can control a thumb in this same way.

Palm Bending

You can easily set up a control for palm bending by adding an attribute for it, rotating the palm joints, and offsetting the fingers to accommodate the bend.

Refer to the files on the companion CD to see how we set this up for an example hand.

Constraining a Hand to a World Object

One of the final attributes to add to a hand is a control that enables objects to be locked to the hand. Once the object is locked to the hand, you can manipulate the palm and fingers and control how the character carries objects. This same control also allows the hand to be locked to world space objects.

1. Create a locator or another object that doesn't render, such as a curve, and center it on the origin. Move it into position in the palm of the hand, and freeze the transformations (Modify > Freeze Transformations). Parent-constrain this world object's null to the MasterCTRL for now. Rename it LHandObject and LHandObjectNull.

 Note: When animating, you will want to parent-constrain the hand to the part of the object that will best suit your hand/object relationship.

2. Rebuild the WorldOrient attribute for your hand control by first deleting it. Also delete the parent constraint for LHandIKCTRL. You must do this before you can set up the new attribute. Now create a new enum attribute. Name it WorldOrient, and give it three values: World, Figure, and Object.

3. Parent-constrain the hand control's null to the clavicle (remember to select "driver then driven") by selecting LClavicle and then LHandIKCTRLNull, and then choose Constrain > Parent. Next, parent the hand control's null LHandIKCTRLNull to LArm and LHandObject. Now open your Set Driven Key Editor (Animate > Set Driven Key > Set), and load LHandIKCTRL as the driver and its parent constraint as the driven.

4. Select the WorldOrient attribute for LHandIKCTRL, and select the three lowest options for the parent constraint. They should be named something like LHandObjectW0, LArmW1, and LClavicleW2.

5. Select the LHandIKCTRL, and make sure the WorldOrient is on LHandObject. Now set the parent constraint to be weighted to the LHandObject by setting the object attribute LHandObject to a value of 1 and World and by setting Figure to 0. Click Key in the Set Driven Key Editor to set a key.

6. Now set the weights for the other two options but respective to the parent goal. Repeat step 5, but select Figure or World as the driver, and then set the parent to the correct constraint target. Figure 8.11 shows the result.

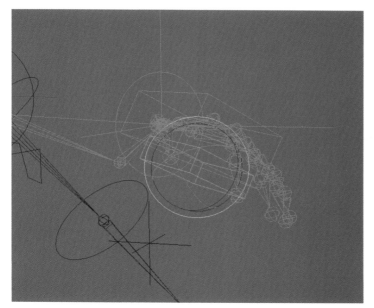

Figure 8.11 The Hand is parent-constrained to an object that has three World orient options.

Conclusion

Although the hands are the most complicated body part you've encountered thus far, using set-driven controls makes them manageable. In this chapter, you learned two techniques for rigging the palms and added several controls for curling, bending, and spreading the fingers. In the next chapter, you'll learn how to rig the neck and head. This doesn't include all the facial controls, which will come later, but just the controls to move the head and neck.

A Head above the Rest: Controlling the Head and Neck

9

Once the body and limbs are rigged and ready to go, you can turn to the neck joints and the head. In this chapter, we'll show how to create two controls, one for the neck and one for the head. A rigged jaw is important for talking, chewing, and biting. We will talk about the differences with using a rigged jaw and without. If the character has a wide mouth, you will want to use a rigged jaw setup. Like with the jaw, you can use blendshapes *(morphs), joints, or influence objects to drive the lips into position for expressions and visemes.*

Chapter Contents
Setting up the neck
Rigging eyes
Rigging the jaw
Creating controls for the head
Creating secondary items on head

Planning Ahead

Before making heads turn, it is best to take a close look at your character to determine the types of head controls you'll need. Once again, time spent planning will save you work later. Figure 9.1 shows what the finished neck and eyes will look like.

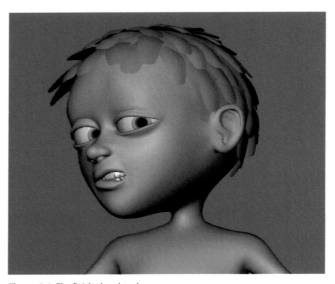

Figure 9.1 The finished neck and eyes

Starting with the Neck

The neck joints can be simply an extension of the spine; however, if you want added precision and extra functionality, you'll want to parent-constrain the neck to your skeleton. This parent constraint allows a broken rig in this area, giving you more movement options for the neck. For example, it allows you to freely move the neck from the spine, and it keeps the scaling isolated to the spine.

The neck should be long enough to separate the head from the rest of the body so that when the character rotates their head, it doesn't collide with the shoulder or with the breastbone. If the neck is small or there is no neck, you still want to create a joint for this rotation. The animator can then show a hint of a neck even when the character has no neck.

Number of Joints

Necks can be as simple as two joints or can include several joints in a more complicated IK setup. The number of joints depends on the articulation required and the length of the neck. For example, you need more than two or three joints to rig a neck for a dragon or a giraffe. Most character necks have one to three joints.

Rotation Centers

Correctly locating the rotation center is key for neck joints. For a photorealistic character, place the center of rotation at the base of the skull, right where the brain stem enters the spine. If you're not sure where that is, check skeletal anatomy pictures. As a general rule, place the joint where the center of rotation is in real life. From this location, the head can naturally move up and down and turn side to side without impacting the overall shape and mass of the neck. In a cartoony character, placement can be less accurate.

Keep two things in mind when placing neck joints: the degree of twisting that the character needs for each joint and the position of the center of rotation for each joint. If you position the rotation center too far forward, the neck will twist more like a cartoon neck. If the joints are placed too far back, then when the head is bent forward, the geometry will crumple.

What Do You Need for Controls?

Some animators prefer a single control located at the top of the head that allows the neck to twist and move around its rotation center. A control like this is easy to grab and allows for quick manipulation of the neck. Using a single control for the head, you can pass rotation down into the neck with an expression, just as the forearm rotation passes rotation values from the wrist up the forearm.

Another option is to create separate neck and head controls. This provides more of an FK type of control. It requires more animation but gives more control.

To Jaw or Not to Jaw

Most character rigs use both a rigged jaw and blendshapes. Remember that it is better to have it in there and not need it than to not have it in there and need it. A character with a jaw rig can talk and drop their jaw to show surprise more effectively. They are also better at showing the chewing and biting motions, such as with a cow that moves its jaw side to side. Visemes, used for talking, look more realistic with a rigged jaw. Blendshapes are used for facial expressions such as smiles and raising and lowering the eyes. For a more comprehensive book on facial setup, check out Jason Osipa's *Stop Staring: Facial Modeling and Animation Done Right* (Sybex, 2007). His book provides a much more in-depth look at facial setups that use both a rigged jaw and blendshapes.

A huge gaping mouth is still possible without a rigged jaw. You just need to keep in mind that this shape will be created with a blendshape that moves each vertex in a straight line; thus, the midpoint results in a shorter jaw. The majority of the figures have rigged jaws. They are a good idea and allow for better deformations later.

Rotation Center

If the character is rigged with a jaw, then a rotation center for the jaw must be defined. Typically, use an axis parallel to the X-axis (if your figure is facing down the Z-axis) that is located underneath and a little in front of each ear. This allows the jaw to rotate in only one direction, causing the mouth to gape. If your character is using only blendshapes to create jaw movement, the blendshapes where the jaw rotates should all be rotated from this same point.

Blendshapes

You can create expressions and speaking gestures using blendshapes. A great way to create specific mouth shapes on characters is to use blendshapes along with a rigged jaw so you can get the movement and look they require. We'll cover how to use blendshapes to create visemes in Chapter 13, "Control That Face of Yours: Working with Expressions and Facial User Interfaces."

Alternately, you can use influence objects as deformers to create predictable and/or exaggerated shapes for the mouth. With this setup, the animator can create the shape of the viseme and then shape specific areas. This setup requires a little more work but adds functionality. As we talk about the blendshapes that are needed in the next few chapters, keep all of these tips in mind, since you will need to duplicate them with the influence objects.

What Do You Need for Controls?

For a character with a rigged jaw, a single control, located in front of the chin, makes it easy to move the jaw down and up. This control drives the jaw joint and has a rotation center at the base of the jaw. This control will supplement your blendshapes. It will make an open mouth as wide as you need.

If your character has only blendshapes, all your shapes will likely be controlled from the place of your choosing. We will address blendshape controls in more detail in Chapter 13.

The Eyes Have It

The eyes provide the view into the character's soul, and as such, they can make or break a character. Creating realistic eye movement is very important to sell your character's believability. The eyes are best represented by joints that are parented or parent-constrained to the head, as shown in Figure 9.2. This allows the eyes to move with the head but also lets them move independently from the head. The eyes themselves will be parented or bound completely to the eye joints.

When animating eyes, it is good to have the eyes move randomly occasionally to add some interest and realism to the character. Building the rig so that the eyes are independent makes it easy to add this type of animation.

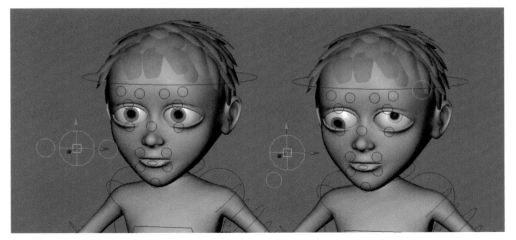
Figure 9.2 Independent eye control

Binocular or Independent Lateral Vision?

Eyes can be linked to rotate together so they are always in sync, looking at the same object. Binocular eyes that move together can be accomplished using constraints or using scripts that let a main control direct where the eyes are aiming. But some characters require eyes that act independently, such as a gecko whose eyes point in two directions at once. These characters need independent lateral vision.

What Do You Need for Controls?

One of the easiest ways to control binocular eyes is to place a control out in front of the eyes and aim-constrain the eyes to look at it. This controls the rotation and orientation of the eyes and offers realistic eye tracking automatically. For lateral vision, you would want to create controls at the eyes that allow for the independent movement. If you have an aim locator in this instance, you would want to make a switch that could aim the eyes either at a single target or at individual targets.

Hair, Ears, and Other Secondary Objects

Some characters have secondary parts linked to the head, such as ponytails or ears. The type of ancillary jointing needed for each of these body parts is different for each separate part. If your character has floppy ears, you might want a dynamic joint setup or a jiggle deformer to help in animating.

What Do You Need for Controls?

The controls needed for head-relative body parts depend on the type of motion you want. For some secondary body parts, it is enough to simply parent the part to the head. Ponytails, for example, can be linked with a simple spline set of joints and attached to the head. This setup gives the ability to animate a whip-like motion as the head is rotated.

Hair spikes might need to be controlled independently. You could set up individual FK controls for them, or you could create a connection between the joints and have the first joint drive and compound the rotation of the others.

Setting Up the Neck

As we said earlier, the neck setup can be as simple as a couple of joints extending from the spine or as complex as another stretching spine set atop the existing spine. For this example, we'll show you how to create a simple neck setup with three joints. These joints can be parent constrained to the spine, which allows the neck, and subsequently the head, to move with the rest of the body.

Creating the Joint

When creating the neck joints, create the first two joints that run from above the base of the neck, in between the collarbone joints to the base of the skull. Create a third joint from the top of the neck to the middle of the head. Once the joints are created, be sure to parent-constrain them to the spine.

Dealing with Rotation Concerns

Positioning the rotation centers is critical to getting the right movement. At the back of your neck, the lowest of the cervical vertebrae is easy to identify because it sticks out from the others. This area represents the rotation center for the first neck joint. The other neck joints can follow the neck, and line to the insertion point in the skull. The neck actually starts low and back, then moves toward the middle, and finally fits into a central location in the skull. Keep this in mind when setting up your joints.

Be careful not to position the rotation center for the neck joint at the front of the neck, or you'll see some serious deformation along the back of the neck as the head tilts. For more uniform neck bending, as in a cartoony character, you can position the neck rotation center in the center of the neck.

The Standard Neck Rigging Approach

To implement the neck rigging approach, follow these steps:

1. Create a separate joint chain with three joints as if it were a continuation of the spine. For more realistic movement, you will want at least two joints for the neck. In a cartoony figure, like the one shown in Figure 9.3, you want to lean toward positioning the joints in the center of the neck for better bending. With a realistic figure, like the one in Figure 9.4, you'll want to be more accurate with the rotation positions. Think of where the vertebral column enters the skull. For this exercise, place the joints in the realistic locations. Test the smooth bind to see how the joints work. If you don't like them, undo the bind, and change their positions. Remember to orient your joints if you move them.

2. Orient the joints (Skeleton > Orient Joints). Use the orientation process described in Chapter 3, "Rigging That's Right: Concepts You Need to Know." Rename your joints to NeckLo, NeckMid, and Head.

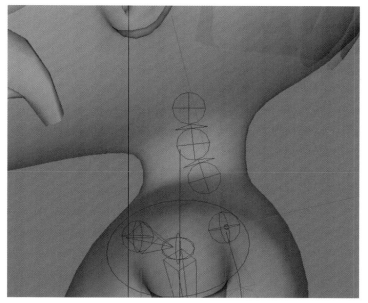

Figure 9.3 Floating neck

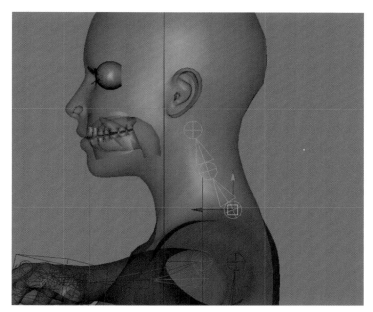

Figure 9.4 Floating neck with anatomical positioning

3. You now can parent your neck null to the last joint of your spine, Bind_SpineJ7 or the extra joint, if you put one there for the purpose of a broken rig, Select "driver then driven," and choose Constrain > Parent. This chain will not echo the scaling of the spine.

4. Add a control curve around the neck, or add one that extends back behind the character for selecting your head and neck. Follow the instructions in Chapter 3 for control creation.

Rigging the Eyes

Since the eyes are separate, individual objects, they could be controlled using completely different controls, but adding the eyes to a single control has its benefits. Animators will want this because of its ease of use. With this setup, animators will be able to easily move the target around the scene. They can even create a lazy eye quickly that will follow the tracking of a target object.

Eye Connection and Orientation

Eyes are rigged using a single joint that extends from the head joint. The eye joint should be located within the exact center of the eyeball. If the joint is placed by "eyeballing" it, then you might be off a little, causing the eye to move out of its socket as it rotates. To avoid eyes that rotate off-center, point-constrain a locator to the eyeball to find its center, and then snap your new joint to the locator by pressing and holding the V key.

As the eyeballs are parented to the eye joint, make sure the eyeball orientation isn't changed. If you watch the eyes as you constrain them, you will see whether they rotate even slightly. Avoid this by aim-constraining your eyes to the target while it is directly in front of the eye, moving the target if needed, and then zeroing (freezing transformations) out the target. You want to make sure the eye is completely controlled and oriented correctly when the figure is skinned.

Note: If the eyes are not spherical, you might want to consider remodeling or controlling the iris by projecting it onto the eye surface with a shader. For a similar effect, you can create the eyeballs as spheres and deform them into the desired shape. You can do this by adding an eye bulge deformer after skinning. We will talk more about this and other eye issues in Chapter 10.

Standard Eye Rigging

To implement the eye rigging, follow these steps:

1. Create a single joint (for the head) in the side view that is in the middle of the head and in front of the ears. Name this joint `Head`. This joint is mainly cosmetic but will be the main joint to which all the head items can be attached. You can rig a character without this joint. The cartoony character example, shown in Figure 9.5, has the joint, while the realistic character, shown in Figure 9.6, does not. It is up to you whether to include the joint in your character. It is nice to have for organizational purposes and for skinning but, again, is not necessary.

Tip: If your skeleton is going to be visible after the character setup, you might want to create a joint that extends beyond the front of the head to show the head's orientation.

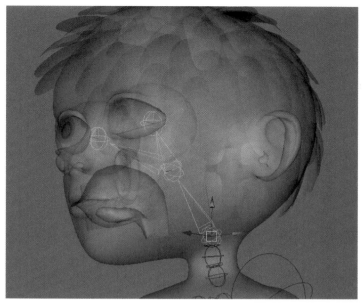

Figure 9.5 Cartoony character eye setup

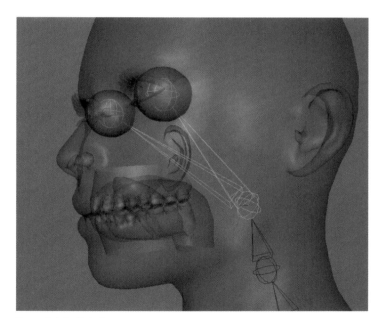

Figure 9.6 Realistic character eye setup

2. From the Head joint or from the top of the neck, create a joint that is in the center of rotation of the left eye. Name this joint LEye. You can find the center of your eye by selecting the eye polygons. Center the pivot (Modify > Center Pivot), and see where the tool indicator is. You can also select a ring of vertices. Create a cluster, snap a joint to the cluster, and then delete the cluster. Cluster handles are often great ways to find the center of vertex groups without scripting complex calculations.

3. Place a joint at the center of the other eye. We will cover eye hookups in more detail in the next chapter.

4. Rename the joints LEye and REye, respectively. Make sure the joints are oriented correctly. Orient their nulls using the methods discussed in Chapter 3.

Rigging the Jaw

Create a jaw using a single set of joints. If the jaw simply needs to move up and down, then use a single set of two joints running from the head joint to the chin. For realistic movement of the jaw and chin, place the main rotation position of the jaw joint directly below and in front of the ears, at the center of the jaw axis. Create a first joint that ends at the rotation axis point, and create a second joint that ends at the chin.

Characters with a jointed jaw need blendshapes, floating joints, or influence objects if they must show facial expressions or speak. If you don't include a jointed jaw, you can use blendshapes or influence objects to achieve a pseudo–jaw rig effect. This pseudo rig is limited to a linear type of movement. A jointed jaw, however, will look good throughout its rotation.

Jointed Jaw Setup

For our example, we'll show how to add a jointed jaw to the existing rig. This will enable the character to display specific expressions.

Jaw Location

When creating the jaw, the most important thing to figure out is the center of rotation of the jawbone. If you look at a skeleton or look at another person, you can see that the jaw rotates from a location that is a little lower and slightly in front of the ear.

The Standard Jaw Rigging

Follow these steps for standard jaw rigging:

1. With the Joint tool (Skeleton > Joint Tool), select the Head joint, and create a new joint at the pivot point for the jaw. This joint placement is extremely important. Make sure this joint is exactly at your jaw rotation center when looking at your model from the side view. This will make for a more realistic jaw movement. Figure 9.7 shows the jaw joints for the cartoony character, and Figure 9.8 shows the realistic character.

2. Create a secondary cosmetic joint that will serve as the guide for the jaw's rotation and orientation. Place the secondary joint at the chin.

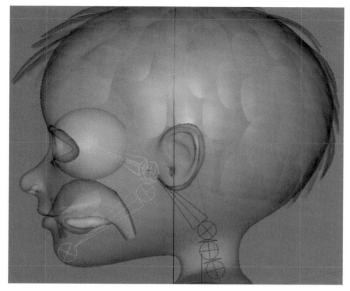

Figure 9.7 Cartoony jaw setup

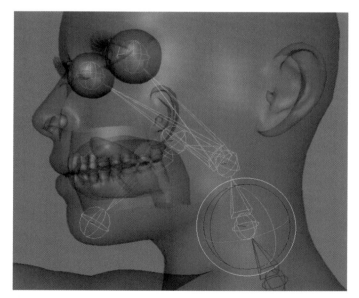

Figure 9.8 Realistic character jaw setup

Nonjointed Jaw Setup

If you are using a nonjointed jaw setup, where all your facial shapes are driven by deformers such as blendshapes or morph targets, you do not need to add any other joints to the head. If you discover that whenever you're animating the character and are dialing up a face blendshape, the face moves back to its default position, it's because you need to reorder the deformation so the blendshape is calculated first and then the skin that's moving in space. You can do this in two ways. The easiest way is to use the reorderDeformers MEL command. For example:

```
reorderDeformers skinCluster1 blendShape1;
```

Remember that this MEL command reflects the default naming, and you will need to substitute the correct node names. The second way does the same thing through the interface:

1. Select the mesh.

2. Click the Inputs to the Selected Object button in the status line of the interface.

3. Now, use the middle mouse button to drag the blendshape under the SkinCluster node in the Outliner.

Controls for the Head

Once you've added the neck and head joints to the rig, you can begin to add the various controls needed to animate them. For the example rig, we'll show how to create two separate controls—one for the neck and one for the head. These controls enable the head and neck to move independently of each other and to move and deform within a desired fashion.

1. Create a curve control for the neck. Follow the instructions in Chapter 3 for control creation. Place it, as we discussed earlier, in a location that is appropriate for your character type, typically at the center of the neck.

2. Now, select the head joint, make sure it is oriented correctly, and attach it as a control. Use the control process we discussed in Chapter 3 to create the head control. Figure 9.9 shows the controls for a cartoony character, and Figure 9.10 shows the controls for a realistic character.

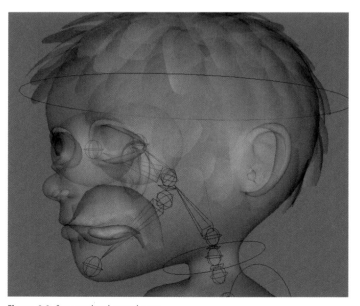

Figure 9.9 Cartoony head control setup

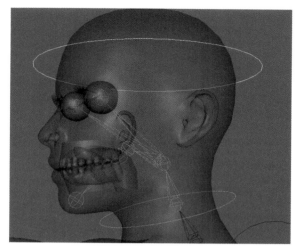
Figure 9.10 Realistic head control setup

Secondary Items on the Head

Ponytails, floppy ears, and hats are just some examples of secondary objects you might need to rig on a head. You can attach these secondary body parts to the head joint, and as we discussed several times earlier in the chapter, they can include multiple joints.

It is often helpful for certain body parts, such as a ponytail, to use a series of joints combined with a spline IK to create a dynamic appendage like a soft body or hair curves. This solution allows an animator to whip the ponytail around the head as the head moves, for example. To create a simple secondary object for the head, follow these steps:

1. Position separate joint chain(s) through the item(s).

2. Rename and orient as necessary. Create controls as necessary.

3. Parent-constrain (Constrain > Parent) the base joint of the chain to the head joint. For a hat or a removable object, parent the object to a world space object, such as a locator, and make an attribute that allows the animator to switch between the two. Refer to the world/local switching we discussed while dealing with feet in Chapter 7, "Getting a Leg (or Two) Up on the Competition: Under- standing Legs and Feet," and with hands in Chapter 8, "Hands That Grab Your Attention: Hand Rigging Techniques."

Conclusion

The head is often the focus of the character, and its actions need to be realistic to hold the audience's attention. The rigging for the neck is fairly simple, but placing the rota- tion centers correctly is critical. Make sure you have the head set up to your liking, since so much will be attached to it. Create it correctly, and move forward with confidence.

Now that the body is rigged, you can turn your attention to the details of the face. The first step is to rig the eyes to make them realistic. Let's move on to the eye setup and deformations of the face.

What Are You Looking At? Realistic Eyes

10

The eyes are central to the look of the character and capture the soul of the character. Realistic eyes can add a lot of believability to both realistic and cartoony characters.

The eyes are capable of some very intricate and quick moves, including rapid darting back and forth, pupil dilation and they also control the lids to an extent. We will go over a few setups to recreate these complex movements.

Chapter Contents
Planning eyes
Controlling eye movement
Working with eyelids
Eye targeting methods
Squashing and stretching eyes
Adding lacrimal ducts
Morphing eyelids
Tying the eye rig to the rest of the rig

Freaky Bird

The main image for this chapter, *Freaky Bird*, by Patrick Beaulieu is a great example of how eyes can communicate emotion even in a "freaky" bird. The iris colors are real and add to the believability of the figure. Notice the construction of the eyelids. How do you think Patrick rigged this figure?

Planning Eyes

Realism is found in the eyes' subtle motions. Each of these motions—eye targeting, random eye movement, eyelid movement, or pupil dilation—needs to be checked to see whether the controls to create such a motion are warranted by the character's role. If they are needed, you need to plan each movement before tackling the eyes. Figure 10.1 illustrates some of the movement you may want your character to be able to mimic.

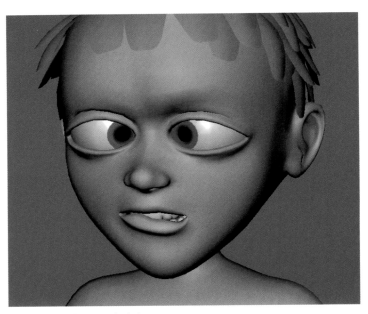

Figure 10.1 Looking outside the box

Considering Character Type

The type of eye rigging required really depends on the type of character you are creating. Is your character an edgy informant who lives in paranoia, requiring a lot of shifty eye movement and twitching? In this case, you might want more interesting lid controls than usual. Or is your character a beauty with lots of close-up shots of her deep blue eyes? For this type of character, control over the iris morphs is essential. The realism in the model will require realism and precision in the rig.

During the planning phase, it helps to know what type of character you'll be working with. We've broken the types of characters down into three categories to help you determine which type of eyes to create. Other categories exist, but these are the eye styles we'll present in this chapter.

Realistic Photorealistic characters need eyes that can handle all the various movements of the eyeballs, eyelids, irises, and pupils that real people have. Even within this category, your eye rigging requirements might change depending on how visible the eyes will be to the audience. If the animation shows the character only from 10 feet away, you will likely not provide iris movement controls. However, if your character approaches the camera and is close at all, you will want to have the ability to add a twitch to one eye or even a wink. Built-in subtleties can bring your character even closer to photorealism. But photorealism takes time and patience. Watch the subtle eye movements in such films as *Beowulf* by Sony Imageworks to see how they worked to mimic the human eye.

Cartoony realistic Another general category is the cartoony-realistic character. This character type is realistic, but the eyes can be exaggerated to show emotion, giving the eyes a hyperrealistic motion. Take a look at the characters in *Surfs Up*, also by Sony Imageworks. All the penguins have spherical eyes. Watch how their eyes convey lifelike emotion while still retaining their cartoony shapes.

Squash-and-stretch eyes Another type of cartoon character is a character with eyes that bulge, squash, and stretch in the recognized way that cartoons do. As an example, take Remy in Pixar's film *Ratatouille*. When Remy is mistaken for a saltshaker and is squeezed, his eyes bulge. We will show you a way to mimic this type of deformation. You can also use this type of deformation for exaggerated expressions.

The squash and stretch controls work by maintaining the volume of the eyeball, so when the eye is pushed together at its middle, the two ends bulge out. This gives the character the smooth, bouncy, fluid movement that is common in cartoons.

Controlling Eye Movement

The controls to enable these subtle, realistic eye movements, as well as the brash cartoony motions, are handled in several ways. One common control for eye movement is a target flag. Using this type of control, the eyeballs are constrained to look at a particular target. Other controls can include a target for both eyes. We'll show how to use a central target to control the two individual targets, and in turn, those will control each eye independently.

Targeting Eyes

The easiest way to control the rotations of both eyeballs is to constrain them to point at a target object, located in front of them. If both eyeballs are constrained in this way to a single object, then the eyeballs will always move and be in sync.

However, for some characters, you'll need independent target objects for each eye. Perhaps you need an offset lazy eye for the character. This setup gives you more control over where each eye looks and lets you create some bizarre and odd eye motions that might be required by some characters. For an Igor-like individual, you could make a *wall-eyed* (slang for Strabismus) appearance using this setup.

Fixed single constraint A fixed single constraint is the easiest method to enable. Simply create a single object on which both eyeballs are focused. Then by moving the target object, both eyeballs will rotate to keep the target in focus.

Independent constraints When using independent constraints, it is helpful to have a control that you can use to lock the target objects together so they move as one object. You should also make an option to unlock and move the target objects independently. You also could do this with the hierarchy of the nodes.

Eye Controls

You can also include other subtle controls to provide random eye motions within a given range or a control to change the iris and pupil size. The random eye movements usually are the eye darting from one thing to another. Animators will want to control this manually. The pupil size is easily adjusted with a morph target and a control, such as an attribute slider.

Lacrimal Caruncle Movement

In the inner corner of the eye is the *lacrimal caruncle*. This pink fleshy body contains modified sweat glands. This soft tissue isn't connected to the eyeball, but it does touch the eyeball and moves along with the eyeball. Moving this flesh along with the eyeball, as well as changing its size and shape in relation to the eyeball position, creates a realistic effect. We will do this by attaching lacrimal caruncle movements to the eye rotation. Look ahead in the chapter to Figure 10.8 to see the pink fleshy representation of the lacrimal caruncle, if you're not familiar with this body part.

Iris Morphing

The final eye motion to consider is creating a blendshape for the size of the iris as the eye's pupil increases or decreases. This happens when the eye focuses on an object or when the eye is exposed to more or less light. For example, when a character is surprised by a bright light in their eyes, their pupils constrict to reduce the amount of light that is striking the cornea. This motion is great for creating ultrarealistic characters, but it is noticeable only if the character is up close. We will not cover this, since it is a fairly easy morph to build. You will want to plan where the control of this morph will be. Remember, you want all your controls to be easily accessible for the animator.

Dealing with Eyelids

Another common eye motion deals with the eyelid. If your character is photorealistic, you might want the eyelid to move. We'll simulate this by hooking a deformer's movement to the rotation of the eye. Adding random blinking to a character is essential for realistic characters. Usually, animators want control over when this happens. You can, however, create a script job that blinks the eyes every so often when the character isn't a principal.

Morphs vs. Jointing

The morph approach creates several morphed blendshapes, and by combining several of these deformers, you can create a blink.

A more realistic approach is to add joints or influence objects to the eyelids that control deformation akin to blinking. This approach, when combined with weight painting, is fairly similar to creating a morph. You can sculpt how the lid looks as it is pulled down. If you parent the lid's joint or influence object to a flag that is easy to control, it will work really well.

Deformations from the Cornea

If you have a realistic character, you might want to consider adding cornea deformations. When the eyelid is closed, the eyeball can continue to move underneath it, and you can still see where the character's eye is pointing. Rapid eye movement, or REM sleep, is common for sleeping characters and will really sell the believability of the character. You can simulate this deformation using either bulge deformers that are parented to the eyeball or, for a more controlled effect, lattices.

Eye Targeting Techniques

The place to start when dealing with eye rigging is with eye tracking since this is the easiest way to recognize eye motion. For eye targeting, there are two common techniques. We'll call these two methods the simple approach and the advanced approach.

The simple targeting setup is easy to create and control, but it doesn't allow you to control the eyeballs independently. The advanced targeting setup gives you more control over each eyeball independently, but this approach can be confusing for animators who mainly work with a single eye targeting control. Table 10.1 lists the strengths and weaknesses of these approaches.

▶ **Table 10.1** Targeting Setup Strengths and Weaknesses

Simple Targeting Setup	Advanced Targeting Setup
Speed of setup	More control
Speed of use	Independent eye control
No independent eye control	Longer to set up

We will give the realistic figure an advanced setup, while the cartoony figure will have the simple setup. You can use either of these setups on any character you want. They are not character specific. All that really matters is that you understand what each setup does and that you choose the setup that meets your character's animation needs.

Simple Setup

To create the simple setup, follow these steps:

1. Use a prebuilt figure, and create a locator that will be the focus of the eyes.

2. Name this locator EyeAim.

3. In the side view, move the locator to a position in front of the eyes by moving up from the origin until you are at the center of the eyes and then out on the Z-axis (this should be in front of the character). As an alternative, you can position the locator in front of your figure and then use the front view to line the target up with the center of the eyes.

Tip: We suggest moving the locator about a figure height in front of the character. You want the target to be somewhat farther ahead so that when the eyes are skinned to the joints, the offset is minimal. To avoid the offset, you can change the setting in the aim constraint to "maintain offset," or you can skin the eyes before you constrain them.

4. Freeze the transforms of the locator so that you can zero it out later as needed during animation.

5. Now, constrain the eyes to the locator, remembering to select the locator (driver), and then to each eye (driven) and aim-constrain (Constrain – Aim) them. If the eye shifts 90 degrees in any direction, open the Attribute Editor, and change the values of the aim axis vector in the aim constraint until the eye aims properly. Also, it's a good idea to make sure the up vector is set to 0 1 0; otherwise, your eyes will roll when the head tilts. This might not be a problem for some cartoons, but it is very bad for blood vessel–textured eyes. It's also good to create another locator as the up object in case your character has to tumble around or do flips. In this case, make sure the up vector object is parented to the head.

Leave the eye controls free. This allows animators the flexibility of being able to move the target wherever they need. As an alternative, you could parent-constrain it to the master control or to the head.

Tip: You can parent-constrain the EyeAim locator to the head, but if you do so, you need to make sure the animator knows to counteranimate to keep the eyes moving. Create this connection by selecting the head joint (driver) and then the locator (driven), and then use the parent constraint (Constrain > Parent) and maintain the offset in the options. The animators will want you to make it possible to aim the eyes at anything. You will also need to parent the control to the other object and animate the weighting within the parent constraint attribute for the locator.

Figure 10.2 shows what the completed simple targeting setup looks like. You can now test the orientation of your joints by moving the EyeAim locator, selecting each eye, and using the Rotate tool. The manipulator will show the orientation of the joint. Figure 10.3 shows the manipulator.

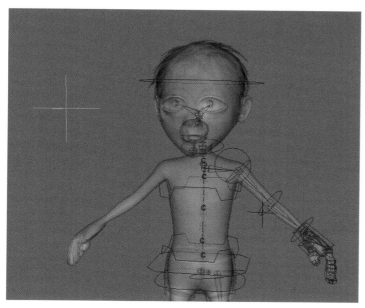

Figure 10.2 Simple eye control setup

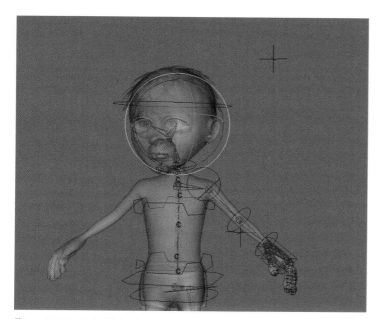

Figure 10.3 Eye test with simple setup

Advanced Setup

Some characters need independent, spherical eyes. The following setup provides those and gives the animator great control.

First, we will address the main control for the eyes. This control is the target for both eyes together. As this target moves, both eyes aim toward it and follow it. Next, we'll add secondary controllers next to the main target. These control each eye independently. Thus, you could emulate one lazy eye but still allow both eyes to track as you move the main target.

Finally, we'll add controls on each eye that allow movement of the actual joint by the group controlling it. These controls are represented as straight lines sticking out of each eye.

1. Create a control curve (Create > CV Curve Tool) that will be the focus of the eyes. This curve needs to represent the target for both eyes, and it is being created to provide the focal point. Make the target visually descriptive. We chose a circle with a cross in it, similar to a crosshair.

2. Center the control's pivot (Modify > Center Pivot), and move it to a location about half the figure height in front of the figure's eyes. This way the locator is not so far away as to be a nuisance, and it is still close enough to grab when working locally. Make sure this target is on the character's midline.

3. Rename this locator or control to EyeAimMaster.

4. Create another curve control. This one will be for the right eye on the right side of the focus point. Each eye will be aimed at its own aim control, and each control will be constrained to the main target. Thus, you will need to make it a child of EyeAimMaster. Create this control with a nurbs circle (Create > Nurbs Primitives > Circle), or choose another shape to represent a target for each eye. We just used a circle for these secondary controls.

5. Move this control into place by snapping to the actual eye joint. Press and hold the V key while you move the control. After it is snapped, you can pull it out, directly along the Z-axis, to the point where the target is.

6. Now duplicate the control, and move it to the exact opposite side of the figure, using the Channel Box. If the X value is negative, then make it positive. Likewise, make it positive if it is negative.

7. Now freeze the transformations on the three curves, and name the side controls to REyeAimCTRL and LEyeAimCTRL, respectively.

8. Create the control for each eye using a curve. Make each a curve (Create > CV Curve Tool) with a curve degree of "1 linear," and use the grid to create a line with two CVs. Make this line parallel with the direction of sight.

9. Center its pivot (Modify > Center Pivot), and then press and hold the C key to move its pivot to the end that is toward the rear of the figure.

10. Snap the line control to the eye joint by pressing and holding the V key, and then freeze its transforms (Modify > Freeze Transformations). Now, repeat this process for the other eye.

11. Name the controls LEyeCTRL and REyeCTRL.

12. Follow the guidelines in the "Creating Controls" section for use on the eye controls in Chapter 3.

13. Now that your flags are driving the eye joints, you can orient them to the flags. Since the flag and the controls are both parent-constrained to the head, you need to create another layer of nulls for each eye.

    Select each flag again, and create another group (Ctrl+G). This creates a null within a null. Name the new nulls LEyeNullAim and REyeNullAim, respectively.

14. Instead of assigning a parent constraint to it, aim constraint this new group to AimFlags for each eye.

15. Select all these flags, and group them together under an organizational group called Eyes.

Figure 10.4 shows the final eye controls for this setup, and Figure 10.5 shows how the eye controls can be moved independently.

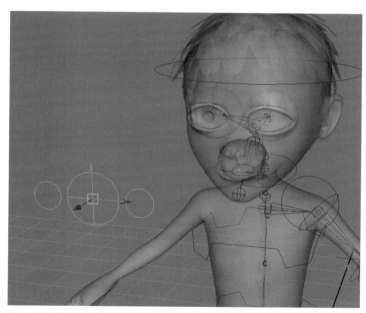

Figure 10.4 Eye controls all set up (preskinning)

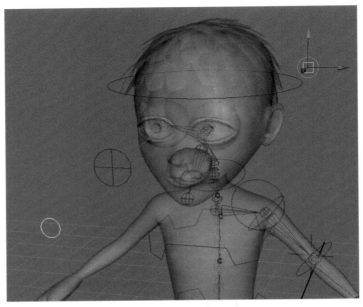

Figure 10.5 Fun test with eye controls (preskinning)

Squashing and Stretching Eyes

For a squash-and-stretch setup, you need a specific character type—one that starts with spherical eyes that cross each other on the X-axis. You need to have a similar character to utilize parts of this tutorial. In this tutorial, we'll show you how to express anger and sadness and other emotions with a lattice deformer that controls the eyes and brow. Later in this chapter, we will show how to create morphs for blinking and separate them into upper and lower eyelids, as well as right and left eyes. We could hook up automatic eyelids and a cornea deformation (we'll discuss those later in the chapter), but for now we'll just go over how to set up a lattice that deforms the entire head.

Note: This is somewhat of a derailment from the rest of the book in that it presents a very stylized and specific type of rigging setup. You probably won't use this type often, but it is good to know when you need it. And, like many rigging tasks, it might spark ideas for solving other problems you might face in the future.

Set up your figure's rig as you would normally with the head and the eyes following a target. This can be a simple target with the eyes aim-constrained, or it can be a complex three-control system. In this tutorial, we will show how to do the following:

- Make the eyes a little cross-eyed for a cartoony feel.
- Add a lattice for the second-tier deformation (after the blendshapes), as shown in Figure 10.6.
- Test the rig.

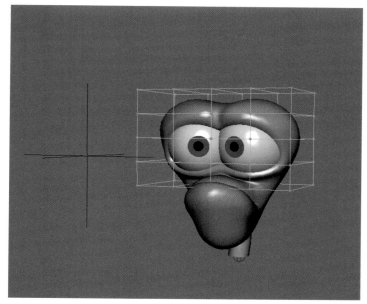

Figure 10.6 Squash and stretch eye controls

Adding the Lattice

To add the lattice, follow these steps:

1. You have created your rig, and you have the joints following an eye target. You might need to adjust for the aiming of the eye joints by turning the eyes inward slightly and not having them aligned with the eye joint. This is needed only to compensate for the size and shape of the eyes.

2. If you haven't done so already, parent-constrain the eyes to the joints. Do this by selecting the joint and then the eye and using Constrain > Parent.

3. Now that you have your eyes ready, establish limits to keep one eye from turning too far into the other eye:

    •   Rotate an eye so that one of the irises is next to the other eye and about to go into it. This is to find its limits.

    •   Select the eye's joint, look in the Channel Box, and get the Y-rotation value.

    •   Open the Attribute Editor for the eye joint, and set a limit for the joint at that value. The limit value that we used for our character is –23.

    •   If you are working on the left eye, select the Rot Limit Y Min box (select Rot Limit Y Max if you are working on the right eye), and put the limit value in the field.

4. Repeat step 3 for the other eye. It will consequently need a max limit.

5. Select all the geometry you want to affect with the lattice. If you want to stretch everything, select the skin and eyes and create your lattice (Create Deformers > Lattice). You will most likely want to have minimum dimensions of 5 by 4 by 2. Lower resolution will not give you the detail you need.

6. Parent ffd1Lattice under ffd1Base (these are easily selected in the Outliner; drag ffd1Lattice under ffd1Base with the middle mouse button). This will allow you to move the lattice to the position that you will want distorted. For this character, we want to distort both the eyes and the lids. Now you can rename your lattice prefixes to something that is representative of your character, such as EyeLattice and EyeLatticeBase.

7. Parent the EyeLatticeBase under the head joint so that it moves with your rig.

 Tip: It is good practice to place your lattices in areas where the geometry will not be affected by other joints.

Figure 10.7 shows an example of the expressions you can create with this type of setup. You can now test the lattices' effect on the character by manipulating the EyeLattice points.

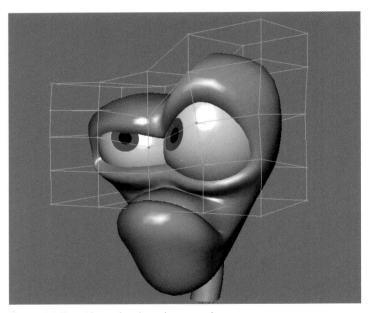

Figure 10.7 Test with squash and stretch eye controls

Lovely Lacrimals

Simulating the lacrimal ducts located in the corner of the eye can really make your eye movement stand out. They help define the eye as a system with soft tissue instead of making the eyeball just a round spinning sphere.

Modeling larcimal carnuncles in the corners of the eyes isn't enough; you need to create the motions of these ducts deforming as the eyeball moves. The best way to create these deformations is with morphs. Figure 10.8 shows how the lacrimal ducts deform into the eyeball space when the eyeball moves to the side.

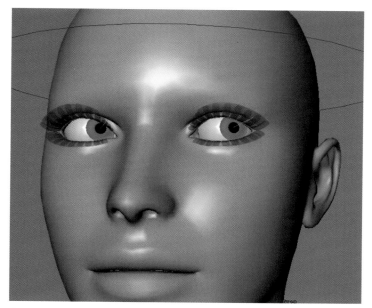

Figure 10.8 Lovely pink lacrimals and their deformations built onto Daz3D's Victoria 4

In the tutorials that follow, we'll show you several specific morphs that are required for realistic lacrimal movement.

LacrimalIn-OutL and *LacrimalIn-OutR*

One of the more difficult aspects of this morph is bidirectional movement. It is best to have your morph work in the positive and the negative, because it will help in setting up the connections. Using a blendshape is somewhat inefficient because your morph target is a linear deformation. Therefore, the lacrimal will not curve around the eye surface. As the blendshape is driven in the positive and then in the negative, make sure it does not leave the eye surface in either direction of travel. You will likely need to have the lacrimal geometry move through the eye geometry slightly to achieve this detail.

We will show how to hook up the deformation with set-driven keys. Using this technique, you can drive the morphs with joint handle rotation.

1. Start by making sure that your eye setup (built in previous tutorials) is working properly and that you can move both eyes with the controllers. You will also need to create both lacrimal morphs that we just talked about as blendshapes. Use someone else's eyes for reference when building these blendshapes for your character since it is challenging to look sideways and see your lacrimals in a mirror. You can name these blendshapes LEyeLacrimal and REyeLacrimal.

2. Open the Set Driven Key Editor (Animate > Set Driven Key > Set), and select the left eye joint as the driver. Now open the Blendshape Editor, and select the list of lacrimal blendshapes. Use the Select button below the morphs. After you have pushed it, go back to your set-driven key panel, and hit the Load Driven button.

3. Select rotateY for the joint, and then select the corresponding lacrimal morph for the driven. The Y rotate now drives the lacrimal morph.

4.   You always need to remember to key the base position before you get started. This will give the set-driven key a base position as well. Now use the Key button to set the base position.

5.   Now, rotate on the Y-axis of the eye to the extreme on one side, set the morph to create its corresponding shape, and use the Key button to set the driven key.

6.   Repeat step 5 for the opposite extreme Y-rotation, as shown in Figure 10.9.

7.   Repeat steps 4, 5, and 6 for the right eye.

Figure 10.10 shows the lacrimal morphs applied to both eyes.

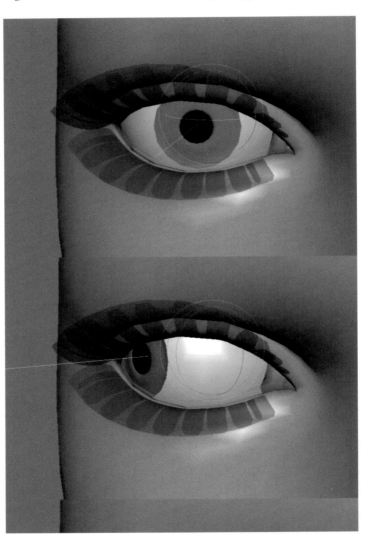

Figure 10.9 Lacrimal in and out position examples

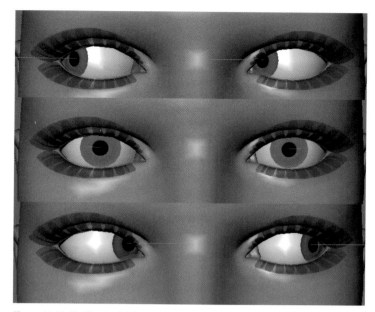

Figure 10.10 Final lacrimal deformations

Eyelid Morphs You Will Need

Eyeball movement is easy to control because it deals with two parented objects that are independent from the rest of the face mesh. The eyelids, however, are part of the face mesh and need to stretch and deform along with the rest of the face. We'll now discuss a way in which you can accomplish automatic eyelid movement. You might not want to set this up because it can expose the eyes to unwanted deformations. However, if you set up automatic deformations correctly, you have the freedom of independent lid movement, as well as automatically driven lids.

The main eyelid motion is that of blinking. You can accomplish this in several ways. One method is simply to deform the eyelids with a morph and connect them to a control that drives how far the eyelids close. Another approach is to use the joint or influence object approach. This approach attaches a control to the outer eye, and it has a center of manipulation at the center of the eye. The weights are painted according to the desired shape of each lid. This creates a realistic curving motion for the lid.

Creating Eye Area Shape Morphs

When dealing with morphs, several specific morphs are useful to create the eyelid motions. You will want to create some of these morphs at extremes and then dial them back to save the shape. This will be helpful when the animator wants to dial the morph beyond its value of 1. If you create these shapes with influence objects, aim for the shapes that follow.

Blink

This will be the morph you can use as a starting point for the others. Build this, and you will have each movement for the eye, as shown in Figure 10.11. Separate it into the lid components, and you're done with building.

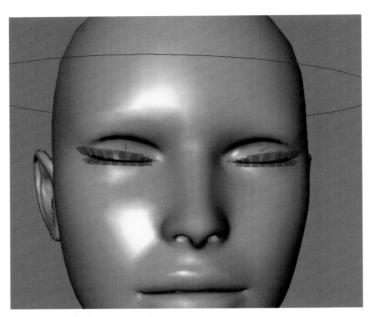

Figure 10.11 Blink morph example

You need to be wary of the dreaded poke-through issues that accompany a blink morph. Because your eye is spherical and the blink morph is linear, you need to make sure there is ample coverage at the 50 percent mark. Dial the morph back to partial values, and make sure the eye is not poking through the lid. If it is, you need to adjust the morph to 100 percent, or you will need to adjust the base shape. Watch the upper lid. You will also want to watch for swimming lashes as you morph. This is caused when the morph is made and the lashes are accidentally moved to emanate from a different insertion point. Thus, when the morph is applied, the eyelashes appear to move. The lashes need to keep the same insertion point as the base, or they will not look real as your character blinks.

UpperLidUpL and UpperLidUpR

The UpperLidUp morphs are used to convey surprise and shock. For the UpperLidUp morph, you want the top lid to come open to about the top of the iris. (You should have built your base with the upper lid at about the midpoint between the pupil and the iris edge and the lower lid at the iris's lower edge.) For more exaggerated characters, you might want to go even further. For realism, subtlety is the key. You do not need large movements to communicate surprise or shock. Small eye movements will show that emotion. Figure 10.12 shows the base position for an eyelid, and Figure 10.13 shows a raised upper eyelid.

Figure 10.12 The base eyelid position

Figure 10.13 UpperLidUp

UpperLidDownL and *UpperLidDownR*

The UpperLidDown morph makes a character look lazy or creates an eyelash flutter. This morph is the one you really need to watch for poke-through. Make sure that as the lid drops, it grows to match the surface of the eye so that it in essence stretches over the surface. Bring this morph farther than halfway down the eye as in reality, as shown in Figure 10.14. You will see how neat this is once you set up the eye automation.

Figure 10.14 UpperLidDown

LowLidUpL and *LowLidUpR*

LowLidUp is perfect for wincing and smiling. This is one of the more fun morphs to see, since it really gives your character life. Make sure this morph is brought up to the point where the lower lid and the upper lid are about the same distance from the pupil, as shown in Figure 10.15. This will create a realistic blink where the upper lid falls just under the pupil in a blink, and the lower lid comes up to meet it. Also, you will need to make sure it works with the UpperLidDown morph for the blink. Apply the UpperLidDown morph to test. You will add the two together to achieve a blink.

Figure 10.15 LowerLidUp

LowLidDownL and LowLidDownR

The LowerLidDown morphs will mostly be used for the automated process. They also can be used to convey anger, surprise, shock, or intensity. Using references, you can see that most of that movement is in the upper lid, as shown in Figure 10.16. The lower lid moves only slightly when opening the eyes wide.

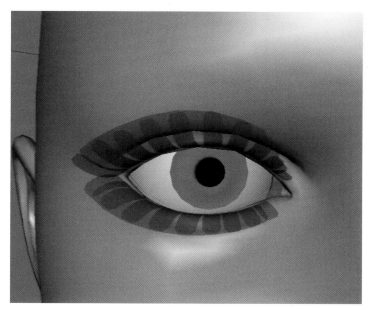

Figure 10.16 LowerLidDown

Automating Eyelid Deformations Using Set-Driven Keys

After all your eyelid morphs are created, you can create a driven keys setup that uses the various movements to correspond with the eyeball movement. This setup uses the Z-axis as its aiming axis. If you want to have the X-axis as your aiming axis, replace the other rotations for your driven values in the tutorial.

> **Tip:** Before you begin, make sure your eye setup is working. You will also need to check your blend-shapes. As you work on this setup, use a friend's eyes for reference, since the eye has subtle movements that you will want to reflect.

1. Open the Set Driven Key Editor (Animate > Set Driven Key > Set), and select the right eye joint as the driver. Now open the Blend Shape Editor (Windows > Animation Editors > Blend Shape), and select the list of the lid targets using the Select button located below the morphs. Now, return to your set-driven key panel, and click the Load Driven button.

3. Select RotateX for the driver, and select all the lid morphs you created earlier as the driven. Click the Key button to set the default position.

4. Select RotateX in the driven and the LowLidDownR morph. Rotate the eyeball until the pupil goes into the lower lid. Apply the LowerLidDownR morph. Set the key in the Set Driven Key Editor.

5. Now select UpperLidDownR for the driven, and then apply the morph and move it down slightly. It needs to cover only the tip of the iris, as shown in Figure 10.17. Set a key for this as well.

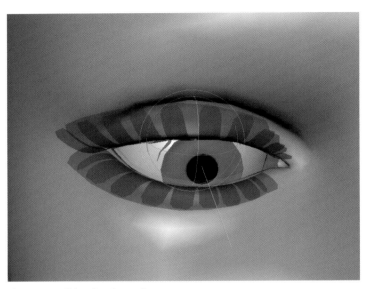

Figure 10.17 Lid settings for eye down

6. Now rotate the right eye up until the pupil is just into the upper lid, as shown in Figure 10.18. Now apply the UpperLidUpR morph, and select it as the driven. Use the Key button to set a key. Now bring the LowLidUpR morph up, and select it as the driven. Use the Key button to set another key.

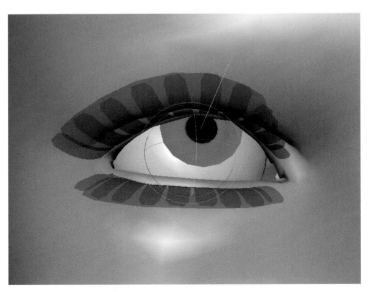

Figure 10.18 Lid settings for eye up

7. Repeat steps 1 through 6 for the left eye. Remember to set the default position and then set the keys. Then test the system by moving the eye target. Figure 10.19 shows the results.

Tip: If you are having any difficulty with your rotation, experiment with different rotation orders until the joint works. Rotation order can provide wrong results if it is not set up properly.

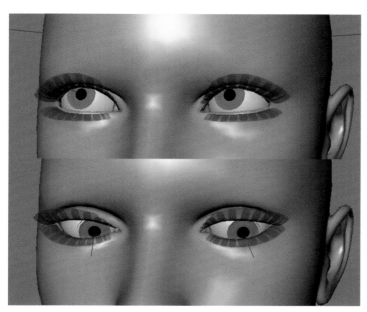

Figure 10.19 The automatic eye setup effect

Automatic Cornea/Lid Deformation

A feature that will really add realism to your characters is a cornea deformation. The cornea sits on the sphere of the eye and causes a slight bump as it moves under the lids; it pushes them out slightly. This becomes very evident when you are sleeping. It also makes it possible to actually see where someone is pointing their eyes, even if they are closed. Here is a way to mimic this movement in your figure:

1. Select the size of geometry that you want affected by the cornea deformation.

2. Create a lattice (Create Deformers > Lattice > Options) with a minimum matrix of 5, 5, 2. This will give you control in the X- and Y-axes, right where you need it. You might want more control than this, so an alternate lattice resolution would be 7, 7, 2 or even 10, 10, 2.

3. In the Outliner, drag the base under the lattice with the middle mouse button (or parent it, child to parent, using the P hotkey).

4

Move the lattice into place, as shown in Figure 10.20.

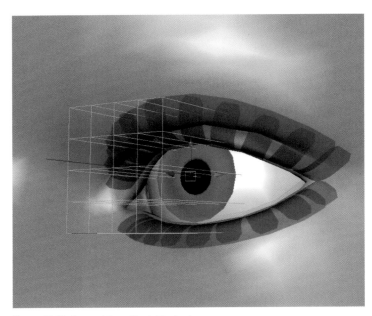

Figure 10.20 Cornea deformation lattice in place

5. Select the various lattice points, and manipulate them to the desired cornea deformation shape, as shown in Figure 10.21 (Right-click the lattice–lattice point.) Figure 10.22 shows the results.

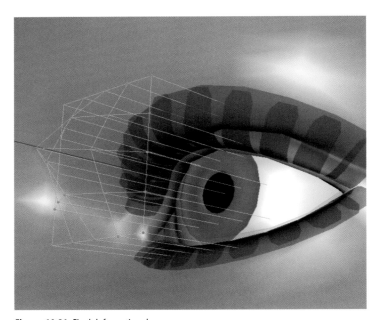

Figure 10.21 Final deformation shape

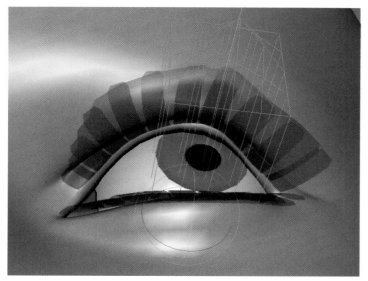

Figure 10.22 We have achieved cornea deformations.

Creating Tears

An amazing little piece of geometry that you can create is the tear. You can simulate tears by creating a surface that runs along the lower lid. You can either follow your morphs or weight it in with your joint of influence object so that it moves with your lid deformation. You can either use a nurbs curve or a little bit of Sub division to create the surface. You might want to create a morph that allows the surface to get thicker, creating a "welling up" effect. DAZ3D's Victoria 4 character is a good illustration of how the tear geometry is used.

Tying the Eye Controls to the Rest of the Rig

Now that you have a bunch of eye controls, you'll need to tie these controls into the rest of the rig so they move when the character moves:

1. Select all the items created in this chapter, and group them under an Eyes group.
2. Check to make sure the group includes the lattice, the right and left eye controls, and the master eye-aim control.

Conclusion

Realistic eye movements are defined by subtle motions. This is especially true when the audience is looking at a close-up of your character. That's when these subtle eye motions are paramount. This chapter covered several important eye motions including eye targeting and blinking. It also covered several less used but essential eye movements, including lacrimal duct deformations, eyelid deformations, and cornea deformations. We also talked about exaggerated cartoon eyes.

In the next chapter, we'll move down from the eyes and begin covering the mouth, teeth, and jaw. We will start with making the general mouth expressions.

Show Your Teeth: Creating the Mouth and Jaw

11

The jaw and the mouth are the defining features of the face. The motions created by what you do in this chapter will define how your character will speak. When it comes to rigging the mouth and jaw, there are essentially three approaches you can take. One approach is to build a rig for the jaw and mouth using joints or influence objects. The second approach is to use a set of morphed expressions with a rigged jaw. The third is using only morphs for the jaw and speech movement. We are also going to go over some of the shapes that will be needed to make believable speech.

Chapter Contents
Jaw rigging techniques
Introducing shapes for the jaw rig
Creating the master morphs
Using morphs in your setup

Jaw Rigging Techniques

The main reasons for rigging the mouth and jaw are speaking and expressing emotions. Most characters who need to speak will likely need to have very subtle visemes and expressions that can be driven to higher morph levels. If the mouth and jaw setup don't work, you can lose the whole illusion of the character. Just think of how bad it looks when, in a movie, the sound is not in time with the film. If you have even the slightest issue with speech, your audience will know there is a problem. With correct jaw and mouth rigging, you can achieve the realism that your character deserves and give the animators the tools to create realistic speech and emotion. Figure 11.1 shows an example of a realistic mouth expression.

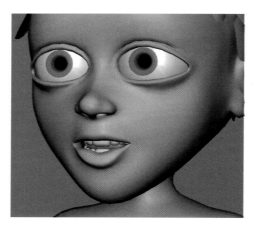 

Figure 11.1 A speaking mouth

Rigged Jaw vs. Morphed Jaw vs. Morphs with Rigged Jaw

The two most common setups for jaws are the morph-driven jaw and the rigged jaw. A head that includes a morph-driven jaw needs only a simple rig that extends up to the eyes. The rest of the head is then weighted to the head joint in the binding process. A rigged or joint-driven jaw can be somewhat more difficult to set up. A third setup adds morphs to a rigged jaw. Table 11.1 lists the main differences in their capabilities.

Rigged Jaw and Mouth	Morphed Jaw	Morphs with Rigged Jaw
Unlimited variability	Linear movement (nonrealistic)	Hinged jaw (realistic)
Easy to set up	Teeth and jaw move in nonrealistic way	Facial morphs need to work with jaw
Will take time to bind	Can create combination morphs	
Need to create morphs with poses		

As you know, we're using two figures for the rigging examples in this book. Our realistic figure will have morphs and a rigged jaw. Our cartoony character will have a rigged jaw with influence objects driving the mouth movement. With both figures, you will need to define mouth shapes. With the realistic figure, they will simply be different blendshapes. With the cartoony runner character, you will need to use set-driven keys with attributes to create sliders for each shape.

As we show how to work with the jaw throughout the rest of the chapter, we'll take an approach that uses both joints for the jaw and morphs for the jaw and mouth. We'll use a rigged jaw for all the major movements of the jaw. A wide-open mouth or the jaw moving side to side are good examples of how you can use a jointed jaw. We'll also show how to make morphs for the mouth, lips, and jaw. By combining both of these approaches, you can achieve a wide array of motions for the mouth and jaw.

> **Note:** If you are using influence objects for your character, make sure the character's mouth can perform the basic shapes discussed in this chapter.

Morphs and Painting Weights

Although we are not going to paint weights at this time (this is discussed in Chapter 18, "The Skinny on Skinning: Effective Surface Attachment"), it is good to see how the weights fall off in order to correctly create morphs for the jaw. You might want to paint your weights with the OpenMouth morph applied. With the mouth open, you can more easily work in areas that are hard to reach. Refer to Figure 11.2 for an example of the falloff you will need to work with in these morphs.

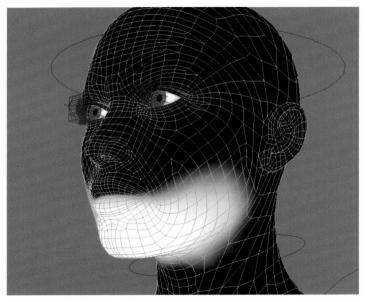

Figure 11.2 Painted jaw weights

Shapes for the Jaw Rig

Combining rig joints and morphs requires some extra planning. You'll need to establish good naming conventions to keep all the morphs and joints straight. We talked about proper naming conventions in Chapter 2, "Getting to Know You: Maya's Interface and Basics." You'll also want to find a tool that simplifies the process of creating morphs. Modo and ZBrush are two excellent choices for making this task much easier. Modo is a powerful polygon and subdivision modeling package with artisan and symmetry tools that are virtually unmatched. It also displays in, and allows you to work on, the subdivision surface. This makes modeling fast and dreamy. ZBrush has similar tools that allow artists to spend more time creating and less time fiddling with tools. We'll show how to use both of these applications to create morphs for the Victoria character.

Morphs

Morphs are a great way to make the surface deform to a predetermined state. If you are working only in Maya, you can create a morph by creating a copy of your geometry (offsetting it) and manipulating it as desired. You then can apply it using the Create Deformers > Blendshape Tool command.

Morphs, like most everything in Maya, can be hooked up to any type of node. A rotation bend of an elbow can drive a morph made to squish the skin in that area. An attribute can drive other attributes, which in turn drive many morphs. The possibilities are endless when setting up controls like this.

You can then modify your character with the morphs in the Blendshapes window (Window > Animation Editor > Blend Shape). Figure 11.3 shows a basic slider list, which is where your shapes are stored. Some animators prefer to use this method of animating because it is simple to key and to set up. When creating your morph targets, you can duplicate your whole figure once for each morph, or you can separate the head and duplicate just the head for each morph. As an alternative, you can use a completely different head as a wrap deformer to the full body geometry and then apply all the morphs to this. For dealing with the same problem, cSmartBlend, developed by Comet Digital, had a workaround for this, but sadly, it is no longer supported.

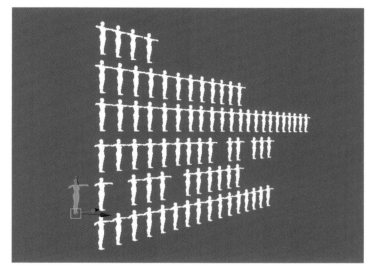

Figure 11.3 Morphs creation

Joints and Influence Objects

Joints and influence objects are both great for free-floating deformations, which can be useful for mouth, eyebrow, and eyelid shapes. We put joints and influence objects together because they can be used in similar ways. Both can be attached to the surface by painting their weights. You can control both by creating layered nulls for control of individual joints or using set-driven controls.

For controlling either joints or influence objects, you'll want the hierarchy to first have the joints, then the controls (per joint), and then the null group for each (set-driven keys can drive the null group that is above the group holding the control). With the runner character, we'll show how to use a UI selection system to select influence object controls and set-driven keys to drive all the visemes.

Naming Conventions

As you create a variety of morphs, it can become difficult to remember which morph goes with which expression, so it becomes crucial that you establish and stick to a rigid naming convention. For mouth morphs, the naming convention should enable you to look at a morph name and know immediately the body part it affects, the side of the mouth it belongs on, and whether it influences the upper or lower lips. An example of this is RLipLowUp.

The naming convention should include the body part first because this provides an easy way to organize the morphs. This should list the local area of the body part such as the lips or mouth corner. The next part of the morph name should be the action. Is the morph providing depth, height, or side-to-side motion? After that, the name should designate whether the morph impacts the lower or upper lips because of local area and alphabetical sorting. Finally, the name should include an L or R for determining the side.

We recommend using a naming convention follows this format:

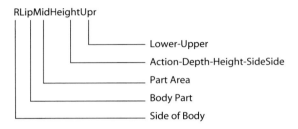

RLipMidHeightUpr

Lower-Upper
Action-Depth-Height-SideSide
Part Area
Body Part
Side of Body

Some examples of how this naming convention can be applied are as follows:

RLipInLow: Lower right lip moves toward the center of the body.

RMouthCornerDepth: Mouth corner right moves in and out in the same morph.

RLipMidHeightUpr: Lip mid is an area of the lips for the upper and lower.

Morph Creation

After you have planned the morphs and have defined the naming convention, you can get down to the business of creating the actual morphs. Although Maya has a robust set of modeling tools, some artists choose another package that provides tools and a workflow they feel comfortable with. This is fine, but be sure to test to make sure you have a good way of importing the geometry into Maya. Maya does not like group designations, so make sure your file doesn't have groups. Also make sure that point order is maintained when you export from your application. This is usually not a big concern since most applications are great with this.

Working in ZBrush

The first tool we recommend after you have gotten a good base shape is ZBrush. ZBrush can quickly distort and create defined shapes without having to model every poly or even use multiple-step falloff tools. ZBrush also calculates changes very rapidly. In this section, we'll cover the basics of morph target creation in ZBrush.

To create a morph in ZBrush, follow these steps:

1. Export the figure from your modeling program as an *.obj file.

2. Open ZBrush, and import the base mesh as a tool (Tool > Import).

Tip: Point order problems can be really nasty, especially after you have taken time to carefully craft your morph. They manifest themselves as portions of your morph exploding like string art straight from the '70s. The vert placement will be correct, but the vertices switch their order. You can avoid this by exporting your mesh from Maya to an *.obj file and then reimporting that same mesh. Once the model has made the journey out and back in once, you can export and import with confidence. There are point order matchers available that can help correct problems, but it's better to avoid the problem altogether.

3. Bring the object into view by right-clicking in the main viewport and dragging to the right. The model scale actually stays the same size. You might want to export your tool now to verify that the model is the same scale as the export. If it is not, simply import your model twice.

4. Go to Edit mode (right-click in the viewport and choose Edit Object, or use the hotkey T), as shown in Figure 11.4.

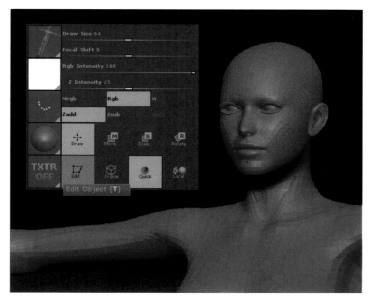

Figure 11.4 Be sure to enter Edit mode.

5. Turn on symmetry in the X-axis (Transform > >X<) so that changes to one side of the face are automatically applied to the opposite side of the face.

6. If you are working with a Subd cage, you can smooth the mesh to approximate changes (Tool > Geometry > Divide).

7. Manipulate the mesh with the drawing and tweaking brushes for the final shape.

8. If you didn't subdivide, move to the next step. If you used the Subdivision in ZBrush, bring the model back to the cage by moving the SDiv level to 1and by clicking Cage. This will calculate the high-resolution representative cage for you.

9. Export the mesh (Tool > Export).

Figure 11.5 shows an example head model that was modified using ZBrush. Notice the symmetry of the model and how smooth the results are when you use the Subd cage.

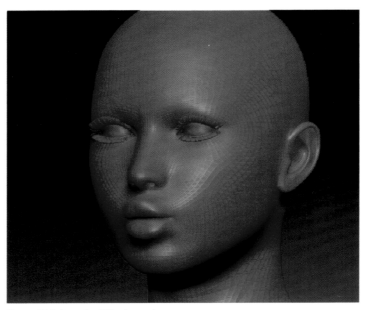

Figure 11.5 Example of ZBrush morph

Working in Modo

There are many amazing scripts and features for speeding up modeling in Maya, but there are also some other packages that are worth exploring. Our weapon of choice for modeling is Modo. The concepts we'll go over in this chapter are partly application specific. Some of the ideas will be easily translated into your favorite package, while others will not. Since these applications are constantly evolving, always be open to the possibility that another tool could make the process even faster.

The main advantage of Modo is that it creates a very manageable morph list and application system. It is simple to apply morphs to other morphs with a falloff, for instance. You can also quickly mask off an area of a morph that you can then clear back to the base shape. Modo also has excellent tools for creating different falloffs and for selecting specific areas of the mesh.

The Master Morphs

If you have chosen to create your facial shapes with joints or influence objects, make sure you can still make these facial shapes with your figure and its deformers. This is an excellent benchmark to hit when creating visemes.

Regardless of the tools you choose to use, concentrate on producing a set of morphs to cover all the possible expressions that your character will need to re-create. The base morphs you create are called the *master morphs* because the animator can combine them to produce all the regularly used expressions and visemes. We will discuss our viseme list in Chapter 12, "Can't You See What I'm Saying? Logical Viseme Creation."

Set up a mirror next to your monitor. Make each of these shapes with the same movement that you observe when you make the shape yourself. Having as much reference as possible makes for better shaping.

The master morphs we'll show you include the following:

- MouthOpen
- MouthCornerDepth
- LipsOut
- LipsIn
- MouthHeight
- LipMidHeight
- MouthCornerHeight
- MouthWidth
- MouthNarrow
- LipsPart

We are also going to go over a few optional tongue morphs. These will help you to achieve more realistic results if you choose to use them.

MouthOpen

The MouthOpen morph is a good place to start. It is very useful in the creation of other morphs. It moves the mouth from closed to gaping open, as shown in Figure 11.6, and is the default morph to use when testing any jaw rigging joints. It also is a good morph to use when you need to see the interior of the mouth and the lips without any overlapping.

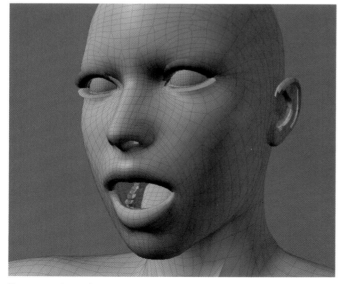

Figure 11.6 MouthOpen

The MouthOpen morph needs to work well with the jaw rig, allowing the jaw to rotate from its center position. For jaw rigs, you need to parent constrain the lower teeth to the jaw. For a morphed-only face, you need to create jaw morphs that mimic the movement of a jaw rig. The teeth need to follow these morphs without deforming.

This morph also represents an extreme position and as such should not be used with large negative values, which would cause the morph to tear apart. You also need to watch the corners of the mouth, when the morph is overdriven, so that they keep their shape as the mouth opens.

To make a MouthOpen morph, follow these steps:

1. Make sure that symmetry is turned on, and then select the center of the lower lip.

2. Next, grow the selection (Shift+up arrow) until it selects the lower lip to the corner of the mouth, and then shrink the selection back about three to four steps.

3. Now, rotate the selection looking from an orthographic view. Experiment with the point of rotation until you find the correct rotation point in front of and below the ear. The center of rotation on our model was about 1.5 inches, relative, in front of and below the ear.

4. Grow the selection, and rotate from the same spot you used in step 3.

5. Repeat step 4 for a gradual pseudo-falloff.

6. Smooth the geometry with the Smooth tool. Go easy with it since it has a tendency to flatten.

7. If you are using a rigged jaw, select the tongue, teeth, and gums, and then use the clear morph command (Vertex Map > Clear).

8. Rotate the jaw into the opened mouth position since it is slightly hidden from the front orthographic camera.

You can expand the OpenMouth morph to create derivative morphs for the left and right sides of the mouth opening, as shown in Figure 11.7. The derivative morphs aren't necessary for the general visemes. For those, only the open mouth usually needs to be used. The derivative morphs, like the left and right, can be used for an added level of asymmetry and realism.

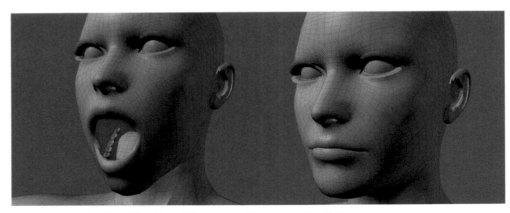

Figure 11.7 Examples of overdriven MouthOpen and a slight negative MouthOpen

MouthCornerDepth

Figure 11.8 shows MouthCornerDepth. The MouthCornerDepth, MouthHeight, and MouthWidth morphs are used together to create the smile expression.

> **Tip:** You should use the negative value of MouthCornerDepth sparingly, or you'll end up with a weird pucker on your character's face.

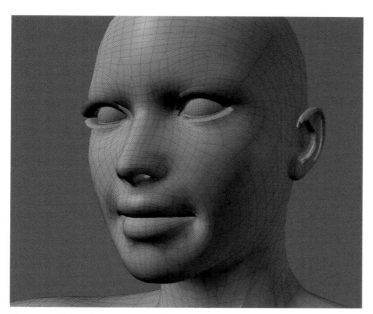

Figure 11.8 MouthCornerDepth

To create a MouthCornerDepth morph, follow these steps:

1. Use ZBrush to move the corners of the mouth straight back. Look at the model from the side, and use the Tweak brush to push back the area. The negative morph should pull the lips straight out.

2. Make sure you have the labial furrows (wrinkles that go from the sides of the mouth to the nose). You might need to pull some of the flesh around the wrinkles to compensate for the pinching.

3. Export your morph using Tool > Export, and then import the file into Modo with the Load command.

4. Clear the teeth to avoid unwanted movement, such as stretching.

5. From within Modo, make two duplicates of the morph (right-click Morph, and then pick Duplicate), and rename the duplicates for use on the left and right sides.

6. Now copy the morph to the duplicates using the Morph tool and a linear falloff to apply it to the appropriate side of the model.

Tip: You can expand the MouthCornerDepth morph to create MouthCornerDepthL and MouthCornerDepthR derivative morphs for the left and right sides of the smile, as shown in Figure 11.9.

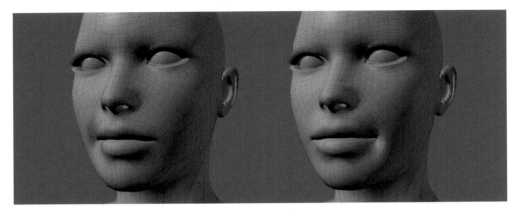

Figure 11.9 MouthCornerDepthL and MouthCornerDepthR

LipsOut

The LipsOut morph is used to show the lips extending outward. It can portray a sad expression, a partial viseme component, and the beginning of a kiss, as shown in Figure 11.10.

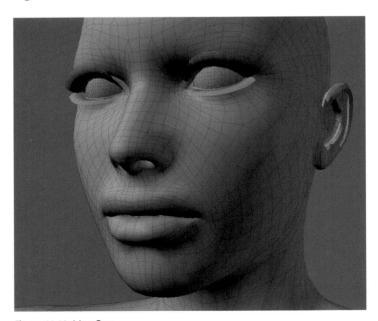

Figure 11.10 LipsOut

This morph should roll the lips outward. It is used with a partial OpenMouth morph to create CH and SH sounds. It makes the lips thicker as they rotate out slightly. The lower lip on this morph makes the character look like they are pouting.

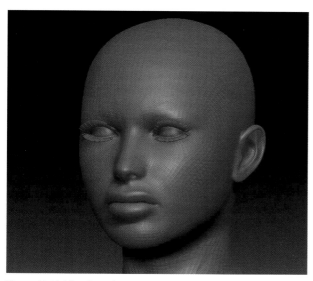

Figure 11.11 LipsOut, shown in ZBrush

To create the LipsOut morph, follow these steps:

1. Move the area of the lips out with an appropriate falloff using ZBrush.

2. Make sure you mimic the rolling of the lips as they move out. Pay attention to the thickness of the lips as they roll. Rolling them can cause unwanted pinching in some areas.

3. Export your morph using Tool > Export, and then import the file into Modo using the Load command.

4. Remember to clear the teeth to avoid unwanted movement, such as stretching.

5. Now, in Modo, separate the top and bottom lips by creating a selection set of points (Select > Assign Selection Set). Select the middle polygons of the lower lip, and increase your selection until it includes the corners of the mouth. Convert the selection to points by pressing and holding the Alt key.

6. Duplicate the morph twice, and rename each morph appropriately for the top or bottom. Copy the morph you just created to the duplicate morphs you just created, clear one with your selection set to get the top version (Vertex Map > Clear), invert your selection (Selection > Invert), and clear the other portion with that selection to get the bottom version.

7. To separate the original LipsOut morph to its left and right sides, make two duplicates of the morph (right-click the morph, and use the option Duplicate), and rename them appropriately to the left and right designations as talked about earlier.

8. Now copy the LipsOut morph to the duplicates using the Morph tool, and use a linear falloff to apply it to each side of the model.

Tip: You can expand this morph to create derivative morphs for the upper and lower left and right sides of the lips also, as shown in Figure 11.12, which are named as LipOutUprL, LipOutUprR, LipOutLowL, and LipOutLowR.

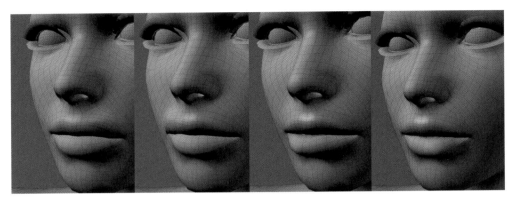

Figure 11.12 LipOutUprL, LipOutUprR, LipOutLowL, and LipOutLowR

LipsIn

The LipsIn morph is the opposite of the LipsOut morph. It is used to portray a biting lip, as shown in Figure 11.13. This morph will also be used to create the mouth shapes for the M and F sounds. Figure 11.14 shows the lips separated into the upper and lower versions of LipsIn.

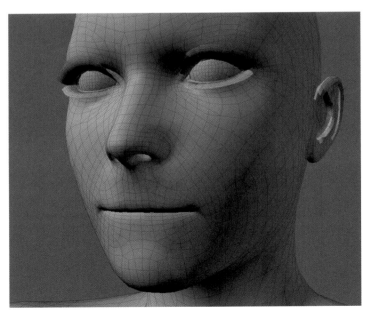

Figure 11.13 LipsIn

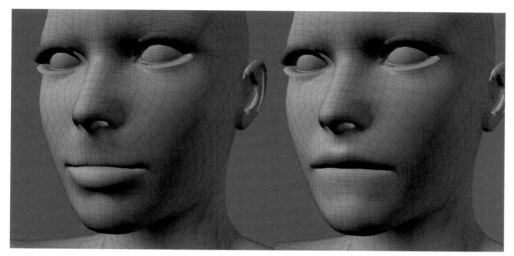

Figure 11.14 LipsInUpr and LipsInLow before separation

To create a LipsIn morph, follow these steps:

1. Move the edges of the lips toward the opening of the mouth using the Tweak tool in ZBrush.

2. As you make the lips smaller, try to approximate the thinness you see in your mirror reference. You might want to give the philtrum area (the vertical groove on the median line of the upper lip) a vertical convex shape.

3. Export your morph using Tool > Export, and then import the file into Modo using the Load command.

4. Clear the teeth to avoid unwanted movement.

5. Now, in Modo, separate the top and bottom lips of this morph first by using your selection set from the previous morph creation.

6. Duplicate your LipsIn morph two times, and rename appropriately. Copy your morph to both morphs, clear one with your selection set (Vertex Map > Clear), invert your selection (Selection-Invert), and clear the other portion with that selection.

7. To separate the left and right sides, make two duplicates of the morph (right-click the morph duplicate), and rename them appropriately.

8. Now copy the morph to the duplicates using the Morph tool and a linear falloff to apply it to the appropriate side.

Tip: You can extend this morph to create derivative morphs for the upper and lower left and right sides of the lips also, as shown in Figure 11.15, which are named as LipInUprL, LipInUprR, LipInLowL, and LipInLowR.

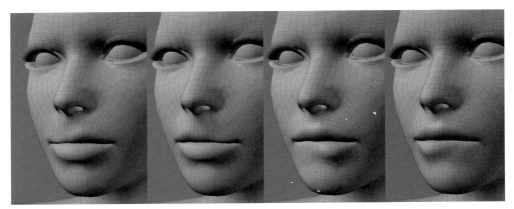

Figure 11.15 LipInUprL, LipInUprR, LipInLowL, and LipInLowR

MouthHeight

The MouthHeight morph is used to make a smile or a harsh frown more realistic. Figure 11.16 shows the morph.

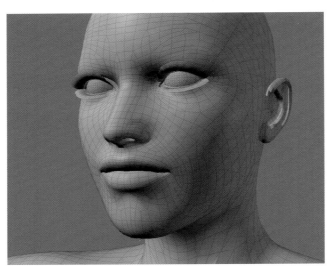

Figure 11.16 MouthHeight

To create the MouthHeight morph, follow these steps:

1. Move the edges of the lips downward using ZBrush. Pay attention to your mirror reference since it doesn't take much movement to create a realistic frown.

2. Export the morph using Tool > Export, and then import the file into Modo using the Load command.

3. Clear the teeth so you do not get unwanted stretching.

4. To separate the left and right sides, make two duplicates of the morph (right-click the morph, and then select Duplicate), and rename them appropriately.

5. Now copy the morph to the duplicates using the Morph tool and a linear falloff to apply it to the appropriate side.

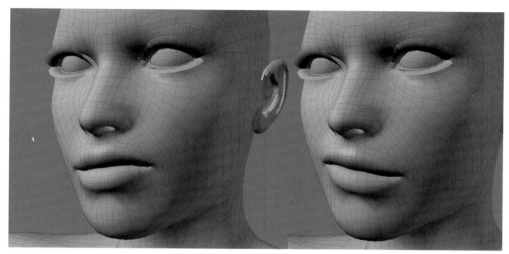

Figure 11.17 MouthHeightL and MouthHeightR

LipMidHeight

The LipMidHeight morph looks like a sneer, as shown in Figure 11.18. You can also use it when opening a mouth in a gaping yell and to aid in flexed cheeks or with scrunching the nose. To make this morph more realistic, you will want to allow the nostrils to fall off a little or to flare out.

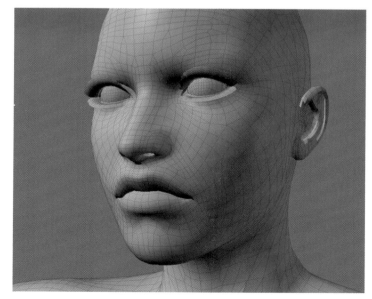

Figure 11.18 LipMidHeight

To create the LipMidHeight morph, follow these steps:

1. Move the area near the corners of the mouth upward, like a sneer, using ZBrush. You will want to create a snarl-like effect. Try to keep your movements only on the Y-axis since the negative morphs can be used as well. Manipulate the top lip, and don't open the mouth with this morph.

2. Export your morph using Tool > Export, and then import the file into Modo using the Load command.

3. Clear the teeth to avoid unwanted movement.

4. Now in Modo, separate the top and bottom using your selection set.

5. Duplicate your LipMidHeight morph two times, and rename appropriately for the upper and lower parts. Copy your morph to both morphs, clear one with your selection set (Vertex Map > Clear), invert your selection (Selection-Invert), and clear the other portion with that selection.

6. To separate the left and right sides, make two duplicates of the morph (right-click the morph duplicate), and rename them appropriately.

7. Now copy the morph to the duplicates using the Morph tool and a linear falloff to apply it to the appropriate side.

Tip: You can expand this morph to create derivative morphs for the upper and lower left and right sides of the mouth also, as shown in Figure 11.19, which are named LipMidHeightUprL, LipMidHeightUprR, LipMidHeightLowL, and LipMidHeightLowR.

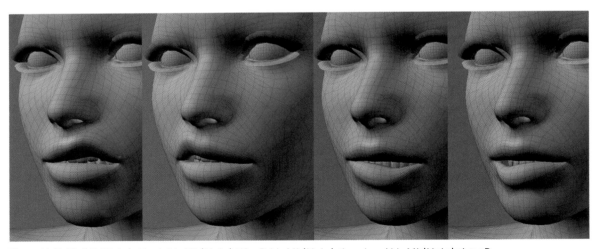

Figure 11.19 LipMidHeightUprL, LipMidHeightUprR, LipMidHeightLowL, and LipMidHeightLowR

MouthCornerHeight

The MouthCornerHeight morph is an interesting morph. When driven in the negative, it looks like a subtle smile, but it shouldn't be used to create a smile expression. Most realistic, and even most caricatured smiles, do not point up at the corners. Create and use this morph for frowns. Then, use the negative (fake smile) with other morphs for an open smile and other mouth shapes. Figure 11.20 shows the frown.

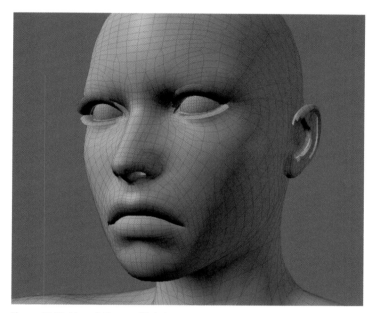

Figure 11.20 MouthCornerHeight

To create a MouthCornerHeight morph, follow these steps:

1. Move the edges of the lips upward using the Tweak brush in ZBrush.

2. Keep the falloff big since this is a simple morph that you will usually use with other morphs.

3. Export your morph using Tool > Export, and then import the file into Modo using the Load command.

4. Clear the teeth to avoid unwanted stretching.

5. To separate the MouthCornerHeight left and right sides, make two duplicates of the morph (right-click morph, and then select Duplicate), and rename them appropriately.

6. Now copy the morph to the duplicates using the Morph tool and a linear falloff to apply it to the appropriate side.

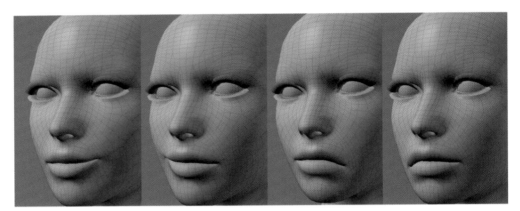

Figure 11.21 MouthCornerHeightL and MouthCornerHeightR in both their negative and positive positions

MouthWidth

The MouthWidth morph is good for helping to create a realistic smile, as shown in Figure 11.22. The MouthWidth morph should mimic the rotation of the lips around the teeth. This morph should also be able to create a type of pucker with the lips.

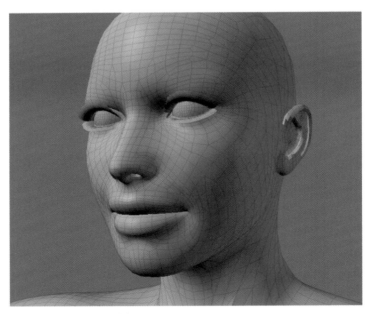

Figure 11.22 MouthWidth

To create the MouthWidth morph, follow these steps:

1. Move the corners of the mouth back and out just a little, using the Tweak brush in ZBrush, so that the negative will pull the lips toward a pucker shape. You do need to worry about getting the mouth wide correct, but remember to keep it simple. You will be combining this morph with others later, and little artifacts can turn into big problems.

2. Make sure you have a hint of labial furrow (wrinkles on the sides of the mouth). You might need to pull out some of the flesh around the wrinkles to compensate for the pinching in the furrows.

3. Export your morph using Tool > Export, and then import the file into Modo using the Load command.

4. Clear the teeth to avoid unwanted scaling.

5. To separate the left and right sides, make two duplicates of the MouthWidth morph (right-click Morph, and select Duplicate), and rename them appropriately.

6. Now copy the morph to the duplicates using the Morph tool and a linear falloff to apply it to the appropriate side.

Tip: You can expand this morph to create derivative morphs for the left and right sides of the mouth, as shown in Figure 11.23, which are named as MouthWidthL and MouthWidthR.

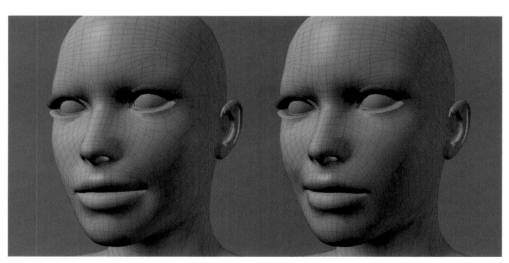

Figure 11.23 MouthWidthL and MouthWidthR

MouthNarrow

The MouthNarrow morph should mimic the rotation of the lips around the teeth. This helps simulate a pucker, as shown in Figure 11.24. When used with the MouthOpen morph, it creates the CH viseme. Make sure you keep the width of the lips at the corners of the mouth on this morph. With many falloff tools, it is easy to get a thin corner of the mouth.

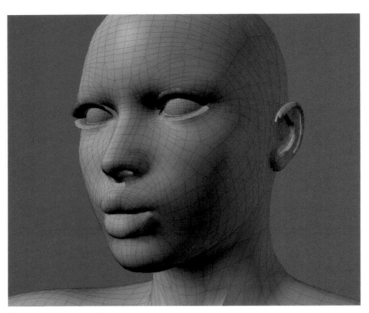

Figure 11.24 MouthNarrow

To create a MouthNarrow morph, follow these steps:

1. Move the corners of the mouth forward to make a pucker, using the Tweak and Add brushes in ZBrush. Really look close at your reference on this one because the thickness of the lips is easy to overlook.

2. Export your morph using Tool > Export, and then import the file into Modo using the Load command.

3. Clear the teeth so you do not get unwanted scaling.

4. To separate the left and right sides, make two duplicates of the morph (right-click the morph, and select Duplicate), and rename them to reflect the right and left sides.

5. Now copy the morph to the duplicates using the Morph tool and a linear falloff to apply it to the appropriate side of the model.

Because of its base importance, this morph doesn't have any derivatives.

LipsPart

The LipsPart morph is the generic resting state for visemes, as shown in Figure 11.25. This morph will become important when we cover visemes in Chapter 12. You will want to use this to create most of your shapes, because the mouth, when speaking, rarely closes. This shape emulates real speech when used between visemes.

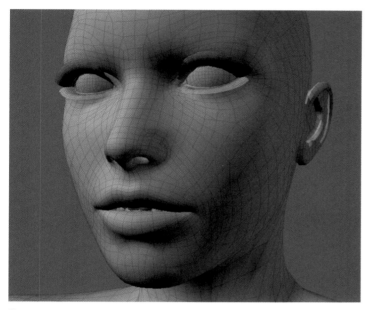

Figure 11.25 LipsPart

To create the LipsPart morph, follow these steps:

1. Using Modo for this one, select the upper lip and increase selection until you have the inside and outside of the upper lip.

2. Move the selection upward, and gradually increase your selection to the next vertices. This is a morph that needs attention to detail. Make a relaxed and subtle opening of the mouth. A good LipsPart is made using your own face as reference.

3. Remember to clear the teeth to avoid unwanted scaling.

Tongue Morphs

The tongue morphs can be really nice *if* the character needs the definition. Tongue morphs can be overkill for certain characters. Some characters don't need any tongue morphs to effectively show emotion and speech. However, it is good practice to add them in just in case. We'll describe these morphs as suggestions, rather than provide step-by-step instructions for creating them. They are optional for most characters. Figure 11.26 shows a tongue in its rigged base position.

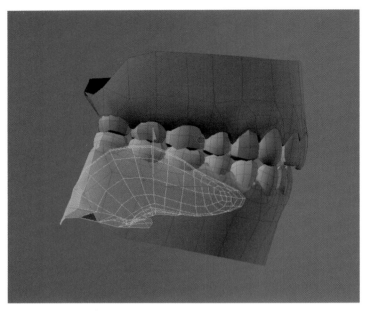

Figure 11.26 Tongue base

TongueHeight This morph will raise and lower the front of the tongue in its positive and negative values, respectively. It, in combination with the TongueWidth morph, mimics the flattening of the tongue needed for such visemes as TH. It is solely responsible for making the shape for the viseme L. Figure 11.27 shows the TongueHeight morph.

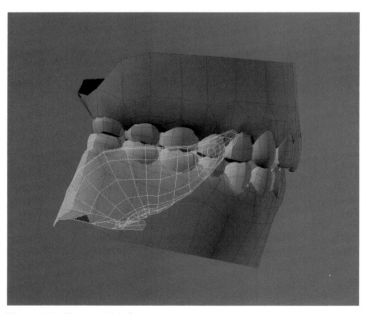

Figure 11.27 TongueHeight

TongueDepth TongueDepth is made for the visemes but can also be used for expressions, such as licking the lips or sticking out the tongue. In this morph, the tongue does not change the width; it merely stretches out with a falloff to the base of the tongue. Figure 11.28 shows the TongueDepth morph.

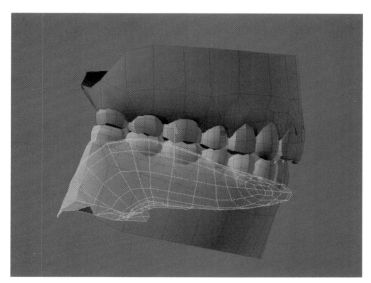

Figure 11.28 TongueDepth

TongueWidth The width morph is used for the TH viseme. The tongue needs to be wide enough to cover the tips of the upper teeth for most of the way around the front of the teeth. Figure 11.29 shows the TongueWidth morph.

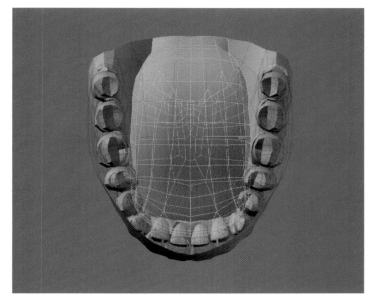

Figure 11.29 TongueWidth

TongueBackHeight TongueBackHeight is a unique morph in that it is used for a very specific phoneme. The "c" in *crane* and the "g" in *grate* both use this shape. Another good example is "uggg." This morph can also be used to show swallowing. The back of the tongue is raised to the roof of the mouth. Figure 11.30 shows the TongueBackHeight morph.

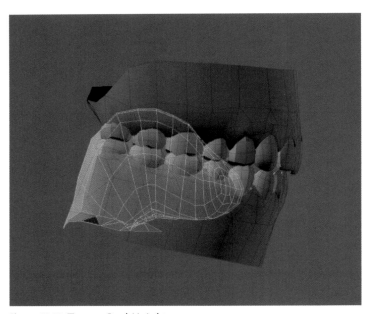

Figure 11.30 TongueBackHeight

Using Morphs in Your Setup

As we talked about earlier, you can use morphs with any type of setup. You might want to create a morph for only your pupil size and do the rest of the facial rig with joints or influence objects, or you could create your whole facial setup with morphs. If you are using morphs for everything, you will want to create a JawOpen morph. Make sure this morph looks good with and without the MouthOpen morph.

If you are going to make a hybrid face that uses a rigged jaw and facial morphs, you will want to create the morphs in this and the next chapters. The jaw morph should affect the jaw and lower lips. This is a very good approach for realism, since the morphs can be created in very specific shapes.

If you are going to create everything with joints, after you have successfully weighted all your joints or influence objects, you can pattern attribute switches to mimic these shapes. You will also want to mimic the shapes from the next chapters.

No matter which approach you take, these shapes are needed for creating readable lip movement for both realistic and cartoony characters.

Conclusion

Jaw and mouth rigging using joints and/or morphs is important for enabling character speech and realistic expressions. By combining both joint and morph rigging approaches, you create a solution that can portray a broader range of facial expressions.

Since the work involved in creating a set of expression and viseme morphs is intensive, search for a modeler that suits your needs. Maya is really the standard right now, but there are other options that offer different toolsets. Find the most efficient, and express yourself.

The next chapter deals with the visemes that are needed to make it possible for your character to speak.

Can't You See What I'm Saying? Logical Viseme Creation

In this chapter, you'll turn your attention to the specific motions involved in making characters speak. For each sound (or phoneme) a character makes, a shape (or viseme) is needed. These shapes are then blended in sync with the audio track. The trick is being able to distinguish all the various sounds and produce shapes for them without duplication, while still providing enough variety to cover all the different speaking possibilities.

12

Chapter Contents

Animating the body
Understanding the difference between phonemes and visemes
Creating visemes
Essential visemes for speech
Secondary issues
Visual viseme reference

Maximus Decimus

Mihai Anghelescu's model of Maximus Decimus from the movie *Gladiator* is an excellent example of a facial rig. Mihai's rig uses both blendshapes and a facial rig to accomplish the realistic facial motion.

Speaking without Saying a Word

Before we begin, let's talk about body language. Great animators start animation with the body before the head. In fact, you can tell what a person is saying more by their body language than by anything else.

You want your character to speak with his arms, posture, and eyes. This conveys believable animation because we as the audience see body language in use in everyday life. If you prefer to work on the mouth first, make a plan of how your character will move. Act the scene out in front of a mirror a few times until you feel comfortable with the performance. If you are animating, you should animate this and then leave the lip syncing for the end. This body language is what makes animation believable. It is good workflow to first convey the meaning with the body and then add the syncing.

Phonemes and Visemes

Phonemes are the smallest, distinguishable unit of sound used in spoken language. The International Phonetic Alphabet (IPA) is composed of 107 distinct letters (representing phonemes) and 56 diacritics and suprasegmentals (representing accents and special pronunciations). These 163 symbols represent all the sounds required for all languages and dialects.

Note: As of this writing, the IPA included 163 symbols. Occasionally, symbols are added, modified, or deleted by the International Phonetic Association, which maintains the alphabet.

Visemes are the basic visual unit of speech that corresponds with the phoneme. They describe the facial movement that is made when each phoneme is uttered, as shown in Figure 12.1 and Figure 12.2.

The Science of the Hidden

You could create a unique shape for each of the 107 distinct audible sounds in human speech. However, making visemes to cover every possible sound is not efficient and would most likely result in overanimation. When lip-syncing, animators want to use basic movements and timing to match the audio track.

Figure 12.1 Cartoony OO viseme

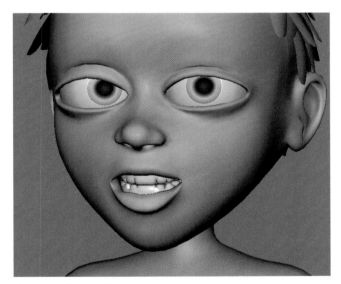

Figure 12.2 Cartoony EE viseme

Consider the F and V sounds. Both are made by bringing the lips close together, but the difference in sound is in the location of the tongue. When animating a character using either of these sounds, only a single viseme is required, and since the tongue is usually hidden inside the mouth, it doesn't even need to be animated. You might want to animate the tongue if you are striving for realism, but in most stylized and cartoony characters, you do not need the animation. We will show you how to rig the tongue so you'll be able to give animators what they need, when they need it.

Recognizing the visemes that can be combined will save you a ton of work. Throughout the rest of the chapter we'll identify those visemes that will represent a complete phonetic set.

It Is Easy to Get Wrong

One of the most criticized areas of 3D is the actual animation, and one of animation's more critical areas is lip-sync. You probably can think of movies where the character's speech looked wrong. Since you are very familiar with speech, you know what looks right and definitely know what doesn't. Ask anyone, with an artistic background or not, to view your viseme animation, and they will tell you whether it looks weird. Don't ask your mother, though—mothers usually are biased. If your visemes don't blend seamlessly or if the timing is off, then others will know immediately that something is wrong, even though you might not. Having the correct shapes gives you the best tools to create believable speech.

You Will Know When You Have It Right

Along with the ability to recognize when a lip sync is wrong comes the ability to know when it is done right. It is a neat moment when you really feel like the character just said what you have been working on. You watch it, and you just know that it is correct; you see the character coming to life.

So, how do you go about getting lip syncing to look right? Here is a workflow that you can follow that will help in this process:

1. *Build the correct shapes*: The first step is to form the correct shapes. The remainder of this chapter focuses on identifying and creating the set of visemes needed to simulate speech.

2. *Break it up*: The process of identifying the needed visemes begins with first breaking down the audio into recognized phonemes. As each phoneme is isolated, map it to a viseme that you'll need to create. We will talk more about this later in the chapter.

3. *Keep the mouth open*: When creating visemes, your instinct will be to shut the mouth, but if you watch yourself in the mirror, you'll notice that the mouth actually doesn't close between sounds. Remember to keep the mouth open. This allows the viseme to take positive and negative values without having the lips collide. An open mouth also makes it easier to blend adjacent visemes into one another.

4. *Add subtle movements*: Once the visemes are created, blending between the various visemes lets you endow the look with subtle movements. These are made possible with the blend amounts that can be negative and/or greater than 100 percent if a little exaggeration is needed. It is these subtle movements that give the characters personality as they speak.

Creating Visemes

In the previous chapter, we showed you the various facial movements that encompass the main movements of the mouth. Visemes are used together with these jaw and facial movements to create character speech. But, building too many visemes wastes your time, and not building enough makes your lip sync appear unrealistic. We will show you how to identify the correct shapes. We also talked about the deformation order. If you have problems with the blendshapes going back to the default shape when animated, look at your deformer order as talked about in the previous chapter.

Building Universal Shapes

You can create a wide variety of phonemes from a subset of universal shapes. By creating and combining these universal shapes, you can create an entire set of diverse expressions and visemes easily and quickly.

In the sections that follow, we'll start with the basic universal shapes and show how to blend these together to create more unique shapes that can be used in turn to create even more visemes.

Using the Correct Tool

The approach you use depends on the software you'll be using. Maya's approach relies on controls, attributes, and blendshapes. Maya controls can be visual, nonrendered controls that are placed within the scene near the character, or they can be external interface controls, such as sliders and check boxes.

Controls Visual controls on the side of the head are a great way to set up animation controls. They follow the head, making the controls easy to reach and use, as shown in Figure 12.3.

External interface controls can be very helpful, since they are easy to grab no matter where you are in the viewport. Since they are separate from the 3D interface, you can place the window so that it is easy to grab and out of the way in any situation.

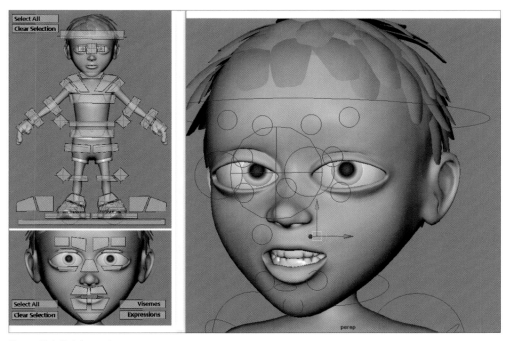

Figure 12.3 Facial controls

Attributes Defining custom attributes to drive your morphs or influence objects is another good way to control facial animation. They give you the benefit of precise numeric control, as shown in Figure 12.4, that is lacking with a visual control. Morphs like the ones created in Modo can also be brought across to Maya and driven with attribute switches that use set-driven keys.

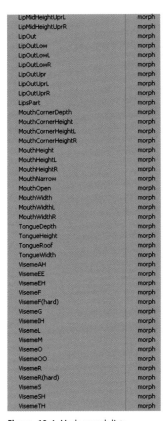

Figure 12.4 Modo morph lists

Breaking It Up

Now, it is time to look at the audio file. You can look at the specific dialogue that the character needs to speak and break it down into speech phonemes. Keep in mind that not every phoneme will form a complete viseme. Some sounds are well defined, and others are passed by quickly.

Try not to break the sentence up into words and parts of words. Look at the sentence as a whole string of sounds. Take the palindrome, "Madam, I'm Adam." These words can easily blend together and be made into simple phonemes. You could find the visemes for *mime* and *mad* in there. Think about sentences as a flow of simple sounds.

Now let's analyze a sentence. Look at yourself in the mirror and say, "You are the best facial rigger ever." We can break this simple sentence into several parts. As you watch yourself say, "You are," you will see that the facial movements can be simplified into OO with a faint hint of R. Your mouth and teeth open slightly and then close slightly. There is not much time for the TH of *the* before the mouth is on the B in *best*. We don't really see any of the S in *best*, but we do see the T. The word *rigger* can be simplified to R, IH, and R and then *ever* consists of EH, F, and ER.

So, we have the following:

OO – R – TH – B – T – F – CH – R – IH – R – EH – F – R
You could even take it a step further and simplify it to this:
R – B – T – F – CH – R – IH – R – EH – R

Note also that the spacing between each sound isn't always equal. Some words are separate, and others run together. There is not a viseme for a pause between words. The mouth transitions from word to word in normal speech.

Keeping the Mouth Open

Remember also to keep the mouth open between visemes, as shown in Figure 12.5. This will make more realistic animation as you begin to sync with the dialogue. The exceptions to this rule are the P, B, and M sounds where the lips are brought together to form the sound.

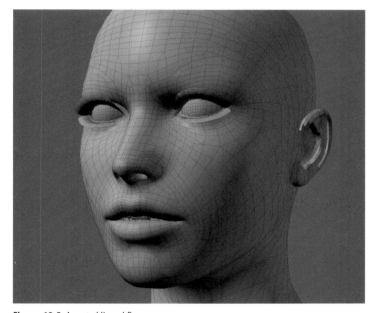

Figure 12.5 A parted lipped figure

Using Tongue Visemes

Tongue morphs might or might not be needed for your character. They add definition to visemes and can be quite useful for realistic characters and facial shapes. On the other hand, they can be overkill, waste time, and unnecessarily consume resources. If you have the resources, add them so they're available if needed.

Adding Subtle Motions

Finally, remember the subtle motions that give your character a personality. Does your character speak with a southern drawl? This may require additional jaw or lip motion. Is your character tight-lipped? Tight-lipped characters speak with small mouth movements. Think about these issues, and you will be better able to anticipate what will be needed for animation.

Realistic Visemes

Visemes can be classified in several different ways. One such group is realistic visemes. These are used when you want to re-create a person's exact speech patterns.

Realistic visemes tend to be more subtle and subdued. They follow the principle that "less is more." If you watch someone speak while relaxed, you will see simple movements. If the person enunciates, you will be able to see more expressive visemes. Your visemes will need to bridge this difference and allow the animator the possibility of anything in between. Make your shapes look good in extreme values, because you can always use less of the shape.

Cartoon Visemes

Cartoon visemes are another common classification of visemes. This group of visemes benefits from exaggeration, but since all visemes are exaggerated, the timing can be thrown off, so keeping the timing correct is essential.

Tips for Great Visemes

Before jumping into the viseme reference, the following tips will help:

Look at your mentors Many companies have set the standard for high-quality expressive visemes. Watch your favorite CG movie, and play a scene you are familiar with in slow motion. See whether you can break apart the different facial visemes they are using. Take notes on how they present each shape. We recommend Sony's *Open Season* and Pixar's *Ratatouille* for amazing visemes.

Watch people People are another great source of viseme references. Notice how different personalities use different visemes to make the same type of sound. Try getting several different people to say the same statement, and notice the variation between them. Another idea is to ask a person to say a sentence in different ways, such as when excited, as a question, or when bored. Notice also the corresponding body motions that accompany such speech.

Watch yourself Finally, get a mirror, and speak into it yourself. When speaking, try to overexaggerate the various facial and mouth movements. This will make it easier to pick up the subtle details.

Reading lips As you complete a lip-syncing animation, you'll want to test your results. One way to do this is to watch your character with and without sound. If you can understand your character by simply reading their lips, then you'll know the visemes are working just fine.

Viseme Reference

The following sections of the chapter provide a visual reference of the common visemes used to create most phonemes. We provide a comprehensive list of phonemes that you could make. We compared many viseme lists and came up with this standard. We believe it is a true reflection of the viseme work that we have done, as well as the thoughts of others on the subject of viseme groups. The list is a melting pot of many lists and ideas:

- Viseme M (P, B, M)
- Viseme OO/viseme O
- Viseme R (R, ER)
- Viseme F (F, V)
- Viseme IH (IH, S)
- Viseme SH (SH, CH, J)
- Viseme EE
- Viseme AH (OH, AH, UH)
- Viseme EH (EH, AW, AA, A, I)
- Viseme TH (tongue)
- Viseme L (N, L, T, D: tongue movement)
- Viseme G (NG, G, K: tongue movement)

Viseme M (P, B, M)

For this position, you can use the character's base mouth shape, if the base has the mouth closed in a relaxed state. If your character has a mouth position that is different from a P, B, M shape, you can make one by closing the mouth into a relaxed look. Remember, however, that your base state is the foundation of your animation, and if it is not at a relaxed position, you might get unnecessary lip movement through your syncing.

Remember that this shape will need to be used to transition into the next viseme. For instance, *mumu* and *theme*, as shown in Figure 12.6 and Figure 12.7, are examples of a wide and a narrow M viseme. Make sure your MouthWidth morph works with this morph.

You can use a small amount of the LipIn shape, if you want the lips to tighten slightly. This can be used for in-between sounds. For this shape, we used the following: LipIn: 10 percent (this should be based on your personal preference).

The viseme P exhales the most air and can be separated into its own viseme. You might need to add MouthNarrow after the closed mouth. The B viseme exhales a lesser amount, and the M exhales no air.

When animating the PBM viseme, it is important to be aware of the neighboring phonemes and viseme shapes. This will help you maintain smooth animation and avoid lip flap. Keep this shape's use to a minimum since the resting state of the lips during speech should be open.

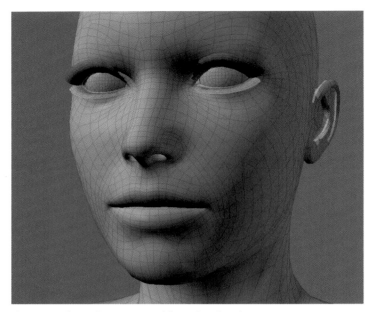

Figure 12.6 The regular viseme M used for words such as *theme*

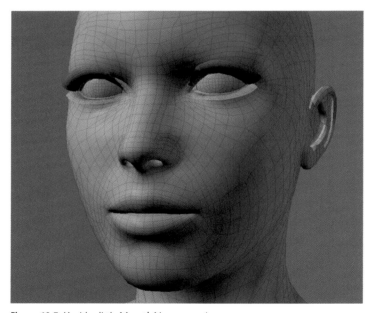

Figure 12.7 M with a little MouthNarrow as in *mumu*

Viseme OO/Viseme O

The shapes for the OO viseme and the O viseme are similar but slightly different. The shape for the OO viseme is a little more pursed. The OO viseme is used for words like *boot* and *tube*. This viseme is mainly built with MouthNarrow and has a little bit of MouthOpen in it, as shown in Figure 12.8.

For the OO shape, we used the following:

- MouthNarrow: 100 percent to 110 percent
- MouthOpen: 40 percent

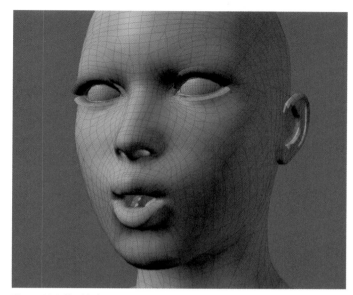

Figure 12.8 The OO shape

The O shape is just slightly more relaxed with the mouth a little more opened, as shown in Figure 12.9. The O viseme is used for words like *boat* and *rope*.

For the O shape, we used the following:

- MouthNarrow: 90 percent
- MouthOpen: 80 percent

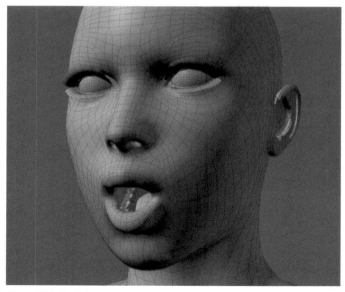

Figure 12.9 The O shape

Since these shapes are so similar, you might just want to combine them into one. Then, you can use the Narrow and Open morphs to tweak the result depending on what is needed.

These shapes are fairly strong shapes in their usage. They will not usually take on the characteristics of their neighboring sounds like some of the other visemes. If these visemes are needed, the other visemes that are near will transition into them.

Viseme R (R, ER)

This viseme stands out as a strong viseme. It has a definite uniqueness to it. You can see that it has a recognizable shape, as shown in Figure 12.10. This viseme uses a few different mouth shapes for its creation. The R viseme is used for words like *rigger*.

For the R shape, we used the following:

- MouthNarrow: 50 percent
- LipMidHeightUpr: 20 percent
- LipMidHeightLow: 20 percent

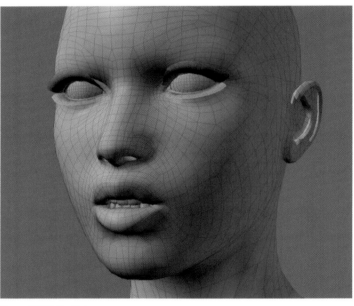

Figure 12.10 The R shape

The hard R shape also has a strong state to it. Because the base and morph work on a linear basis, you cannot just add the morph to itself and expect it to look good. To get a hard R viseme, add some more Lipup, which will add to the intensity of the morph. Also, add a little bit of narrow into the mix, as shown in Figure 12.11.

For the hard R shape, we used the following:

- LipMidHeightUpr: 10 percent
- LipMidHeightLow: 10 percent
- MouthNarrow: –10 percent

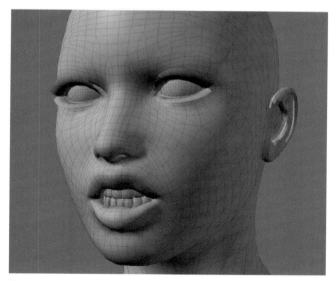

Figure 12.11 The hard R

This hard R viseme approaches the CH and SH shapes. If you look in the mirror and say "<u>R</u>an<u>ch</u>" or "<u>Sha</u>re," you can see that the shapes are quite similar. Even the lesser value of the hard R looks similar to the R. The major difference is the way the mouth starts into the R viseme. It is much more narrow when compared to the CH viseme.

Viseme F (F, V)

This is a fun shape because it is expressive and easy to create. The F shape is made by bringing the mouth a little more narrow than the default and raising the upper lip. The lower lip is also raised to meet the bottom edge of the upper teeth. You will not want to use too much MouthNarrow here, because you do not want the corners of your character's mouth moving too much during lip sync, as shown in Figure 12.12.

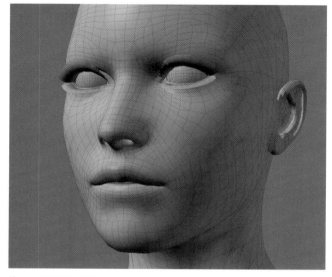

Figure 12.12 The F viseme

Here is our recipe for the viseme F:

- LipsPart: 100 percent
- LipInLow: 60 percent
- MouthNarrow: 20 percent
- LipMidHeightLow: 30 percent (to bring the low lip to the upper teeth)

There is also a hard F counterpart that you might want to add if the animation warrants it. The F viseme is used for words like *favor* and *vapor*. You can use all the "hard" examples to really plus (enhance) a character with expressive visemes, as shown in Figure 12.13. To add to your character's F morph, you can do the following:

- LipInLow: 20 percent (from the default)
- LipMidHeightLow: 40 percent

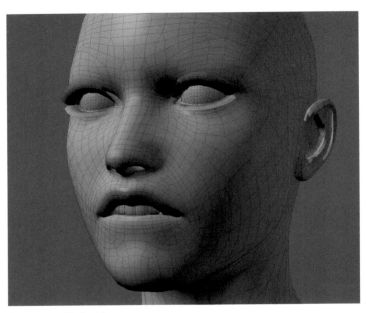

Figure 12.13 The hard F

Viseme IH (IH, S)

IH may sound very different from S, but as you look at the shapes made by your mouth when you make those sounds, they are actually very similar. The S viseme is the one we will tackle first. It is used for words like *sassy*. It partially opens mouth without the teeth moving. Add a little bit of opening between the upper lip and the lower lip, and you are pretty much there, as shown in Figure 12.14.

- LipMidHeightUpr: 50 percent
- LipMidHeightLow: 70 percent

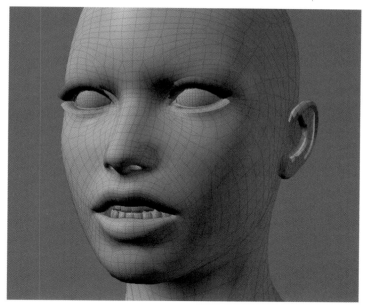

Figure 12.14 The S viseme

The IH shape has the similar shape, so let's start with the S viseme. All you really need to do is open the mouth just slightly, and you have the IH viseme. This shape is used for words like *fist* and *rigger*. These two are so close that they could easily be one morph with the option to add MouthOpen, as shown in Figure 12.15.

- MouthOpen: 10 percent

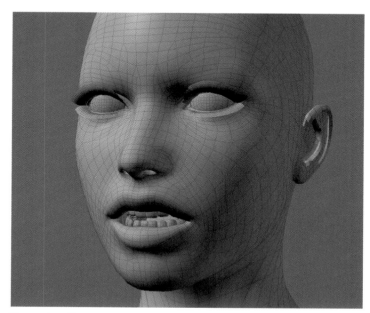

Figure 12.15 The IH viseme

Viseme SH (SH, CH, J)

The SH and CH viseme is one of the classics. Almost everyone has this viseme in their to-do list, and it is always a good giveaway when someone is not doing an adequate job on their morphs. This viseme actually rolls the lips forward and pushes the sound from them. This viseme is used for words like *josh* and *chide*. The J viseme fits nicely along side the other two in that the phoneme emanates from a similar positioning of the mouth, as shown in Figure 12.16.

The SH viseme is made with the following:

- MouthNarrow: 80 percent
- LipMidHeightUpr: 100 percent
- LipMidHeightLow: 100 percent

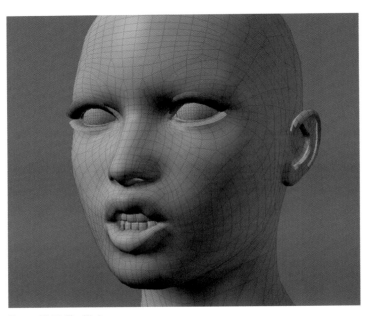

Figure 12.16 The SH viseme

Viseme EE

The EE viseme is a good traditional one; everyone seems to use it. But it can easily be blown out of proportion. The tendency is to make a hard EE and leave it at that. The realistic and cartoony EE morph is a subtle shape that shows some teeth but in a relaxed way. It is used for words like *leap* and *jeep*. It uses just a pinch of MouthOpen and mainly uses the lip height morphs for definition, as shown in Figure 12.17.

Here are the morphs used for the EE shape:

- LipMidHeightUpr: 60 percent
- LipMidHeightLow: 60 percent
- MouthCornerDepth: 20 percent
- OpenMouth: 5 percent

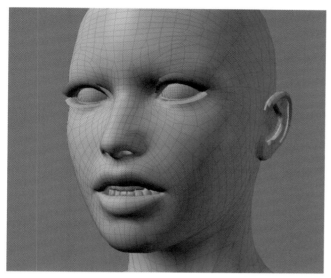

Figure 12.17 The EE viseme

Viseme AH (OH, AH, UH)

The AH viseme is interesting because it is one of the closest shapes to an open mouth. It is closer than any other viseme. The OH shape has been added to this list, because it needs only slight modification from the AH, and you can usually get away with using an AH shape, as shown in Figure 12.18. This shape is used for words like *mow* and *huh*. The OH variation can have a little of MouthNarrow added to get slightly closer to the pucker shape.

For the AH and UH shapes, here's the recipe:

- LipMidHeightUpr: 40 percent
- MouthOpen: 70 percent

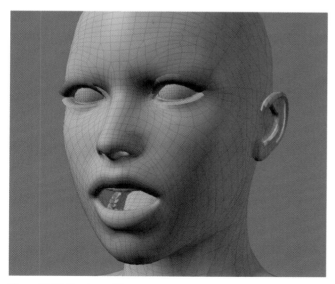

Figure 12.18 The viseme AH

Viseme EH (EH, AW, AA, A, I)

This seems to be the catchall shape since it can make so many phonic sounds. It is almost a relaxed open mouth and has little alteration, but it still needs to be on its own, as shown in Figure 12.19. This shape is for words like *wet* and *bought*. As other shapes transition into this shape, it will need to be able to stay consistent. Thus, this will be like a resting state for many of your words.

This shape is made with the following:

- LipMidHeightUpr: 50 percent
- LipMidHeightLow: 60 percent
- MouthOpen: 25 percent

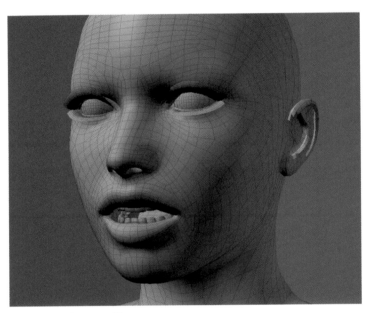

Figure 12.19 The viseme EH

Viseme TH (Tongue)

You are now ready to tackle the TH shape. If you look in the mirror and say "these three things," you can see the tongue getting wide as it presses to the back of the primary incisors on the top jaw. You need to replicate this with your tongue morphs. The TH viseme is shown in Figure 12.20.

Here is the quantity of each morph that worked for this shape:

- TongueHeight: 60 percent
- TongueDepth: 100 percent
- TongueWidth: 100 percent
- MouthOpen: 20 percent

- LipMidHeightUpr: 50 percent
- LipMidHeightLow: 50 percent

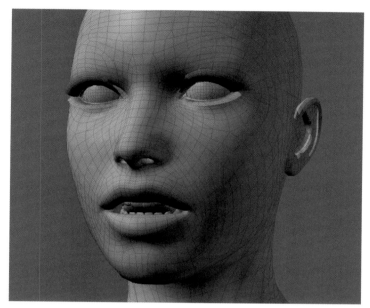

Figure 12.20 The TH viseme

Viseme L (N, L, T, D: Tongue Movement)

Start this morph off with the open mouth that the TH viseme used. Apply the lip and mouth shapes to the viseme. The mouth shapes are those that precede it or those that follow it. For example, "ooloo" and "eelee" both use this shape, but there are separate visemes attached to it. Now the difference is in the tongue. This viseme has the tongue touch the top of the mouth, but it does not press against the back of the teeth. It points to the front of the roof of the mouth. For N, T, and D, it widens slightly in that same area to slow the flow of air, as shown in Figure 12.21. You can break these out into separate visemes when needed for realism; otherwise, it is good to lump them into this one viseme for ease of use. The tongue height needs to be a little higher than in the TH viseme.

Here are the values from the default position:

- MouthOpen: 20 percent
- LipMidHeightUpr: 50 percent
- LipMidHeightLow: 50 percent
- TongueHeight: 100 percent
- TongueDepth: 100 percent

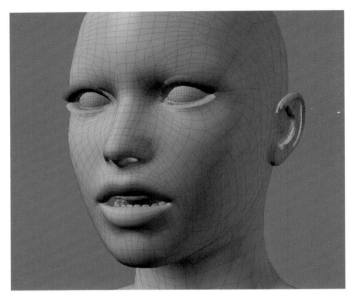

Figure 12.21 The L viseme

Viseme G (NG, G, K: Tongue Movement)

Depending on the amount of detail you want to put into your figure, you might want to make this viseme with no morph at all. We are getting to a level of detail that some (or most) will not see. This viseme may be combined with the N, L, T, D viseme because it has to do with the tongue touching the roof of the mouth. The only difference here is that the back of the tongue is touching in this instance, as shown in Figure 12.22. The audience might not see this if the mouth is slightly closed or closed entirely. It is up to you, your supervisor, or your animators to determine how much detail should go into this viseme. Figure 12.23 shows the G viseme.

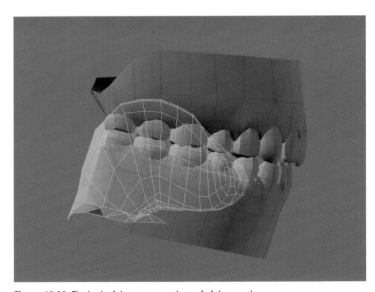

Figure 12.22 The back of the tongue on the roof of the mouth

- TongueBackHeight: 100 percent
- MouthOpen: 20 percent
- LipMidHeightUpr: 50 percent
- LipMidHeightLow: 50 percent

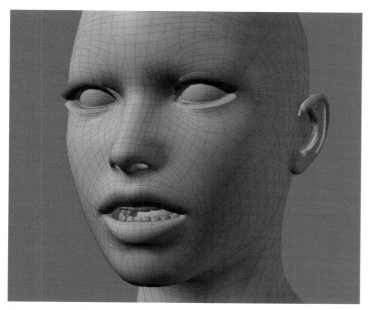

Figure 12.23 The G viseme

Secondary Issues

Once your set of visemes is complete, you should consider several secondary issues:

Relaxed open state When animating with visemes, it is best to maintain a simple relaxed open state. This creates a more relaxed realistic and identifiable animation. If you can create the character speaking in this manner, then you can later add emotion. However, if you don't get the lip sync looking good using a relaxed state, then adding more emotion will just make it worse. More emotion on a bad lip sync is just covering it up.

Previous and follow-up sounds Often transitions between certain sounds aren't complete. If you try to break a word such as *betcha* up into phonemes of B, E, T, CH, and A, you'll see that many of the phonemes are combined, so you really end with a B phoneme transitioning to a CH sound. When rigging or animating, you have to think in these terms.

Emotions and visemes If you can complete the lip sync with a normal relaxed state, then inserting emotion is simply a matter of exaggerating the visemes and adding the necessary body language. This is why it is good practice to make something more exaggerated and then tone it down for the saved morph.

Conclusion

Learning the difference between phonemes and visemes allows you to create the shapes that are needed to simulate speech. When creating visemes, it is important to build the correct shapes, to break down the speech patterns in phonemes, to keep the mouth open between visemes, and to allow for subtle movements.

Remember also to use a mirror and to watch others as they speak when learning the look of various visemes. The chapter also covered a base set of visemes that can be used to simulate speech.

Keeping track of all the various facial controls can be a difficult task. In the next chapter, we'll cover several user interfaces that make animating facial expressions easier.

Control That Face of Yours: Working with Expressions and Facial User Interfaces

13

The face is the part of your character that will draw the most attention. It is also the part of the body that will have the most deformation. In this chapter, we will finish our morph creation and go over how to manage this area with specific control systems.

Chapter Contents
Working on expressions
Planning deformations
Using joints, influence objects, and morphs
Creating UI controls, attribute controls, and facial representations
Exploring facial control systems

Facial Expressions

Let's finish the list of the needed facial expressions that we started in Chapter 10. As always, you will need a rigger's best friend for help with this: a mirror. To complete the facial expressions, you need the following:

- BrowMidHeight
- BrowOuterHeight
- BrowSqueeze
- NoseWrinkle
- CheekFlex
- Squint
- CheekBalloon

What Do You Want to Separate?

Characters need brow shapes to express anger and worry. But, before you begin building, you need to ask yourself, "Should the brows be separated, right and left? Or would a single control for the mid-brow and separate controls for the outer brows be a better choice?"

Typically, the answer is a matter of the animator's personal preference.

Also, think about the cheek flex. Do you want to separate the cheek flex into its left and right components? If they are separate, you can add asymmetry and realism to the face.

Think about the separation options while you work through these examples. Understand that animators like options when trying to be expressive.

 Tip: As a rule of thumb, if there are two of anything (right and left eyebrows, nostrils, cheeks, upper and lower lips, and so on), make two controls. The exception? You don't need to make two controls for these items when a character is in the background and requires minimal or no control.

Choosing Morphs or Deformers

As you go through the shape descriptions, remember that they are suggested end shapes that you should be striving to accomplish with your mouth and face setup. And there are a variety of methods for building the shapes. You can use painting weights on your blendshapes to split them. This is a great way to split apart morphs. The Paint Blend Shape Weights tool gives you weighted blendshape capability. If you use influence objects, make sure the influence objects have the ability to create the necessary shapes. You can use attributes and set-driven keys to drive the multiple objects into the positions that make the shapes. Perhaps you'll choose to leave them free-floating and parented to the head joint. You will probably want to use the SDK for controlling multiple objects at one time.

BrowMidHeight When creating a BrowMidHeight shape, think about the way the brow travels as it moves vertically in the center. When you lift your brow, notice that the center of the forehead does not travel quite as high as the outer brow. You might want to add extra detail by driving a bump map or a separate morph target. This allows you to wrinkle the brow as it raises.

Create all the brow morphs together in one morph, and then separate them. This approach gives you the predictable end result you modeled initially when you add the parts together for a brow up. Test the morph in both the positive movement and the negative movement. In Figure 13.1, you can see the positive BrowMidHeight morph, and Figure 13.2 shows the negative version of the blendshape.

Tip: You might want to isolate the sides of this morph so you can lift one eyebrow without losing a ruffled brow capability. The other optional derivatives from this shape are BrowMidHeightL and BrowMidHeightR.

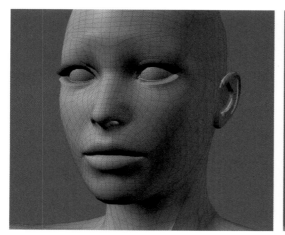

Figure 13.1 BrowMidHeight

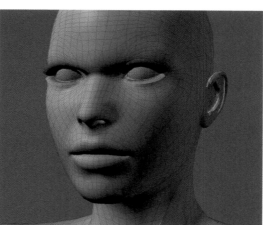

Figure 13.2 BrowMidHeight in the negative

BrowOuterHeight Since the outside of the brow generally moves more dramatically than the inside does, it is a nice touch to add a thickening of the brow tissue just above the eye. Add the thickening with care so it doesn't take away from the illusion of a skull underneath the brow as it travels in the positive and thins the area. Here too, wrinkles can be driven with additional morph targets or maps.

To create this morph, you need a model created using a full-brow approach and a reverse-falloff-capable modeler. With those in place, the reverse of the falloff used for BrowMidHeight will create this morph perfectly. Otherwise, you will have to re-create a matching (or close to) falloff used for the previous morph. Both morphs applied together should make a collective brow up and brow down.

 Tip: Derivative morphs, BrowOuterHeightL and BrowOuterHeightR, can be created from this morph.

Figure 13.3 shows the BrowOuterHeight shape, and Figure 13.4 shows its negative value. If you look closely at the mesh layout, you can see the left and right variations in Figure 13.5.

Figure 13.3 BrowOuterHeight

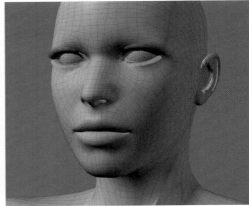

Figure 13.4 Negative BrowOuterHeight

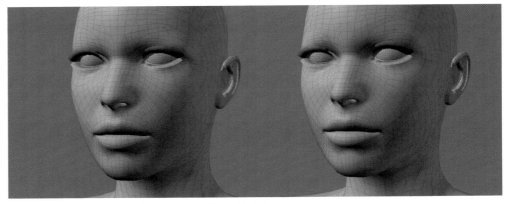

Figure 13.5 BrowOuterHeightR and BrowOuterHeightL

BrowSqueeze This shape is needed to squeeze the middle of the brow to emulate a furrowed brow. The BrowMidHeight movement is made for vertical movement. This shape is made for horizontal movement.

If this shape is created with a morph, you will want to make sure it works with the brow up and brow down. The resultant combination could be a very angry brow or a very worried brow. You might also drive a map or morph with this shape to create wrinkles. Use a set-driven key connection driven by an attribute to drive the strength of a bump map. Figure 13.6 shows the BrowSqueeze shape.

NoseWrinkle This shape mimics a sneer. It can be used with the BrowMidDown and BrowSqueeze shapes. Include a little thickening of the skin under the eyes and add a little nostril flare to show the pulling by the cheek muscles. Be careful with the nostril flare, though, because the nostril area will be affected by the movement of the lip-up shapes.

Take a look in the mirror. Notice that you can wrinkle your nose and still move your brow independently. That's why NoseWrinkle needs to be a separate shape. You can also add a driven morph or map for realism with the wrinkles that are created with NoseWrinkle. Figure 13.7 shows the shape.

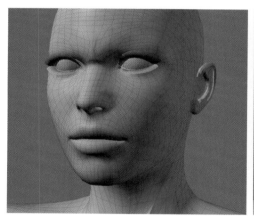
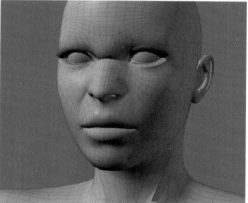

Figure 13.6 BrowSqueeze

Figure 13.7 NoseWrinkle

CheekFlex The CheekFlex shape is used in conjunction with the lip shapes to create the kind of big smile that affects the cheeks all the way up to the eyes. This shape is meant to be used with both the open smile and the closed smile. You can also use it to define the nasolabial fold. Make sure the shape is additive and works with MouthWide and MouthRaise. If you create it as a morph, divide the shape into its parts, CheekFlexL and CheekFlexR, or use the Paint Blend Shape Weights tool to create two different blends. Figure 13.8 shows CheekFlex, and Figure 13.9 shows the left and right versions.

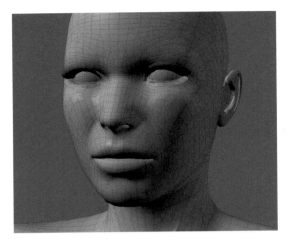

Figure 13.8 CheekFlex

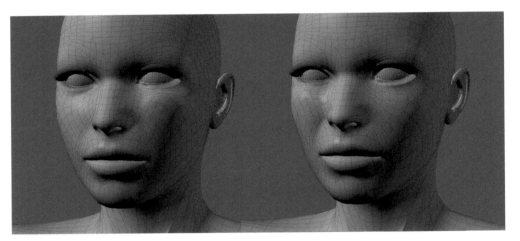

Figure 13.9 CheekFlexL and CheekFlexR

Squint You can use Squint for a few different expressions. Shock and wince both use this shape. It combines a slight closing of the eyes with a tightening of the outer eye. You can use normal maps, displacement maps, or bump maps to add wrinkles that aren't too deep, or if your geometry has high enough resolution to allow it, you can add crow's feet with another driven morph.

If you are adding Squint to eyes with morphs for the automatic movement, you can add the morph on top of the automatic movement. You might want to add it in degrees so the lid doesn't cover too much of the iris or pupil in the blink movement. If the eye closes too much, it gives an unrealistic look to the lid. Figure 13.10 shows the Squint shape.

Tip: You can separate the shape into SquintL and SquintR, as shown in Figure 13.11.

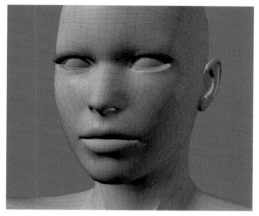

Figure 13.10 Squint

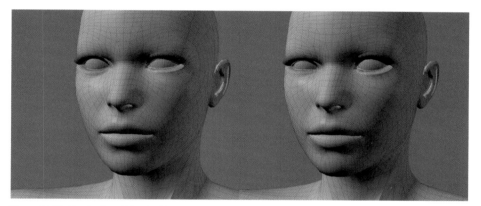

Figure 13.11 SquintL and SquintR

CheekBalloon This is a somewhat unique shape; it may or may not be needed on your character. If you are striving for realism, this is a much-needed shape. No other morphs can provide this unique deformation. When the animator needs it, it is nice to have this option. The shape can be made with a couple of variants. Usually, the shape is made by puffing up the cheeks, as if the character were blowing up a balloon. A more realistic version puffs up the lips as well. Figure 13.12 shows a CheekBalloon shape.

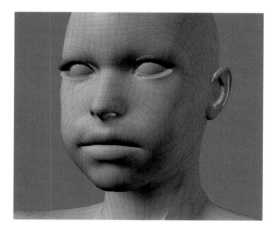

Figure 13.12 CheekBalloon

Avoiding Lower Teeth Problems

If you created a jaw joint for your rig, parent the lower teeth to that joint using a parent constraint. This allows your geometry to stay in the same structure for organizational purposes.

If you do not have a jointed jaw, make sure that when the jaw moves, the rotation center stays consistent. Since morphs are linear, you will not get perfect results driving the morphs at higher values. Linear morphs move vertices in straight lines. This will eventually create unwanted deformations.

Planning the Deformation Control System

Our cartoony runner character is joint-based with a MEL UI. As you decide the setup for your character's facial UI, remember that your character can use any combination of the systems discussed in this chapter. Whether your model uses morphs or joints and influence objects for expressions, you can use any one of the control systems mentioned in this chapter. You are not limited to the choices we made for our characters. These systems can work together, so your character can have a jointed jaw with morphs driving the mouth shapes and influence objects controlling the brow and eyes. Choose the controls that work best for your character. Figure 13.13 shows some isolated expressions.

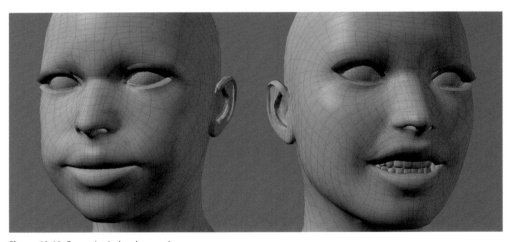

Figure 13.13 Expressive isolated expressions

Joints, Influence Objects, and Morphs

Our runner character uses influence objects for all of his facial expressions. You could use weighted joints, as shown in Figure 13.14. We used individual controls for each influence object, as shown in Figure 13.15. We'll talk about these in Chapter 14, "Deforming, Organizing, and Bomb-Proofing Your Rig." We'll show you how to create them and how to make a separate window that allows animators to easily select any control on his face and body.

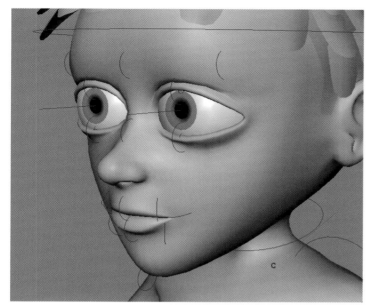

Figure 13.14 A jointed face with controls on each joint

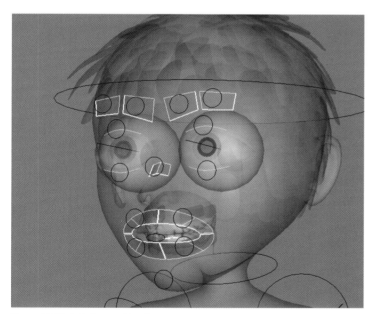

Figure 13.15 An influence object face

Daz3D's Victoria4 is controlled mainly by morphs. The actual (high-resolution) figure employs a part-based rigging system with falloff. The figure has a rigged jaw with the morphs, which creates a dynamic and realistic look for the figure. Figure 13.16 shows a morph on the character.

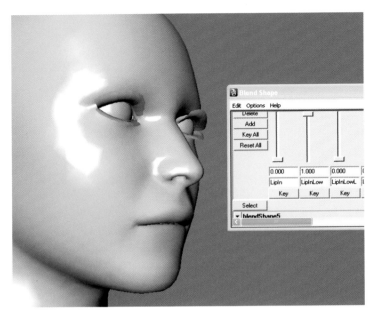

Figure 13.16 The LipInLow morph

Table 13.1 describes a comparison between using morphs or influence objects for facial deformations.

▷ **Table 13.1** Morphs and Jointed Face Features

Morphs	Joints and Influence Objects
Linear in their movement Cannot rotate from point A to point B	More control over falloffs and extreme movement (independent control of joints)
Easily defined	Handles all mouths and shapes—very wide to very small
Easily made (fast)	Allows teeth to be added to the jaw in a realistic way
Easy to hook up	

UI Controls, Attribute Controls, and Facial Representations

When considering the controls to use to drive the expressions, you have several choices. Here are some options to consider when creating a facial setup:

- UI joystick window (Figure 13.17)
- UI selection windows (Figure 13.18)
- Setups involving morphs and attributes only (Figure 13.19)
- Facial representations (Figure 13.20)

Each has its advantages and disadvantages and some animators prefer one over another, but we recommend you choose one of these setups and run with it. If it is done well, any animator will be pleased.

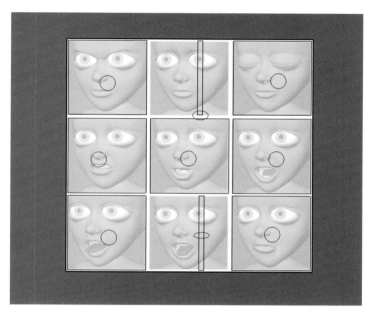

Figure 13.17 UI joystick controls

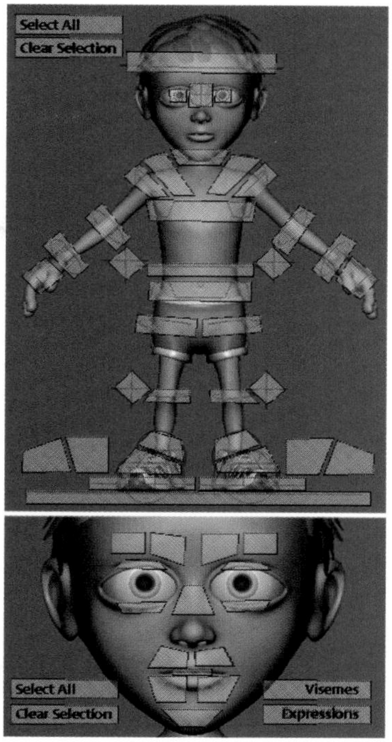

Figure 13.18 UI selection controls

Figure 13.19 Attribute controls

Figure 13.20 Facial representation for the Tadeo Jones character

As you prepare to create your facial controls, ask yourself the following questions:

- What do I really want?
- Does the character need a quick setup or a complex system?
- Who will be using the controls, and what do they need?
- How much time do you have for creation?
- Will a facial animation system that is parented to the head provide the functionality that the character needs?
- Will a facial UI be enough?

Table 13.2 is a quick comparison chart of the benefits of each of the UI setups.

▶ **Table 13.2** UI Comparison

Attributes/Morphs	Facial Representation	UI Controls
Easy/no setup	Medium build time	Long build time
Organized (attributes)	Direct facial representation	Easy-to-read facial representation
Sliders (middle mouse drag in viewport)	Easy to understand	Joystick
	Can be in separate window or next to character	Easy to understand
		Can be in separate window or next to character

UI Joystick Controls

The UI joystick controls shown in Figure 13.17 are examples of the types of joysticks you might want for your character. They are simple control curves with limits that extend to another square curve that makes up the boundary. We will talk about how to create these later in the chapter. Each joystick you create performs a specific function. For example, you can create one joystick that moves just the upper lip up and to the right and create another for moving it down and to the left. Facial joysticks really are an intuitive way to control a character. You can use them wherever you need them. You can parent-constrain them and place them to the side of the character's face. You can also use them in a facial representation's rig.

There are three main types of joystick controls. We'll show you how to create each one. The main control can be used for whatever you want. Since the setup is made with set-driven keys, you can have the top right of a control make the face get angry, and the bottom left of the control can make a gentle face. Anything is possible. We recommend you manipulate only a portion of your figure with each control. A control could make a mouth wider or narrower in the right and left, open and close, and up and down positions. The possibilities are limited only by your imagination.

UI Selection Controls

The UI selection controls work together with the facial controls to provide ease of selection. These controls allow you to select any control on the figure. This setup is great for restricting the selection to controls only. If you hide the controls in your main viewport, all the animator sees are the control representations in the UI selection window.

UI Window

We'll cover this setup in Chapter 15, "MEL Scripting: An Introduction." We're mentioning it here because it is important that you decide what you want for your character. This setup, as shown in Figure 13.18 earlier, is made for the animator who doesn't want to have to select from a control on the figure. This animator wants to manipulate only the hidden controls there. So, you would use this by selecting the part of the figure in the selection window, and then you would manipulate the joint from the 3D window. The control would be hidden. This is a great way to give the animator easy access to the controls without having them visually represented in the shot.

Facial Control Using MEL

You can use a MEL script to create a window and load a camera view into it. The camera you use will have a background that is representative of the character's visemes and expressions. Within this window you can use joysticks to manipulate your character. The windowCreator.mel script, which is included on the accompanying CD, shows how to code a simple UI window with tabs. For this window you will need to create a background for the camera that is in turn locked onto the controls (joysticks) that are parent-constrained to the head of the figure. Figure 13.21 shows this type of setup.

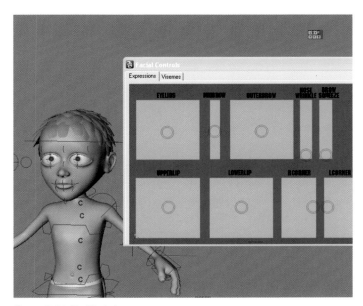

Figure 13.21 The UI window setup

Facial Representation

For a facial representation setup, you will re-create the face using curves for controls. This is a popular way to represent the facial features quickly. For quick understanding, these controls echo the positions of the actual facial controls. Figure 13.22 shows this type of setup. The X and Y movements of these controls control the movement and rotation attributes, as well as their translation attributes. This can easily be done with set-driven keys. You can then set your controls as you want. The control's translation is hooked to the morph's value or to a joint or an influence object's rotation.

Figure 13.22 Facial representation of Tadeo Jones by Enrique Gato

Attribute Controls

You can use attribute controls with any setup. They work really well alone, too. Remember that we showed how to set up the finger movement with attributes. You could set up your figure to have only attributes that drive morph targets. A list of morph targets will look like Figure 13.23. The attributes then could drive multiple morph targets across the face to produce full facial expressions such as happy or angry. When using morphs, you can drive them either from the Channel Box as in Figure 13.24 or from the Blend Shape window. For major expressions such as happy, sad, and angry, you can use attributes and set-driven keys to control many morphs. The Channel Box provides an excellent, concise view of your morphs and attributes. You can also group the blendshapes in the Blendshape Editor as shown in Figure 13.25.

As you have seen, you can set up most anything as an attribute. You can also drive morphs and influence objects. You can use a single attribute slider to control many morphs at once. You can use an attribute to move influence objects.

BrowMidHeight	MouthCornerDepth
BrowOutHeight	MouthCornerHeight
BrowOutHeightL	MouthCornerHeightL
BrowOutHeightR	MouthCornerHeightR
BrowSqueeze	MouthHeight
CheekBalloon	MouthHeightL
CheekFlex	MouthHeightR
CheekFlexL	MouthNarrow
CheekFlexR	MouthOpen
EyeSquint	MouthWidth
EyeSquintL	MouthWidthL
EyeSquintR	MouthWidthR
LacrimalR.InOut	NoseWrinkle
LacrimalL.InOut	TongueDepth
LidBlink	TongueHeight
LidLowDownL	TongueRoof
LidLowDownR	TongueWidth
LidLowUpL	VisemeAH
LidLowUpR	VisemeEE
LidUprDownL	VisemeEH
LidUprDownR	VisemeF
LidUprUpL	VisemeF(hard)
LidUprUpR	VisemeG
LipIn	VisemeIH
LipInLow	VisemeL
LipInLowL	VisemeM
LipInLowR	VisemeO
LipInUpr	VisemeOO
LipInUprL	VisemeR
LipInUprR	VisemeR(hard)
LipMidHeight	VisemeS
LipMidHeightLow	VisemeSH
LipMidHeightLowL	VisemeTH
LipMidHeightLowR	
LipMidHeightUpr	
LipMidHeightUprL	
LipMidHeightUprR	
LipOut	
LipOutLow	
LipOutLowL	
LipOutLowR	
LipOutUpr	
LipOutUprL	
LipOutUprR	
LipsPart	

Figure 13.23 List of morphs

Figure 13.24 Attributes in the Channel Box

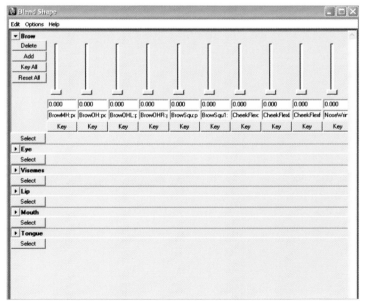

Figure 13.25 Morph slider grouping

Morphs and Attribute Lists

If you are building all your deformations with morph targets, you will want to figure out how to best represent and organize the many targets in your figure. Morphs lists and attribute lists can assist you in this task.

Morphs lists are automatically created when morphs are generated. This list shown in Figure 13.26 can be oriented vertically or horizontally in the Blend Shape options. If you click the Select button in the Blend Shape window, it selects the set of morphs that are over the select button. The morphs now populate the Channel Box. Within the Channel Box, you can now control these morphs. From within the Blend Shape window, you can set the sliders to overdrive the morphs by adding a number such as 2 or –1. You might want to overdrive morphs for exaggerated features.

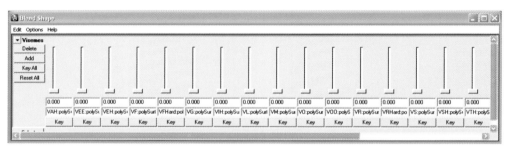

Figure 13.26 Blend Shape window

The next step up from the morphs list is the attribute list. This list simply drives morphs by using set-driven keys. Using an attribute list places all your controls in a vertical format, which is much more manageable than the space-hungry default display of the Blend Shape window.

You can edit the attributes easily by selecting one and dragging with the middle mouse button in the main workspace. Figure 12.23 (shown earlier) shows the attribute list morphs.

Meet Enrique Gato

Enrique Gato is a one of our favorite character setup artists. He has created realistic cartoony figures and produced many award-winning short films. The Tadeo Jones character, featured in the most recent of these shorts, uses a facial representation system that drives morph targets.

What is your background?

I was born in Valladolid, a small city in the north of Spain, but I've always lived in Madrid. Since I was a kid, I've always loved two main areas: animation

and computers. When I first had a computer, I realized that I really loved technology, and I learned to program my own little video games, where I also made all the graphics and animation. So, when

continues

I had to decide what to study at the university, I had no doubts, and I entered computer science engineering. There, I specialized in computer graphics, where I could develop some simple 3D engines and graphic tools to understand the basics of 2D and 3D software. During these years, I entered a computer graphics association called Artek, where I created my first animation shorts. They weren't especially good, but they helped me get my first job as character animator at Pyro Studios, a quite well-known video-game company. That's where I started my career as a professional.

What software do you use? What software do you prefer and why?

I've always used 3D Studio Max as the main tool, just because that's the tool that all the studios I've worked with had. In recent years, I've also worked with Maya, and I have to say that it's a really nice tool, with a very powerful and versatile core. But there's something that I never liked about this software: it's extremely slow. Maybe it's that Max is an extremely fast tool; you can make anything in less than half of the time of other packages. Although there are a couple of things that Max hasn't achieved yet, nowadays you can reach whatever you have in your mind with this software.

What did you do on Superlópez and both Tadeo short films?

Well, since I started developing my own animation shorts, I've been in charge of all the development areas. I did 100 percent of the work for Superlópez (including sound and music) and about 80 percent of the work for the first Tadeo Jones short. In this last short, I finally had some help from three old mates from Pyro Studios. They worked on the backgrounds. Apart from that, a musician and a sound FX engineer were hired to make the sound work more professionally. For the second part of Tadeo Jones, *Tadeo Jones and the Basement of Doom*, we had some more money, and I could put out more work. So, about 35 percent of it was made again by five old mates from different companies. It's quite difficult being involved in a work of this size; you don't have time to think a lot about how to make things. But it had its good points. I've always wanted to have a deep knowledge of all the development areas for this industry so I can afford big projects without doubts about the workflow. Well, I think I'm getting that, and there's a possibility that I will be able to start my first animated feature within the next year.

What was the hardest part of Tadeo's current rig for this latest installment?

Rigs for Tadeo's shorts are based on a very well-known tool for Max users: Character Studio. We didn't have time to develop our own skeletons and rigs, so I decided to use stock skeletons and rigs, as I had for previous shorts. But this time I wanted to go further with the deformation system. I didn't want to use skin morph tools to reshape the joint areas of the characters when, for example, the arms and legs bent because they were quite unstable. So, I developed a muscle-bones system to make deformations work better. The final result was a Character Studio skeleton with lots of additional muscle bones everywhere. This system was applied to all the characters in the short. Anyway, the most complex rigs weren't for the characters, but for some other animated elements, like a squared structure full of chains with shackles that traps Tadeo. There're about 300 independent links for the chains, and each one moves to follow the rest. Apart from that, each chain rolls up and down in its own structure. The idea was to automate each link's animation so the animator could manage the system in a simple way. In the end, the animator had to move only five handles for each chain to shape it; the rest is absolutely automatic, including the roll-up system.

continues

Meet Enrique Gato *(continued)*

What are a few "best practices" when rigging?

Rigging is by far the most technical area in visual productions. I really encourage riggers to have a deep knowledge of the tool they're using to get the best results but also look to other packages. Each software package has a very different base philosophy, and the best you can do is open your mind to see different ways of rigging in other tools. This will give you new ways to work in your traditional software.

I also encourage riggers to study all the mathematics they can, especially algebra and computing geometry. They're incredibly useful when you need to solve problems in a much more direct way than complex script controllers that can slow your rigs.

How do you deal with changes or fixes that are needed after the character is fully rigged?

Through the years, I've learned to develop a two-way pipeline that allows me to go back into any part of the work, fix anything, and automatically update most areas, depending on the change. In the case of rigging, I've developed some tools that, for example, store a character's skin information to a file. If the information changes, you have to overwrite only one file and load it anywhere you need (like an animation file you already started with the old rig).

Tell us about the facial setup on Tadeo.

It's a morph-based system, except the jaw deformation, rigged with a bone that I manage with an external animation interface connected through expressions (wire parameters in Max) with the morph targets and bone rotations. It is a typical build with splines that you move to get the different gestures of the head, with a total of about 60 different gestures. It also includes the tongue and eyes control. Maybe the most interesting things about this rig are the eyes controls. It's not the typical look-at system. Well, the eyes follow a look-at target, but the position of the target is managed through the facial animation interface. You don't need to select the target and move it so it follows the character. This gives you a good example of why I said learn mathematics; it can help you solve problems in an easier way. The expression to connect the facial eyes control with the target is not especially complex, but it's very useful.

What advice would give to future animators?

I always say that animation is observation. I remember my first years as an animator, and I can't forget how I was always watching the way everything moved, from a person walking to a paper falling to the floor. Animating is the art of building appealing movement, a very abstract job. It's not like sculpting, where you can see the figure, turn it, push it.... Working with movement is different from any other thing, and that makes it really special.

Creating Facial Control Systems

Now that we've discussed the various interfaces that you can use, we'll get down to business and show you how to create some. We'll start with a simple joystick and slider setup because it is one of the most powerful interfaces.

Simple Joystick and Slider Setup

To build a joystick, you start by building a control box. Control boxes are noneditable boundaries for the joystick. Creating the control boxes is a simple process. Draw a plan of the controls and control arrangement you need. Figure 13.27 shows a facial joystick setup.

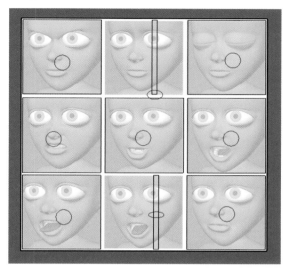

Figure 13.27 Facial joysticks

Let's go over the background control boxes and the joystick creation process:

1. Go to an area slightly offset from the head, the area where you want to place your controls. Make the controls fairly small. You want these controls to be out of the animator's way, but you also want them near the figure.

2. Use your front orthographic camera, and create a square with the CV curve tool set with the option 1 linear. Make sure your curve is constrained to the grid by pressing and holding the X key. It will need to be 2 by 2 for this example. You should have a control like in Figure 13.28.

Figure 13.28 Square control box

This type of control is used for moving areas of the face, such as the upper lip. As you move the joystick to the upper right, the upper right part of the figure's lip moves up. The left and down portions would create similar deformations. If the slider is moved into the middle of the top, it will make the left and right portions of the upper lip go up. If it were in the middle of the lower part of the control, it would make the right and left sides of the upper lip go down.

3. For the next slider type, duplicate the square (Ctrl+D), and move it to the next grid spacing by using the grid snap (pressing and holding X). You might have to center your pivot if you are away from the origin. Select the two CVs at the bottom of your square, move them up, and snap them to the grid. You have just created a 1 by 2 rectangle control, as shown in Figure 13.29.

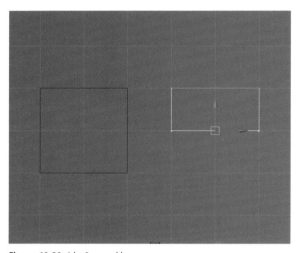

Figure 13.29 1 by 2 control box

This type of slider is typically used for controls that need only one type of movement. For instance, CheekFlex needs only positive values. If this control were driving CheekFlex, it could control the right cheek, left cheek, or both.

4. For the next slider type, duplicate the original square curve, and move it next to the rectangle you just made. Center its pivot, and snap it to the grid, as shown in Figure 13.30.

    This last control is a basic slider that can be used to drive morphs or defined joint shapes. These three are the basic controls you will want in the background of your user interface controls.

5. For a nicer look, duplicate and offset the edges.

6. To create your joysticks, create two circle curves in the center of the first box. To make sure the circle is in the exact center, snap the circle to the grid. Duplicate this circle, and offset it for a nicer control look. The circles should look like the ones in Figure 13.31.

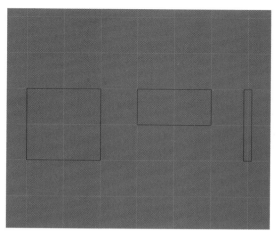

Figure 13.30 Linear control

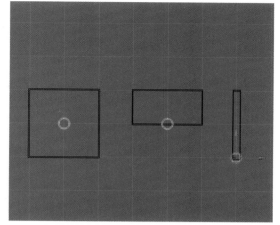

Figure 13.31 Controllers

7. To make these curves act as one single control, select the shape node of the secondary curve and the transform node (regular selection) of the first curve, and enter this MEL command:

```
parent -r -shape;
```

8. Now delete the unused transform node of your second curve.

9. Duplicate this node, and set it in the areas shown in Figure 13.31.

10. Remember to snap them to the appropriate grid intersection and freeze transformations on these controls. The joysticks are snapped to the grid for a purpose. They need to have definite values that they can move within the UI boxes. These values are for the limits for each control. You can also now move these control boxes and joysticks together to another location, since they are relative to each other. Freeze transforms on the joystick, and use the following limits.

11. To set the limits, select the transform node, and set the limits accordingly. The first control would have translate x limits of min –1 and max 1 and translate y limits of min –1 and max 1. Figure 13.32 shows these values.

12. For the second control, select the transform node, and set the limits of translate x to min –1 and max 1 and translate y limits to min 0 and max 1. Figure 13.33 shows these values.

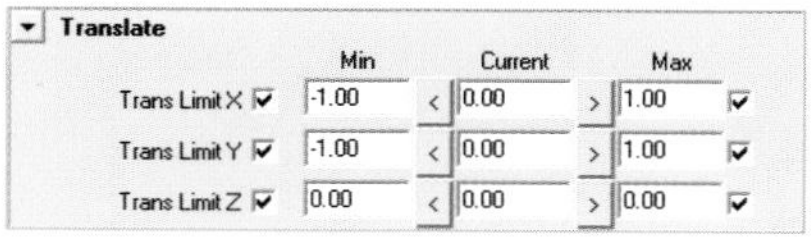

Figure 13.32 Facial joysticks limits

Figure 13.33 Facial joysticks limits

13. For the third control, select the transform node, and set the limits of translate x to min 0 and max 0 and translate y limits to min 0 and max 2. You can also have this control zeroed in the middle and work in the positive and negative. Figure 13.34 shows these values.

Figure 13.34 Facial joysticks limits

14. All these control backgrounds should be grouped together and made to be visible but not selectable. You can do this by going into the Layer Editor at the lower portion of the Channel Box and creating a layer, adding the control backgrounds, and clicking twice in the second column to get *R*. This will make your controls visible but not selectable.

Facial Representation

Creating the facial representation is fun because of the variety of shapes you can use. Make them intuitive and not too busy. Controls are efficient only if they are easily selected. Here is how to set up a facial representation:

1. For a facial representation setup, you will need to re-create the face using curves for controls. Be sure the controls echo the positions of the actual facial controls.

2. Set the X and Y movements of the controls to control the movement and rotation attributes, as well as their translation attributes. You can easily do this with set-driven keys. Create these keys in with the Set Driven Key tool (Animate > Set Driven Key > Set). Load the control in as the driver and the morph, joint, or influence object in as the driven.

3. Set your controls as you want. Hook the control's translation to the morphs value or to a joint or an influence object's rotation.

4. Lock the Z-axis on the controls, and give them limits for movement. This will keep them stationary and more predictable. You can use some of the facial joystick ideas in setting a facial representation rig.

Facial Control Positioning

Now you need to place the facial controls. These controls could go to the side of the head, or if you're using a UI window, you could make them small and inside of the head. They are parent-constrained to the head.

1. It is recommended that you have a camera fixed on the UI controls. To do this and to have your controls move with the head, group all your controls and the camera into a null group and parent-constrain that group to the head joint of the figure.

2. To make your scene even cleaner, you might want to make the controls on a separate scene and have your MEL facial script create the controls by calling that separate scene. A quick way to create facial controls is with a control setup that is parented to the character's head, like our friend Tadeo Jones, as shown in Figure 13.35.

Figure 13.35 Facial representation of Tadeo Jones by Enrique Gato

Conclusion

You have finished creating the needed expressions, and you've gotten to the end of our morphs and shapes list. You also learned about the options of the several user interfaces that you can employ. You now should have a good idea of what the final user experience for your rig will be like. In the next chapter, we'll discuss a few advanced techniques for the deformation of your character.

The rig is now complete and ready to go, but before you throw it over the wall to the animators, you can do a number of things to test the rig to see whether it works like it should. The testing process can reveal some potential problems and give you a chance to fix them.

Deforming and Organizing Your Rig

You've made it to the deformation chapter. This is where the fun begins. So far, you've set up a good, solid foundation rig. Now we'll introduce stretchy joints, a trick to get bendable bones, and new ways to influence or fix the skinned mesh, and then we'll wrap up with the final riggable joints and deformations. There are some neat types of deformations in this chapter, but you might need to modify them to fit your rig. Think of the unique portions of your rig and how you can adapt them for these setups. The best approach is to think outside the box. Let's get deforming!

14

Chapter Contents
Stretchy IK
Rivets
Influence objects
Riggable joints and broken rigs
Final organization

Stretchy IK

Stretching joints is one of the more common advanced features that you can apply to a rig. The stretchy setup is great for animators who want that squash-and-stretch feel. It is also great for extending the arms when the animator needs to do so. For example, say you have a character with short arms that needs to reach the top of his head but can't. With stretchy IK, your character can stretch just a bit to reach something (see Figure 14.1) or really elongate for a style similar to Elastigirl in *The Incredibles*.

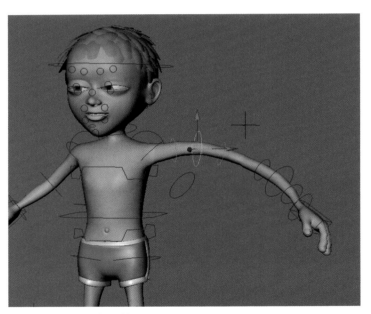

Figure 14.1 The stretchy and bent arm

Think about issues such as forearm rotation and knees with two joints when applying these tutorials. You can easily fix these issues, but it may take a little figuring. For forearm rotation, you simply need to have a plan. Either you have a secondary joint or cluster or you add one using the advanced rivet technique that we will show you. For double-jointed knees, you can simply add the stretch to the extra joint.

In this book, we stress scripting to save time. Setting up a stretchy script is a great idea for automating the setup of stretchy options on the limbs. Keep secondary joints and the placement of your stretchy controls in mind as you approach your script.

Note: We will show how to build some stretchy code in Chapter 15, "MEL Scripting: An Introduction." As you go through the stretchy tutorial in this chapter, watch the Script Editor to see what Maya is doing and how it is hooking up connections. You will be able to see how you can use MEL to efficiently set up attributes. You will also see how you can control the efficiency of the setup and connections.

The tutorial that follows can be used on leg or arm joints. To start, create a test scene to use as you build this setup. Make sure you're familiar with the process before adding it to your rig. Also, organize all your stretch nodes into a group. This will keep things nice and organized in whatever portion of your rig you are adding this function.

For simplicity, the tutorial takes you through the process using left arm joints. Once you've finished and understand the process, you can use it for any appendage; simply change the labels. You can use the technique to add a stretchy IK to the appendages of prebuilt characters as well.

Tip: You can apply this technique to the leg by replacing the shoulder with the thigh, the elbow with the knee, and so on.

1. In the side orthographic view, create a distance dimension node (Create > Measure Tools > Distance Tool), and then snap one of the locators to the shoulder and the other to the wrist joint. Remember that pressing and holding the V key snaps the locator to the joint.

2. Name the locators that were created with the distance dimension node LHandIKDistLoc and LShoulderIKDistLoc. (When you use the process again, you'll use similar names that describe the area on which you're working.) Name the distance dimension node LArmDist or something representative of the area. Now, point-constrain the shoulder locator to LShoulderIK and the wrist locator to LHandIK.

3. Add two attributes to a permanent control, such as the LWristIK. Do this by adding each attribute (select Attribute > Add Attribute, or right-click any existing attribute and choose Add Attribute from the pop-up menu).

   Give each of these attributes the following values, as shown in Figure 14.2:

   Name: Stretch

   Type: float

   Min: 0

   Max: 1

   Default: 1

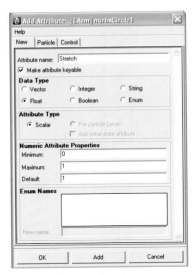

Figure 14.2 The stretch attribute settings

Give the attributes the following values, as shown in Figure 14.3:

Name: IKLength

Type: float

Min: 0

Max: 10

Default: 1

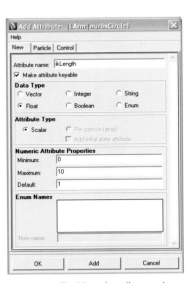

Figure 14.3 The IKLength attribute settings

4. In the Outliner (Window > Outliner), select the LArmDist node. Now switch to the Hypershade (Window > Rendering Editors > Hypershade), and add the node to the graph (Hypershade > Graph > Add Selected to Graph).

5. Create another multiply-divide node, and name it LArmMD. Next connect the distance attribute of the distance dimension node to the Input1X attribute of the multiply-divide node. Make sure that the node is set to multiply.

6. Select the control over the LWrist from the main viewport, and add it to the Hypergraph. Now, grab the outgoing Stretch attribute, and connect it to Input2X in the ZZ. This is the scaling switch. When it is set to zero, the distance is multiplied by zero, which, in turn, makes the stretch equal to zero.

7. In the Hypergraph, double-click the distance dimension node, and copy the distance. Enter the distance value into the InputY2 field of the LArmMD divide node.

8. Hook the IKLength of the control curve to the Input2X of LArmMD. This amplifies the IKLength attribute to accommodate long stretches. Figure 14.4 shows the multiply-divide settings.

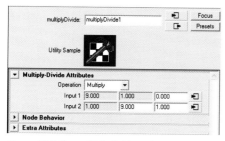

Figure 14.4 The multiply-divide settings

9. Create a condition node. Hook up the outputX of the LArmMD node to the first term and the ColorIfTrueR (you will have to reselect the outputX) of the condition.

10. Hook the outputY of the LArmMD node to the Conditionals second term and the ColorIfFalseR.

11. Create another multiply-divide node. Name the node LArmMD2.

12. Connect outputColorR to the LArmMD2 InputX. Figure 14.5 shows the condition settings.

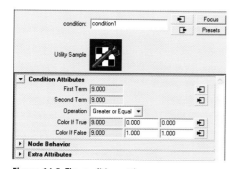

Figure 14.5 The condition settings

13. Select both the shoulder and the elbow, and bring them into the Hypergraph.

14. Hook outputX of LArmMD2 to the joint's scalex.

The resultant Hypergraph should be similar to the one shown in Figure 14.6. You will find a MEL script for stretchy joints on the book's companion CD. It works from the preexisting joint setup. The stretch.mel script uses a distance node, showing the distance between the joints. This distance node returns the same result as the distance dimension node.

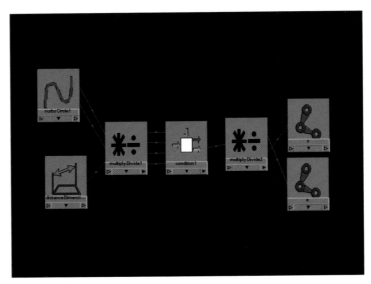

Figure 14.6 The Hypergraph stretch

Rivets

rivet.mel is a MEL script that hooks a locator to a poly or a NURBS surface. This idea comes from Michael Bazhutkin. You can find the script at www.geocities.com/bazhutkin/. No matter what that surface does, the locater will be weighted to the ends of the surface. Think about a ribbon, and imagine that you twist it from both ends, in opposite directions. At a point in the center, the ribbon will fold at a specific angle, and that angle will be perpendicular to the surface. Anything attached with a rivet will always reflect what that surface in the center is doing. The surface is what orients the riveted object. That makes rivets a great tool for attaching any nondeforming object to a deforming one, for example, buttons on a shirt or scales on a lizard.

Rivets, Ribbons, and Follicles

The rivet idea is similar to what the ribbon spine does with a follicle. The locator or joint would use the follicle to determine its world up. One of the more famous uses is the ribbon spine by Aaron Holly of Fahrenheit Digital. It creates a ribbon that has joints that follow the orientation of the surface. Arm deformers, such as the ones in this book, have been created using follicle-based systems.

In this book, we describe the process to create this deformation specifically with rivets and pointOnSurface nodes. Thanks to Jared Fong for the help with that idea and Geordie Martinez for creating a local orientation on the surface that bypasses the follicle and rivet usage. His setup was implemented in the rivet code supplied on the accompanying CD. You'll find Geordie's script, ggmRibbonJoints_v2.mel, there as well. (It is designed to work with joints aiming down the X-axis. For versions that work on the Y-axis and the Z-axis, go to http://www .negative13.com/.) The script opens the usage up to Maya Complete users and is the basis for the deformers that we use.

The Power of the Rivet

An actual rivet, like the one on your jeans' pocket, gives a good approximation of what the rivet script does. This script places a locator in the middle of a surface that appears to be weighted (riveted) to the surface upon which it resides. Rivets are very useful, because they will efficiently take the orientation information from their neighbors and correctly and quickly solve their relative position and orientation.

Polygon Rivets

When used with a polygon, the rivet script creates two curveFromMesh nodes and then creates a loft between the two nodes. This creates a U and V directional surface that can be used to place a rivet. Let's run through a quick tutorial to understand polygonal rivets:

1. Create a single polygon plane, and select two adjacent edges, as shown in Figure 14.7.

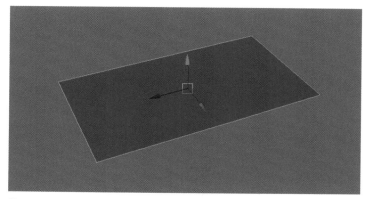

Figure 14.7 The prerivet polygon

2. Run the rivet script from the in-shelf icon.

Select and move/rotate your edges and points to test the workings of the rivet. Now imagine the possibilities of having a string of these that all work off each other. You can parent joints to these locators and create chains of free-moving joints that follow their parents. We will show how to build a string of these to influence the arm joints. We will also explain how to use a rivet to create fore-arm rotation, as shown in Figure 14.8.

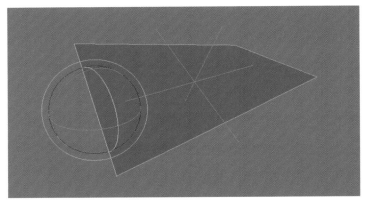

Figure 14.8 The polygon-based rivet

NURBS Rivets

When attached to a NURBS plane, a point on the NURBS surface needs to be defined for the script. After that, the rivet script is run, and you have a resultant rivet that is seemingly controlled by the point on the surface. Follow this exercise to experiment with this:

1. Create a single NURBS plane, and give it three patches in the V direction. Right-click the surface, and select the point on the surface where you need your rivet, as shown in Figure 14.9.

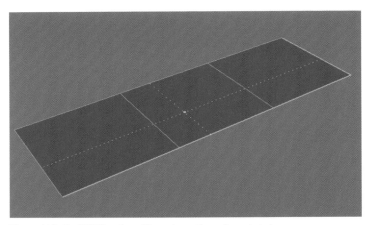

Figure 14.9 The NURBS surface with a point on the surface selected

2. Run the rivet script from the in-shelf icon.

3. Select the CVs to manipulate the surface and to test the rivets and their ability to follow the surface. This is how the ribbon spine was built. There are a few more connections, but this is the basic principle of the rivet setup that is not dependent on follicles. Figure 14.10 shows multiple rivets placed on the three NURBS patches.

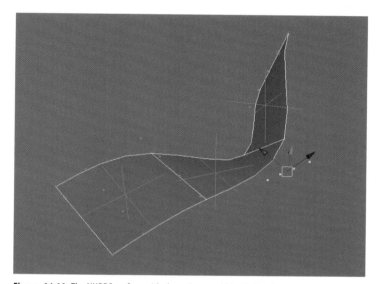

Figure 14.10 The NURBS surface with three rivets and bit of a bend

Where Can You Use Rivets?

You can use rivets wherever you need a deformation that follows its parent joint. For instance, the forearm roll issue, facial expressions, and a spine creation are all prime examples of areas that need major definition and need falloff as well. All these deformations need to be controlled by a parent joint, and they all could utilize the free-form movement that a rivet-based system offers.

You can also use rivets for holding things to a surface without deforming them. If you parent a button onto a shirt with the correct weighting, the button will then move with the surface and not deform.

Lastly, you can use rivets to create Gumby-style deformations. We will show you how to add this type of deformation to character's limbs. You will learn to use the pointOnSurface node with a NURBS patch and layer them for even more control.

In the tutorial that follows, you will create a rivet setup for use with a left forearm. We will show how to create a single patch that will extend from one joint to another. You then will create a rivet. You need to have the rivet.mel script loaded for this tutorial. As you work on this, be sure to name everything. Keep in mind that names need to be unique and descriptive of the body part. Let's get to it.

Rivet-Based Deformation for the Arm

Follow these steps to create a rivet-based deformation for the arm:

1. Create a NURBS plane that is 1×1 at the origin, and then go to the makeNurb-Plane1 node in the Attribute Editor. Change the degree to Linear. This will make the NURBS plane about as simple as it can get with a minimal number of control vertices. Rename the NURBS plane to LForearmMainPatch. Use MEL for creating the NURBS surface by typing the following into the MEL command window that is below the 3D viewport:

   `nurbsPlane -p 0 0 0 -ax 0 0 1 -ch 1 -o on -po 0 -w 1 -lr 1 -d 1 -u 1;`

2. Let's create two clusters that will drive the patch. Select the two control vertices on the left side of the patch, and create a cluster for them (Create Deformer > Cluster). Create another cluster for the other control vertices on the right. Name the clusters LForearmMainClusterUp and LForearmMainClusterDwn.

3. Now you need to create a pointOnSurface node in the exact center of the NURBS surface. Right-click the patch, select Surface Point from the pop-up menu, and then click an edge of the patch and drag inward.

> **Tip:** Type the code that follows into the MEL command line to create a point in the exact center of the patch:
> `select -r LForearmMainPatch.uv[0.5][0.5] ;`
> As an alternative, you can place the point manually when the rivet doesn't need to be exactly on center.

4. With the pointOnSurface selected, create your rivet by clicking the shelf icon that was created when you installed the rivet.mel script. Name your rivet LForearmMainRiv.

5. Create a control for the rivet. You can use any control shape. For this exercise, create a simple NURBS circle. Name it LForearmMainCTRL. Freeze its transformations so the animator can zero it when needed in animation later.

> **Tip:** Use a MEL command to create the circle at the origin. The code for creating a circle at the origin is as follows:
> `circle -ch on -o on -nr 0 1 0 -r 0.5 -d 1 -s 32 ;`

6. Select the control, and create a group (Ctrl+G). Name this group LForearmMain-SecNull. Place LForearmMainSecNull into another group (Ctrl+G) to create the main null. Name this new group LForearmMainNull. Rotate the control so that the X-axis faces the clusters, as shown in Figure 14.11.

7. Parent-constrain LForearmMainNull to the rivet (select the rivet, select LForearmMainNull, and then use Constrain > Parent).

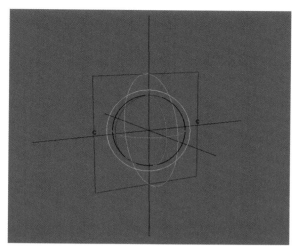

Figure 14.11 The NURBS surface with a point on the surface selected

8. Create a new joint, and move it to the origin. The new joint should be right on top of your rivet now. Name the new joint LForearmMainJointBND. Parent LForearmMainJointBND under LForearmMainCTRL. (Select the control, then select the joint, and finally choose Constrain > Parent).

9. Create a group to organize everything you just created. Name the group LForearmDef for "left forearm deformation." Do this by selecting the clusters, surface, null, joint, and rivet and hitting Ctrl+G.

10. Orient-constrain LForearmMainClusterDwn to the elbow joint, and then delete the constraint. You will find it with the cluster in the Outliner.

11. Orient and point-constrain LForearmMainClusterUp to the elbow joint.

12. Orient and point-constrain LForearmMainClusterDwn to the wrist joint. Make sure that Maintain Offset is checked in the Orient options.

13. Hide the clusters, rivet, NURBS patch, and joint. You will use the joint later when you bind. You can see what it looks like before it is hidden in Figure 14.12.

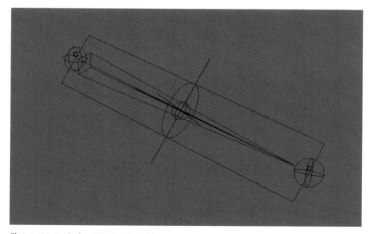

Figure 14.12 Before the rivet is hidden

You will need to run through this process three times, once for each bone in the target limb, to achieve the setup that we have included in the script as well as the figure on the accompanying CD. Use the process on the elbow and against the wrist initially, then on the elbow and LForearmMainJointBND, then the forearm mid-joint (the one you just created), and finally on the forearm midjoint and wrist. We have included a MEL script that runs through this process automatically on the book's companion CD; the script is called deformableLimb.mel. You need to run the script three times, just like the tutorial.

Tip: You should always know exactly what a script does before you use it. Spend some time and figure out where the commands are located in the script and why it was written that way. We will dive deeper into MEL scripting in the next chapter.

Influence Objects

Influence objects are objects that are skinned along with the joints. Influence objects can be used to correct a knee, to fix a shoulder, or even to make facial movements and expressions. Influence objects are treated as objects and can be scaled, rotated, and moved to influence another skinned surface. Influence objects can be polygons, NURBS, or curves. For the most part, they all give you the same performance, except curves don't twist as well as surfaces and therefore are limited in that regard. Experiment to see what works best for each rig.

Half of the work of building influence objects is figuring out what they should look like; the other half is assigning weights for these objects. The object's shape should help you recognize the working shape of the deformation. When you skin the shapes to the surface, start them with a weight of zero and then use the Add brush to assign weight. You need to skin to the influence objects to determine whether you have enough geometry in the influence objects to affect the amount of change you want. So, add the object, paint its weight, detach if it's not right, and then apply weight again until it's giving you the desired results. You can do this to one side, and then if you named the other side correctly, you can mirror weights to the other influence object. So, you have to paint only one side.

In the tutorial that follows, we are going to show you how to make facial expressions. We will create mouth movement, lid movement, and brow movement all with influence objects. As you work through the tutorial, focus on the number of movements you need for your character's face. You can use any model you'd like for the tutorial.

We will detach the lip shape and separate it into four pieces. This gives you good control for sneers and other facial movement. After you get the hang of it, you may want to even have six or eight controls, depending on the facial deformations you need. Also, you need to keep the musculature and the direction of movement in mind each time you create a control. The influence objects will mimic muscles pulling. We will show how to use NURBS surfaces for the lips because you need to be able to move and rotate the lips. For the brows and lid deformations, we'll show how to use NURBS curves as well because they can be very descriptive and look good too.

Mouth Influence Objects

Lets spend some time now to create our influence obects for facial deformations.

1. Make your model's polygon surface live so you can draw on it (select Surface > Modify > Make Live).

2. Create two curves (Create > CV Curve Tool) around the mouth. These curves should follow the curvature of the mouth. They will be lofted and then split apart to create your influence objects. Use the same amount of CVs so they can be lofted. One curve needs to be a little bigger than the other. You can see the result in Figure 14.13.

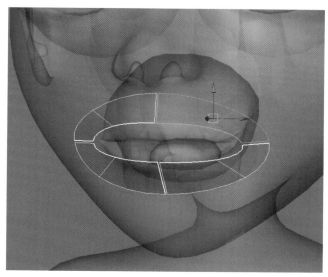

Figure 14.13 Detaching the curve where needed

Tip: Isoparms are divisions in a surface. Make sure your CVs are in the areas that you want to divide to make isoparms that you can separate. The divisions will be cut to make the influence objects.

The curves you create now will be divided to make your influence objects, so make sure your CVs are in the places where you will want to divide later:

- For four influence objects around the mouth, make CVs on the top, sides, and bottom.
- For six points of movement, create CVs on the top and bottom, as well as above and below the corners of the mouth.

For the simplicity of this tutorial, we'll show how to create four points of movement on the surface, as shown in Figure 14.14.

Tip: You may want to have six points of movement. This creates a nice setup because it gives you control over the corners of the mouth.

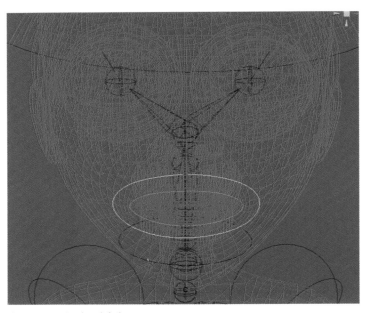

Figure 14.14 Ready to loft the curve

3. Close the curves using the Open/Close Curve Tool (Edit Curves > Open Close Curves > Option Box > Blend .5).

4. Loft between the curves by selecting one and then the other and choosing (Surfaces > Loft).

5. Select the isoparms on the ends, top, and bottom of the surface (Edit Surfaces > Detach).

6. If you want, you can do a temporary test with the influence objects; save the scene first so you can return to this point. Temporarily skin the geometry to a single joint, and then skin the geometry to the influence object. (Select the object to be influenced, select the influence object, and then select Skin > Edit Smooth Skin > Add influence Object.)

Lid Influence Objects

For lid influence objects, you can simply use curves. To create the curve in the eyelid area, turn the model surface live again. (Select the surface, and select Modify > Make Live.) Now, create a simple curve (Create > CV Curve Tool) with three to four CVs on both the top and bottom lids.

Brow Influence Objects

To create brow influence objects, follow these steps:

1. For the brow, make the model surface live. (We talked about how to do this earlier in the chapter.)

2. Create two pairs of curves, each curve having three CVs, and loft across them to create NURBS planes with two separate patches each.

3. Detach the patches to make separate brow pieces. The pieces will be used to make brow expressions.

Controls for Influence Objects

Now, let's create controls for each influence object. These controls will be easily selected once the influence objects and everything else is hidden. For this example, we've used NURBS circles for controls. As an alternative, you can use representative shapes or curves.

1. Select the influence object, and create a group (Ctrl+G). Name each group. Use the influence object name, and add the suffix Null.

2. Freeze transformations on the controls (Modify > Freeze Transformations).

3. Run this MEL command for each control:

```
parent -r -s $influenceObject $Control;
```

4. Now parent the curve to the null (in the Outliner, select the null and then the curve, and choose Edit > Parent).

    Figure 14.15 shows the influence objects.

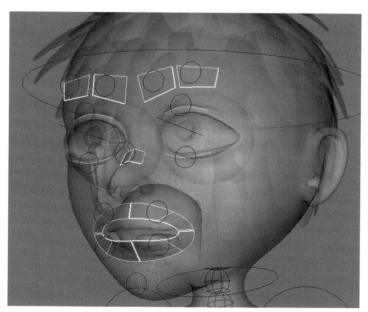

Figure 14.15 The influence objects of the face

Keep in mind that attaching influence objects is somewhat intense for Maya. The software has to calculate the weights as it attaches each object to the surface. You may need to lower some of your settings in the options box, if the default settings are too much for your computer to calculate. Also, remember to check the Use Geometry option in that same option box, or the surface will not recognize your influence objects.

You may also want to use the Use Components setting in the skinCluster. This setting allows you to apply even more deformers to affect the surface.

Riggable Joints and Broken Rigs

You need to have riggable joints and nonriggable joints in your advanced setup because the actual skeleton, when selected, creates an undesirable binding. For instance, you do not want to bind the wrists because they will not rotate with the hand. They will provide positioning only for the hand. You want to bind to the hand joint. All joints are riggable, but we'll show how to use some as placeholders only because their rotations are not wanted in the skin. They serve to direct other joints. So, in order to skip the wrist joint and to have a broken rig that can be manipulated after binding, you need to isolate the correct joints needed for the bind. Also, we'll show how to add another layer of joints that are directly driven by their parent joints.

By this point in the book, you know that a figure consists of sets of joints that were created for the sole purpose of driving other joints. The FK/IK arms that we made had two chains of joints that drove a third and final chain. This final chain is even bound to both of those chains. For this exercise, you'll want to parent-constrain new floating joints to some of the joints on that main chain. You will parent-constrain the clavicle, shoulder, elbow, thigh, and knee joints. The animator won't see any of this, but the setup will still allow for individual tweaking that may be needed later. You can manipulate the floating joints after the skinning process.

With a traditional joint setup, you are constrained to the hierarchy of the skeleton and any additional constraints that you created. With floating joints, you will be independent of the hierarchy, while still echoing its influences. In some areas, this is not really needed. Take the hands, for example; you will not need to create floating, riggable joints for each joint in the hands because you already have that functionality in your setup.

You'll need floating joints in the following locations:

- The top and bottom of the spine (for stretch isolation)
- Along the main joint chain in the arm (shoulder and elbow)
- Along the main joint chain in the leg (thigh and knee)
- Facial setup (if joints are the preferred method of deformation)

To create floating joints, follow these steps:

1. Create a single joint, and snap it to the target joint by holding Ctrl+V. Also, orient-constrain it to the target joint.

2. Now delete the orient constraint you just made. This gives the joint the same initial rotation as its soon to be parent joint.

3. Freeze transformations on the floating joint (Modify > Freeze Transformations).

4. Parent-constrain (Constraint > Parent) the floating joint to its parent joint.

5. Rename these joints so they each have a BND suffix.

6. Now, if you want to hide the floating joint but still be able to manipulate it, you can create a control. To create the control, follow the instructions in the "Control Creation" section of Chapter 3, "Rigging That's Right: Rigging Concepts You Need to Know."

> **Tip:** Create a control for the joint if you think it's necessary for the animator to have free control of the joint. The purpose of this type of joint may require a little explanation before the animator can use it effectively.

Final Organization

Organization is key in rigging. If you hand over a rig with hundreds of connected nodes all on the base level of your scene, you will likely lose popularity with your peers. It is not good practice, and it's very hard to work with. To avoid any of these unwanted social issues, it is best to keep a tight ship.

To reiterate what we mentioned in Chapter 3, be sure you have a base group that is named for your character. This is beneficial for a couple reasons. In scenes with many figures, this will keep the figures organized. Animators and others further down the pipeline will readily know which figure is which. A base group and descriptive naming provide your character with a solid organizational foundation.

Next, make sure you divide the character into body parts and major elements. Dividing by body part is simple. Look at the runner.mb figure that was included on the book's companion CD to see what we mean. The sections of the body are grouped by area of the rig. For instance, LLeg, RLeg, Spine, and Head are all groups. If you grouped and descriptively named body parts as you worked through the previous chapters, your work should be done. The feet often are put into the leg groups but do not have to be. They can be their own separate group. Organize your figure in a way that best suits the animator's needs. Be sure you group the other major elements of your figure. For our figure, these parts included the master control and the actual geometry. These are not exactly body parts, and they can't be broken into body parts; however, they do need their own grouping.

Grouping for Organization and Hierachy

When you create groups, make sure you keep similar items together, and make sure you are prepared for hiding joints and unneeded nodes, such as clusters and IK handles. Then, go through and test your skeleton to make sure you don't have any controls that are hidden or obscured by any other objects. Look for controls that are children of joints. If you want to be able to hide your joints without hiding controls, you will need to make sure the controls are constrained to the joints but not controlled with a child-parent relationship. The joints can then can be hidden, without the controls being affected.

Naming Conventions

Go back through your rig, and make sure you've named things in a like manner. If you followed the conventions we taught you earlier in the book, the controls, FK/IK chains, and body parts are named accordingly. Take a few minutes to verify that your character naming conventions are consistent across the figure. Be sure you named all the bindable joints with a suffix of BND. Review the material in Chapter 2, "Getting to Know You: Maya's Interface and Basics." Verify the naming of your nodes. Remember, you can use MEL to select every node that includes a particular prefix or suffix in the name. For example, for our runner character, we named all the influence objects using a suffix of INF. This allowed for easy multiple selecting with a simple MEL command.

Make sure there are no duplicates in the naming structures. This is extremely important for referencing, which we will cover in Chapter 19, "Optimizing Your Character Pipeline Using Character Pipeline Tools." Make sure all names are unique, even across different nodes. For instance, an arm group and an IK handle cannot both be named LArm. To quickly check to see whether any names are duplicated, run this MEL command in the MEL field at the bottom of the interface:

```
print `ls -type joint`;
```

The resultant list is populated in the log portion of the Script Editor. As you look through your structure, the duplicates are indicated with a pipe that precedes the name, for example, |LArm. Find the duplicates in your Outliner or Hypergraph, and change the names so each is unique. Unique names prevent hierarchy overlaps when the namespaces are created in the referencing process.

Conclusion

In this chapter, we showed you different approaches for deforming, such as the rivet driven arm, the leg deformation, and the stretchy arm and legs. We have touched on good organization practices and broken rigs allowing for correct binding.

You are now ready to move on to the MEL chapter. MEL scripts can help automate specific rigging tasks and ensure that you don't miss critical steps. The next chapter provides a brief introduction to MEL scripting and then shows off some advanced rigging scripts that will make your life easier.

CONCLUSION

Mel Scripting: An Introduction

This chapter was contributed by Jared Fong, a technical director resident currently working at Pixar Animation Studios.

15

One day, when surfing the Internet, I came across a job posting for a technical artist. The ad was for someone with a personal mantra of "Doing something once is artistic, but doing it twice is a pain—just script it!" I couldn't agree more. Scripting a rig has the advantage of being stable, shareable, and repeatable. Stability comes from the fact that your scripts can completely rebuild your rig if something breaks. If a script is written well, it can easily be shared between multiple characters/productions. With the ability to rebuild completely and share rigs between characters, you have a repeatable rigging pipeline that is consistent and easily maintainable.

Chapter Contents
Deciding what to script
Scripting basics
Script planning
Basic procedural rigging pipelines

Good Things to Script

The idea of rigging a character in code seems counterintuitive—why should you script something that can be done with a few simple clicks? Although this sounds good at first, what if you have to do the same thing once for many different characters? What if it needs to be done multiple times per character? Obviously, the few clicks that it took to get the job done at first grows into a lot of tedious work. If you instead scripted the process, the whole thing would be faster and have a guaranteed level of consistency.

Deciding what to script is very important. It doesn't make sense to script a rig for a simple prop with three bones. However, it does make sense to script the creation of limbs, facial rigs, or anything that is complex, that is tedious, or that might go through many iterations. For example, let's say you have a scene that needs a flower in a vase to wave back and forth. You can just throw a few bones in there and a controller and be done with it. Now imagine you have a character who has to interact with the same scene. Your animator will probably need new features and a bug fixed somewhere down the line. These are elements that would be good to script.

The Basics

Many good books and websites are dedicated to mastering MEL. If you want a more in-depth look at how to use MEL, I suggest *MEL Scripting for Maya Animators*, Second Edition, by Mark R. Wilkins and Chris Kazmier (Morgan Kaufmann, 2005). If you are using Maya 8.5 or newer and you prefer Python, Maya's documentation will help you get started. Since MEL is available in older versions of Maya, this chapter will cover it.

MEL scripting is the internal language of Maya. Everything that is done with the interface in Maya can be accomplished with MEL scripts. Since MEL is a scripting language, it is perfectly suited to the one-time building of complex systems such as rigs.

Running MEL Scripts

There are various ways to run MEL scripts. The most common are sourcing external .mel files or using the Script Editor. To source a file, you can manually type the script path in the MEL command line:

```
source "c:\melscripts\helloWorld.mel";
```

Another alternative is to drag and drop the script into Maya's Script Editor. You can open the Script Editor (Window > General Editors > Script Editor) or click the Script Editor (bottom) icon, shown in Figure 15.1.

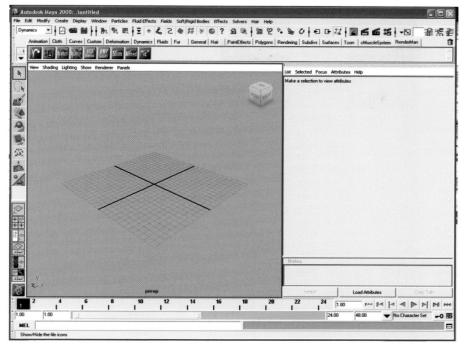

Figure 15.1 The Script Editor icon

To see these two methods for running scripts in action, open the Script Editor, and type the following into the bottom pane of the Script Editor:

```
print "Hello World";
```

Note: The bottom pane is the input section where you can type commands and save/load MEL scripts. The upper pane is an output history, showing scripts entered and other useful feedback.

Now, click anywhere in the bottom input section of the Script Editor, and press Enter; alternatively, press Ctrl+Enter to run the script. Figure 15.2 shows the Script Editor UI.

Tip: You can select portions of scripts and execute only the selected portions of the script. Also, selecting a script before running it prevents the script from being cleared once it is executed. It is not a good thing when a script that you have been working on accidentally gets deleted.

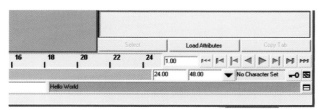

Figure 15.2 The Script Editor UI

After you run the script, look in the command feedback line in the bottom-right corner of the Maya interface. You should see these words:

```
Hello World
```

Now, look in the output history, which is the top section of the Script Editor. There you should see the following:

```
print "Hello World";
Hello World
```

Another way to run a MEL script is by making an external .mel file. To do so open a text editor, like Notepad, and type the following:

```
print "Hello World";
```

Save the file as test.mel to your desktop. You can now drag and drop the file into the Script Editor or source the script to see the same results as the first method.

 Tip: You can use any text editor to write MEL scripts. EditPad is one of the better text editors. EditPad Lite is a free editor. When you purchase EditPad Pro, you can download a syntax highlighter that will highlight your MEL commands for you. The syntax highlighter is available at www.highend3d.com.

Sourcing MEL Scripts

Open test.mel from the desktop by entering the following code into the Script Editor. For Windows, you might have a path that looks like this:

```
source "C:/Documents and Settings/Administrator/Desktop/test.mel";
```

Sourcing allows you to run a script from a user-defined location.

Variables

Variables are containers; they hold information. The information is undefined until the script is run. For example, if you needed to print the name of the selected object, there would be no way to know beforehand what the user selected, so you would use a variable in the script. The script would look something like this:

```
string $name[] = `ls -sl`;
print $name[0];
```

$name is just a placeholder; it has no starting value, but it will hold the information returned by the `ls -sl` command. Remember to use a tick mark (`) here instead of apostrophes ('). No matter what object is selected by the user, the script will print the name of that object. This comes in handy when you have a process that runs on differently named objects but performs the same tasks for each of them. The string name with brackets is used to designate an array. I will talk about string names later in the chapter.

Variable Types

These are the most common variables used in rigging scripts:

- Integers
- Strings
- Floats

Integers are whole numbers, positive or negative (–3, –2, –1, 0, 1, 2, 3). They are useful for counting.

Strings can be a sequence of letters, symbols, and numbers, such as "this is a string"; they are useful for storing names and using commands to get the names of objects. Strings can also contain full commands.

Floats are numbers with decimal representation (such as 3.14159). Floats are useful for controlling attributes, such as translation and rotation information. Since they can include positive or negative decimal values, they are perfect for attribute values.

Variable Declaration

Each variable that you use in a script must be declared before it can be used. Each declaration must follow this basic form, no matter what type of variable it defines:

```
<type> $<name> = <value>;
```

To declare a string with the name of a joint, do this:

```
string $myjoint = "rootbone";
```

Here are a few more examples:

```
int $count = 0;
float $amount = 3.001;
```

Once a variable is declared, it can be assigned a different value, but only of the same variable type. For instance, once $myjoint is declared as a string, you can't assign a float value or int value to it. After you set up a variable, later you can retrieve the information that is stored in that variable. It is a best practice to reuse variables where possible. One of the most common things you can do is save the names of joints and controllers into variables. Then, if the name changes, you have to change the name only in the declaration, rather than changing every instance of the name in the script. Here is an example of using a string to store the name of a controller and then move it to the correct location:

```
string $handControl = "boyLHandCTRL";
string $handJoint = "boyLHandJNT";
float $loc[] = `getAttr ($handJoint + ".t")`;
move -a $loc[0] $loc[1] $loc[2] $handControl;
```

The $loc[] variable is an array used to store the translation information for the joint to which you are moving.

Avoid Dependent Variables

Make each variable that you use nondependent. This means you will use a string that represents the node. For instance, you want to avoid any naming that might prevent your script from remaining viable for the next person. It is best to store all your nodes as variables so the script is not dependent on names within a particular scene.

Whenever you run a command, a value is returned in the output pane. If you type the code:

```
spaceLocator;
```

it will return the result of // Result: locator1 //. This is the return value.

It is better to have the user define the nodes to be manipulated. So, instead of this code, which is dependent on the name locator1, like this:

```
move -r 0 0 2 locator1;
```

you could have your script ask the user to select the object (locator1) and then run the following script, which will build an array of the selected objects and then move the first one. Array entries always start at 0, as in the $sel[0] code. I will also talk about the ls -sl command later in the chapter.

```
//select the object to be moved and run script
string $sel[] = `ls -sl`;
move -r 0 0 2 $sel[0];
```

You can also declare your variables prior to going into a procedure. A *procedure* is a series of commands. I will talk about procedures a little later in the chapter. Just remember that good coding is independent of node naming.

Commenting and Concluding

You can add comments to your code by prefixing the line with //. You can add comments for your own benefit for indexing or for the benefit of others to help them understand your script. You can comment out lines of code with /* */ to prevent them from being executed without having to physically remove them from the script.

```
//this line will not be processed by Maya
/* These lines
will be ignored
by Maya*/
```

You always need to end a line of code with a semicolon. Commented lines do not need a semicolon because Maya ignores any line that begins with comment symbols.

Arrays

Arrays are basically containers that store multiple variables or a list of items. Rather than declaring a separate variable for each value you need, you can store those values in a single container known as an *array*. Imagine an array as a box of canned soups. The box (array) can store many cans of soups, but each can might have a different type of soup. You could have a box of many different soups. An array is the same idea;

although you have one array (box), each element (can) has a different value (flavor). For example, rather than declaring this:

```
string $soup1 = "Tomato";
string$soup2 ="Chicken Noodle";
string$soup3 ="Cream of Mushroom";
```

you can use an array to store the same thing:

```
string $soups[] = {" Tomato"," Chicken Noodle"," Cream of Mushroom"};
```

Once the array is defined, you can access the contents using the number index:

```
print $soups[0];
// Result: Tomato //
print $soups[1];
// Result: Chicken Noodle //
```

Arrays in MEL always begin with the first element indexed as 0 and continue, increasing by 1 each time.

Commands

Commands are the building blocks of MEL scripts. Everything that is done in Maya requires a command call. In the previous example, you encountered the print command. The print command is simple; it takes a single input and prints it in the Script Editor. Not all commands are this simple, however. Commands often have flags or parameters that define how the command behaves. One of the most common commands is the ls command, which is shorthand for list. The ls command lists different nodes in Maya depending on the parameters it is given. One of the most common uses is with the -selected flag. Entering **ls -sl** tells the ls command to return only the objects that are currently selected. Most commands have a few flags that can be used.

Commands are usually expressed in the following format:

```
Command [flags] objects;
```

For example:

```
ikHandle -startJoint joint1 -endEffector joint5;
```

You can easily dissect this command by the flags that are called. If you look at the MEL documentation (Help > MEL Command Reference) and search for the IK Handle command, you will find a list of flags that the command supports. If you look for the flag -startJoint, you will see that it looks something like Figure 15.3.

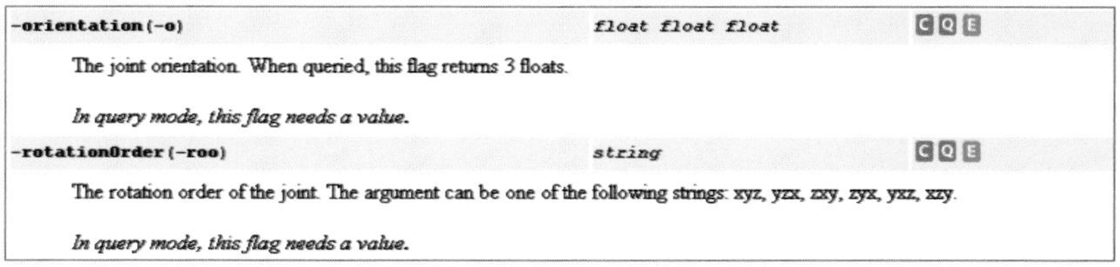

-orientation (-o)	float float float	C Q E
The joint orientation. When queried, this flag returns 3 floats.		
In query mode, this flag needs a value.		
-rotationOrder (-roo)	string	C Q E
The rotation order of the joint. The argument can be one of the following strings: xyz, yzx, zxy, zyx, yxz, xzy.		
In query mode, this flag needs a value.		

Figure 15.3 MEL commands and flags

In the previous example, you saw that the -startJoint flag can be shortened to -sj. Commands almost always have a short name and a long name. You can see that the -sj command is really the same as -startJoint, which defines the starting joint during the creation of an IK handle, and it has one parameter, a string that specifies the start joint of the handle's chain. Now, if you look up the -ee command while you are here, you'll see that it is the -endEffector flag, a string that defines the ending joint for the IK Handle command.

Command Modes

Commands often have three usable states:

Query (-q) Query returns values from a preexisting object based on the flags given to the command.

Edit (-e) Edit mode edits the values or attributes of the preexisting nodes, depending on the flags that are specified.

Create (-c) Create mode is usually the default for commands that create an object of some sort.

If you look to the right in the Figure 15.3, you can see three boxes that contain a Q, a C, and an E. This shows that the –sj flag supports all three modes. So, you could use these commands to change the IK handle that was created earlier. The following command:

```
ikHandle -e -sj joint2;
```

sets the IK Handle command into Edit mode and changes the startJoint to joint2.

Now consider this:

```
ikHandle -q -sj;
```

This set the IK Handle command into query mode, and since the -sj flag is defined, it prints the current start joint for the IK handle. The result looks something like this:

```
// Result: joint2 //
```

You now can create, edit, and query the nodes that you need to manipulate with commands. However, not all flags and commands support all modes, so check the MEL Command Reference when you are unsure which modes are supported.

Getting Information from Commands

Commands often return useful information related to the nodes created or manipulated by the command. Let's return to the previous command mentioned in this chapter:

```
ikHandle -sj joint1 -ee joint5;
```

If you execute the command, the command feedback should output something like this: // Result: ikHandle1 effector1 //. That information can be stored into variables for later use. Or perhaps you need the name of an IK handle and its end effector stored in a string array, like so:

```
string $ik[] = `ikHandle -sj joint1 -ee joint5`;
```

The $ik array now contains information returned by the command. In this instance, $ik[0] contains the IK handle created by the command, and $ik[1] contains the effector created. You can then use the information stored in the array to perform other actions on the IK handle, such as parenting it to a control or hiding it from the animators.

Conditionals

One of the fundamental parts of scripting is the ability to write scripts that can make decisions. Most of the time in MEL scripting these types of scripts are used to define special cases and times when you don't want a script to run before an action to a node.

Boolean Expressions

Boolean expressions are simple statements that check the relationship between two values and then return either a 0 or a 1 depending on the results, 0 being false and 1 being true. Table 15.1 lists the operators available in Maya.

▶ **Table 15.1** Boolean Operators Available in Maya

Operator	Operation
==	Compares two values for equality
!=	Compares two values for inequality
<	Compares two values and returns a 1 when the first value listed is less than the second
>	Compares two values and returns a 1 when the first value listed is greater than the second
<=	Compares two values and returns a 1 when the first value is less than or equal to the second
>=	Compares two values and returns a 1 when the first value is greater than or equal to the second

For example:

```
(20 == 20)       : returns 1
(10 == 20)       : returns 0
(10 != 20)       : returns 1
(10 != 10)       : returns 0
(10 < 20)       : returns 1
(10 > 20)       : returns 0
(10 <= 20)       : returns 1
(10 <= 10)       : returns 1
("Ninja" == "Ninja")    : returns 1
("Ninja" != "Ninja")    : returns 0
```

Conditional Statements

The if statement is the most common way to make decisions. The syntax looks like this:

```
if Boolean expression
{
    statements
}
```

If the expression evaluates as true, then any statements between the brackets ({ })
will be performed. A simple if statement can check whether a number is within certain
ranges:

```
int $a = 10;
int $b = 20;
if($a < $b)
{
      print "a is smaller than b";
}
Output:
a is smaller than b
```

Also, you can add an else statement to if loops to define a different resulting
task when the if statement evaluates as false:

```
int $a = 10;
int $b = 20;
if($a > $b)
{
      print "a is smaller than b";
}
else
{
      print "a is bigger than b";
}
Output:
a is bigger than b
```

A common thing to check using a conditional statement is the name of an
object. If you have a consistent naming style, then you can easily apply commands or
change attributes to objects of a certain type, such as controllers. If you need to hide
everything except controllers, you can easily check against the naming convention
before you hide an item. Let's assume that the naming convention is *nameCTRL*, so
every control name has the suffix CTRL:

```
string $control = "hipCTRL";
if(`endsWith $control "CTRL"` ){
    //do something
}
```

The endsWith command evaluates the string to see whether the ending matches
the second string using the $control parameter.

Also, you can check the type of objects:

```
string $control = "hipCTRL";
select $control;
string $type[] = `ls -st -sl`;
if($type[1] == "transform"){
    //do something
}
```

This script simply checks whether the $control object is a transform. If it is, then the script can continue and do something useful.

Loops

Loops are an easy way to repeat a task multiple times. Rather than slowly typing everything for each node, you can write a script that will do it for you. The most common type of loop is the for loop. The for loop has two different syntaxes. The first is a for in:

```
string $names[] = {"Jared", "Chad", "Alina", "Brian", "Kim"};

for($name in $names){
    print $name;
}
Output:
JaredChadAlinaBrianKim
```

The syntax for these loops always includes a variable that changes (in this case, $name) and an array of some sort (in this case, $names) that it loops through. With the previous example, it takes the array $names[] and loops through the array, each time replacing $name with the current value until it comes to the end of the items in the array.

The second version, the for loop, should be familiar to you if you have programmed before. Note that this script uses $i, which reminds you that you're incrementing:

```
string $names[] = {"Jared", "Chad", "Alina", "Brian", "Kim"};


for($i = 0; $i < size($names); $i++){
    print $names[$i];
}
Output:
JaredChadAlinaBrianKim
```

This version of the for loop depends on three parameters. Although it's more cumbersome to type and to plan out because it involves more information, you have more control over the pattern of the loop. The basic structure is this:

```
for( initial parameter ; end condition ; iteration statement){
        //do something
}
```

In the previous example, the initial parameter sets the integer $i to zero. When the script starts the loop, it initializes $i to zero. The end condition is the statement that is checked every time the loop finishes executing the commands contained in the brackets. When the end condition is true, the loop ends, and the script continues. In the previous example, $i < size ($names) is the end condition. The statement to the right of the less-than sign evaluates the length of the array $names so that the script always loops the correct number of times. In our example, it evaluates to a 5. Each time through the loop, if $i is less than 5, then Maya loops back and evaluates again. If it isn't, then Maya exits and moves on to the next line in the script. The third statement is used when you change the variables to actually make the loop do something. In this case, $i++ adds 1 to the current value of $i; $i = $i + 1 is equivalent. Every time the loops comes to the end of this statement, the value of $i increases by 1.

This pattern allows for more complex iterations. For example, if you needed to loop backward through a list, you'd use this:

```
string $names[] = {"Jared", "Chad", "Alina", "Brian", "Kim"};
int $i;
    for($i = size ($names); $i > 0; $i-){
        print $names[$i];
}
Output:
KimBrianAlinaChadJared
```

Even more complex patterns are possible, but if you need to loop through a list only, stick with the first type. If you want to learn more about loops, Maya's MEL documentation has more examples of the for loop and also the while loop.

Procedures

Procedures are insanely useful; they put a block of code into a single repeatable section that can be used over and over again. Anything that has to be done many times should be put into a procedure so you don't waste time writing the same code over and over. For example, often things need to be locked off from the animators so they cannot select bones or other things that could break a rig. Done once, the script would look something like this:

```
setAttr "joint1.overrideEnabled" 1;
setAttr "joint1.overrideDisplayType" 2;
```

This simply enables joint1's drawing overrides and then sets the Display Type to Reference (making it unselectable), which makes it impossible for animators to select when they are grabbing controls. This same code is needed for each joint in the scene, so a better way is to create a procedure that performs this task on multiple items based on a name you specify. The procedure would look something like this:

```
global proc makeReference(string $name)
{
    setAttr ($name + ".overrideEnabled") 1;
    setAttr ($name + ".overrideDisplayType") 2;
}
```

The $name variable is declared and passed on to the other commands. The previous procedure can now be called using this:

```
makeReference("joint1");
```

This procedure would be even more useful if it looped through all joints in the scene and applied the procedure:

```
// this procedure references all joints in a scene so they can't be selected
global proc lockAllJoints(){
```

```
    // get a list of all joints in the scene
string $joints[] = `ls -et joint`;

// loop through and apply the procedure to reference them
    for($joint in $joints){
        makeReference($joint);
    }
}
```

Planning a Script

Planning a script beforehand makes writing it a lot easier. If you map the script out, or at least think about everything that is needed, you will find that your script will be more organized and the work will be less overwhelming.

Here are a few basic tips:

- Keep scripts divided by limbs or large sections of rigging, and use the same procedures for all characters.
- Have a main build file for each character that calls the limb procedures and binds everything together.
- Import assets through code in the build file.
- Keep scripts abstract and not dependent through a good use of variables.
- Create smaller procedures for common steps shared throughout the rig.
- Have an update file for character-specific changes and/or revisions.
- Try to make things vertex/edge independent. It is likely that models will change, and it's easier if those things are found dynamically.

Basic Procedural Rigging Pipeline

Most animation projects include several characters. Usually, the characters are similar in anatomy and animation requirements. There are usually some differences, such as limb size, hair length, geometry names, or smaller additions such as tassels or spikes. So, when you are writing your scripts, make them size and name independent. That way you can use them for multiple characters.

It is a best practice to keep the geometry, skeleton, and controls for each character in separate files. When you build the character, you import the files and then move the controls to the location of the joints. Then, if the model file changes, you have to change only the skeleton to match and rebuild the character. Each time you add something, you script it, rebuild the character, and save the scene, overwriting the currently referenced rig file. Once the file is overwritten, the animators will be able to use the new updates. It is usually a good idea to save a backup copy of any file you plan to overwrite. That way, you can return to the original file in the event that something goes wrong.

FK/IK Script

One of the most common things in rigging is an inverse kinematics to forward kinematics switch (FK/IK switch), which allows the animators to switch between IK animation and FK animation. Almost every limb I have ever scripted has had this feature. Wouldn't it be great if you didn't have to individually rig these switches every time you rigged a character? Well, if you script the switch well and make the script automatically detect names, sizes, joints, and controls, you'll be able to reuse it and drop FK/IK switches into your rig in seconds. In this section, I'll break this tedious job down into sections, and I'll include the full script of the example. Here we go.

At the beginning of the script, you need to create a way to get the names of the joints and the controllers that will be part of the FK/IK switch. You can do this either by passing the objects into the script (such as procedure variables) or by using a standard naming convention and just replacing the suffix. In this case, you will pass it in with a procedure (this is a single line of code):

```
global proc ikFk(string $name, string $joint1, string $joint2, string
$joint3, string$ikControl, string $pv, string $switchControl){
```

As you can see, with this code you created a variable for naming new nodes. The script accommodates a shoulder, elbow, wrist setup or a hip, knee, ankle setup. With this script, it doesn't matter. Also with this code, you created variables for the IK control, a pole vector, and a switch control.

Next, you need to create two more joint chains, one for IK, and one for FK, and then you will use the original chain as the actual bind chain (Be aware that some of this code wraps when it is a single line. You can also find this code on the CD):

```
//fk joints
select -cl;
float $pos[];
float $orient[];
//put the joints from the input into a single array
string $joints[] = {$joint1, $joint2, $joint3};
//loop through the new array
for($joint in $joints){
//get the translate values of the current joint
    $pos = `joint -q -p $joint`;
//get the rotation values of the current joint
    $orient = `joint -q -o $joint`;
//create a new joint that matches the old values
    joint -n ($joint + "FK") -p $pos[0] $pos[1] $pos[2] -o $orient[0]
$orient[1] $orient[2];
/*the new joints automatically have the same hierarchy because the joint
command places the new joint under the currently selected object. In this
case the previously created joint is still selected*/
}
select -cl;
```

```
//ik joints. Same thing as above.
for($joint in $joints){
    $pos = `joint -q -p $joint`;
    $orient = `joint -q -o $joint`;
    joint -n ($joint + "IK") -p $pos[0] $pos[1] $pos[2] -o $orient[0]
$orient[1] $orient[2];
}
```

In the previous code, you used the joint command both to create new joints and also to get information from existing joints. A useful thing to know is that the joint command can create a new joint under the previously selected object. Once a joint is created, it is automatically selected. For this script, you clear the selection and then create the first joint in your new chain. Once the first joint has been made and selected, you make a second new joint that goes under the first joint, and so forth. Then you repeat the process to create the IK joints. You now have three joint chains: the original, an FK chain, and an IK chain.

After all the joints have been created, you need to create an IK handle, move an IK control to the end of the joint chain, and move the pole vector to the correct location. Let's look at the code (Be aware that some of this code wraps when it is a single line. You can also find this code on the CD):

```
string $ikMain[] = `ikHandle -n ($name + "MainIK") -sj ($joint1 + "IK") -ee
($joint3 + "IK")`;
group -em -n ($ikControl + "NULL");
parent $ikControl ($ikControl + "NULL");
// what do these next two commands do.
// temporaraly constrain the $ikControl to the end joint
string $tempConst[] = `parentConstraint $joint3 ($ikControl + "NULL")`;
/*delete the constraint. The control is then in the correct
position*/
delete $tempConst[0];
// make the ikhandle constrained to the controller
parentConstraint -mo  $ikControl $ikMain[0];
```

In the previous block of the code, you create a null group for the IK handle so that it can have the same translation space as the third joint. You then parent the $ikControl under the null group and move the null group to the wrist with a parent-Constraint. After the parentConstraint is deleted, you then attach the IK handle to the control (Be aware that some of this code wraps when it is a single line. You can also find this code on the CD):

```
//get the location of the middle joint
float $pos[] = `joint -q -p $joint2`;
//create a group for the pole vector
group -n ($pv + "NULL") $pv;
//move the group to the location of the middle joint
move $pos[0] $pos[1] $pos[2] ($pv + "NULL");
```

```
/*get the pole vector values from the ikhandle. This allows for limbs that
are not perfectly straight.*/
float $pos[] =  `getAttr ($ikMain[0] + ".poleVector")`;
//increases the distance of the pole vector from the limb
float $scaler = 3;
// move the pole vector out. It will stay in the correct position.
move -r ($pos[0] * $scaler) ($pos[1] *$scaler) ($pos[2] * $scaler) ($pv +
"NULL");
//zero out the control
makeIdentity -apply true -t 1 -r 1 -s 1 -n 0 $pv;
//applies the pole vector constraint
poleVectorConstraint $pv $ikMain[0];
```

To place the pole vector in the correct location for the new IK handle, no matter what the angle of the joints, you began by getting the current pole vector values from the IK handle. Next, you moved the pole vector control to the second joint and out away from that second joint by the amount specified in the pole vector attribute. Since a pole vector is just a direction, you can increase the distance away from the joints by multiplying all three attributes by the same number. In this case, you used $scaler = 3. Using $scaler places the control further back from the arm, without affecting the vector.

You could create a control for every FK joint, but in the interest of brevity, you will allow the animators to animate directly on the bones. To do this, you have to make the bones visible by enabling the display handle:

```
for($joint in $joints){
    setAttr ($joint + "FK" + ".displayHandle") 1;
}
```

The next block of code is the most important part of the FK/IK switch (Be aware that some of this code wraps when it is a single line. You can also find this code on the CD):

```
for($joint in $joints){
     //for every joint, enable the display handle
     setAttr ($joint + "FK" + ".displayHandle") 1;
}
//add the switching attribute
addAttr -ln fkIk -at double  -min 0 -max 10 -dv 0 $switchControl;
setAttr -e -keyable true ($switchControl + ".fkIk");
//loop through the joints
for($joint in $joints){
   //orient constraint the original joints to the fk joints
   string $const[] = `orientConstraint -mo ($joint + "FK")
$joint`;
   //orient constraint the original joints to the ik joints
   orientConstraint -mo ($joint + "IK") $joint;
   /*make a setdrivenkey to control the blending between the constraints*/
```

```
    //sets the fk to be on at 0
    setAttr ($switchControl + ".fkIk") 0;
    setAttr ($const[0] + "." + ($joint + "FK") + "W0") 1;
    setDrivenKeyframe -cd ($switchControl + ".fkIk") ($const[0] + "." +
($joint + "FK") + "W0");
//sets the ik to be off at 0
setAttr ($const[0] + "." + ($joint + "IK") + "W1") 0;    setDrivenKeyframe -
cd ($switchControl + ".fkIk") ($const[0] + "." +($joint + "IK") + "W1");
    //sets the fk to be off at 10
    setAttr ($switchControl + ".fkIk") 10;
vsetAttr ($const[0] + "." + ($joint + "FK") + "W0") 0;
    setDrivenKeyframe -cd ($switchControl + ".fkIk") ($const[0] + "." +
($joint + "FK") + "W0");
//sets the ik to be on at 10
    setAttr ($const[0] + "." + ($joint + "IK") +"W1") 1;    setDrivenKeyframe
-cd ($switchControl + ".fkIk") ($const[0] + "." +($joint + "IK") + "W1");
    }
```

First you added an attribute to the switcher control (most of the time it's the wrist control), and then you looped through the joints chains and constrained the rotations to the original skeleton. Next, you created set-driven keys to control the blending between the two different constraints that control rotation, using a newly added attribute on the switcher control.

The only thing left at this point is cleanup. You don't want animators to grab the IK handle or the joints (except for the FK joints) directly, and you also don't want them translating the FK joints. So, you need to start locking things down and organizing the groups (Be aware that some of this code wraps when it is a single line. You can also find this code on the CD):

```
//turn off the things the animators don't need to see
setAttr ($ikMain[0] + ".v") 0;
setAttr ($joint1 + ".v") 0;
setAttr ($joint1 + "IK.v") 0;
//lock the attributes that shouldn't be changed on the fk joints
for($joint in $joints){
setAttr -lock true -keyable false ($joint + "FK" + ".tx");
setAttr -lock true -keyable false ($joint + "FK" + ".ty");
setAttr -lock true -keyable false ($joint + "FK" + ".tz");
setAttr -lock true -keyable false ($joint + "FK" + ".sx");
setAttr -lock true -keyable false ($joint + "FK" + ".sy");
setAttr -lock true -keyable false ($joint + "FK" + ".sz");
setAttr -lock true -keyable false ($joint + "FK" + ".v");
}
//create a master group for organization
group -em -n $name;
//create a group for constraining to the main rig
```

```
group -em -n ($name + "moveMe");
//parent all the necessary parts for movement under moveMe
parent ($joint1 + "FK") ($joint1 + "IK")  $joint1 ($name + "moveMe");
//parent everything else under the master group
parent $switchControl ($name + "moveMe") $ikMain[0] ($ikControl + "NULL")
($pv + "NULL") $name;
}
```

Although the previous script's structure looks like a limb script, it is a simple script. It runs through the following the basic steps:

1. Gets the names of the base objects involved in the rig

2. Moves the controls to the correct locations

3. Sets up the core components of the limb

4. Cleans everything and organizes the limb

Once you have your base down, you can start adding features, such as a stretchy IK setup, wrist controls, and any other feature that you or the animators can imagine.

Stretchy IK Setup

A stretchy IK is a common feature for cartoony characters. It gives the animators ability to place hands and have the arms stretch to keep the hand in the right place. The basic concept is this:

> If the length of the IK handle is longer than the length of the two joints combined, then scale the joints to match the length.
>
> Else
>
> If the length of the IK handle is shorter than the length of the two bones, then don't scale the joints.

I'll show how to create the functionality you want through a series of utility nodes. You'll add the stretch setup code to the previous IK/FK example:

```
...

//create two spaceLocators to plug into the distanceBetween node
string $loc1[] =  `spaceLocator`;
setAttr ($loc1[0] + ".v") 0;
//rename the node to something better
$loc1[0] = `rename $loc1[0] ($name + "ArmStretchDis1")`;
string $loc2[] =  `spaceLocator`;
setAttr ($loc2[0] + ".v") 0;
//rename the node to something better
$loc2[0] = `rename $loc2[0] ($name + "ArmStretchDis2")`;
//move the first locator to the beginning of the limb
```

```
//move the second locator to the end of the limb
string $tempConst[] = `pointConstraint $ikControl $loc2[0] `;
//create the distanceBetweenNode to get the length between the locators
string $mainDist = `createNode -name ($name + "ArmMainDist")
distanceBetween`;


//connect the translate values from the locators to the distance node
connectAttr -f ($loc1[0] + ".translate") ($mainDist+".point1");
connectAttr -f ($loc2[0] + ".translate") ($mainDist+".point2");


//create the condition node
    string $cond = `createNode -n ($name + "LengthCon")
  condition`;
//get the length of the limb from the joints.
    float $length =  `getAttr ($joint2 + ".tx")` + `getAttr
  ($joint3 + ".tx")`;


//set the condition node to greater or equal
    setAttr ($name + "LengthCon.operation") 3;
//connect the distance node to the condition
    connectAttr -f ($mainDist + ".distance") ($name +
  "LengthCon.firstTerm");
// enter the length of the joints into the condition
    setAttr ($name + "LengthCon.secondTerm") $length;
    connectAttr ($mainDist + ".distance") ($name +
  "LengthCon.colorIfTrueR");
//connect the length into the outputs of the condition
    setAttr ($name + "LengthCon.colorIfFalseR") $length;
//create a node to normalize the length to 1 for scaling
    string $norm = `createNode -n ($name + "NormLength")
  multiplyDivide`;
//set the multiplyDivide to divide
    setAttr ($name + "NormLength.operation") 2;
    setAttr ($name + "NormLength.input2X") $length;
//divide the distance between the two by the length of the limb
    connectAttr ($name + "LengthCon.outColorR") ($name +
  "NormLength.input1X");
//connect the ouput into the scale of the two joints
    connectAttr ($name + "NormLength.outputX") ($joint1 +
  "IK.sx");
    connectAttr ($name + "NormLength.outputX") ($joint2 +
  "IK.sx");


...
```

The previous code creates two locators that are attached to the first and third joints and then connects their translation information to a distanceBetween node. The script gets the length of the two bones and sets a condition node to react based on the distance between the controller and the first joint. If the distance is shorter than the length of the two joints, then the rig does nothing. If it's longer, then the script feeds the information to a multiplyDivide node that divides the distance by the original length of the two joints to get a suitable scale value.

The problem, now, is that the scale has no effect on the bind joints. You can fix this by changing the constraint type from an orientConstraint to a parentConstraint. Here is the updated code:

```
//exactly the same as the previous code, but changed to parentConstraint

for($joint in $joints){
    string $const[] = `parentConstraint -mo ($joint + "FK")
    $joint`;
    parentConstraint -mo ($joint + "IK") $joint;
    setAttr ($switchControl + ".fkIk") 0;
    setAttr ($const[0] + "." + ($joint + "FK") + "W0") 1;
    setDrivenKeyframe -cd ($switchControl + ".fkIk") ($const[0] +
      "." + ($joint + "FK") + "W0");
    setAttr ($const[0] + "." + ($joint + "IK") + "W1") 0;
    setDrivenKeyframe -cd ($switchControl + ".fkIk") ($const[0] +
    "." +($joint + "IK") + "W1");
    setAttr ($switchControl + ".fkIk") 10;
    setAttr ($const[0] + "." + ($joint + "FK") + "W0") 0;
    setDrivenKeyframe -cd ($switchControl + ".fkIk") ($const[0] +
    "." + ($joint + "FK") + "W0");
    setAttr ($const[0] + "." + ($joint + "IK") +"W1") 1;
    setDrivenKeyframe -cd ($switchControl + ".fkIk") ($const[0] +
    "." +($joint + "IK") + "W1");
}
```

You have a few new locators from the distanceBetween node that need to be organized. The updated script would look like this (Be aware that some of this code wraps when it is a single line. You can also find this code on the CD):

```
parent $loc1[0] $loc1[1] $switchControl ($name + "moveMe") $ikMain[0]
($ikControl + "NULL") ($pv + "NULL") $name;
```

You now have a script that will get most of your limbs set up. The usual way to call this script is as follows:

```
ikFk("test", "joint1", "joint2", "joint3", "locator1", "locator2",
"locator3");
```

At this point, try to add some features of your own. For instance, the script doesn't have a wrist setup or finger controls (I suggest making a separate procedure for each).

UI Coding

UI coding can be tedious, but with the addition of web browser support to the newer version of Maya, it isn't quite so bad. The basic idea of using a web browser to do your character UI selection is the simplicity of creating an interface in HTML. Maya supports the mel:// protocol, which replaces the regular http:// or ftp:// protocol. This means you can use a web browser to pass MEL commands into Maya. This is how you would write the HTML code:

```
<html>
<body>
<a href="mel://select -cl">clear selection</a>
</body>
</html>
```

This web page creates a hyperlink that performs the MEL command clear selection. The way you can use this is with Maya's webBrowser command. In Maya 8.0 or earlier, you can call the browser with the following script. Figure 15.4 shows the resultant window.

```
string $browser;
window;
columnLayout;
    $browser = `webBrowser -width 800 -height 600 -url "www.autodesk.com"`;
showWindow;
```

This creates a web browser window pointed to www.autodesk.com.

In Maya 8.5 and newer, the webBrowser is replaced with a plug-in that allows a regular browser to control Maya. You don't have to create a window; you just call the file you want manually from the Script Editor. Use the script that follows. Compare the results with the browser window shown in Figure 15.5.

```
system("load " + "c:/mayaFiles/runner.html" );
```

The system command is like calling something directly from the DOS prompt; you can use the load keyword to launch the web page with the default application.

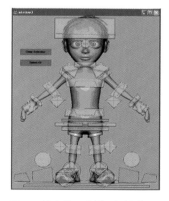

Figure 15.4 Maya 8.0 (and older) browser window

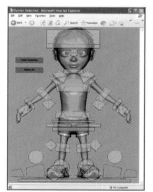

Figure 15.5 Maya 8.5 (and older) browser window

One of the simplest ways to set up a selection UI is to use an HTML image map. The idea is that you use an image of your character as a background and set up hotspots.

Creating an image map usually involves selecting the areas that are going to become links. You really need the image mapper only to define the areas that are selection areas. After you've created the image map, the only things you need to worry about are that the <img> tag has the correct location and the <area> tag has the correct MEL command in the href attribute. You should save this code as an .html file (Be aware that some of this code wraps when it is a single line. You can also find this code on the CD) Your HTML code should look something like the following:

```
<html>
<body>
<img src="runner.jpg" width="559" height="710" border="0" usemap="#Map" />
<map name="Map" id="Map">
    <area shape="poly" coords="369,325,414,268,439,287,398,340"
href="mel://select LElbowCTRL" />
    </map>
</body>
</html>
```

You can see that the link is set up with the mel:// protocol and the command to select LElbowCTRL. After you have your HTML code for the image map, just replace each tag with the appropriate MEL command.

Although selecting something by name is easy, in Maya you cannot always guarantee that LElbowCTRL will always be named the same after referencing. Depending on how your character is referenced and named, LElbowCTRL could actually be named Runner:LElbowCTRL or Runner_LElbowCTRL. You want to create code that is functional in cases where the name includes a prefix, as well as those where it does not. Here is how you can do it:

```
select "*LElbowCTRL";
```

The * character is a wildcard that allows you to select any object with a name that ends in LElbowFlag, so all cases of whateverLElbowFlag will be selected when the script is run. This works if you have good naming conventions and no other character has the same control names but instead has a different prefix. You can accommodate characters with the same control names, if you know the prefixes for each of the characters added by namespaces and referencing:

```
string $prefix = "Runner";
select "*LElbowCTRL";
```

```
string $sel[] = `ls -sl`;
select -cl;
for($object in $sel){
    if(`startsWith $object $prefix`){
        select $object;
        break;
    }
}
```

This code evaluates all object names that end in LElbowCTRL, checks for a speci-fied prefix, and then selects the object and breaks if it finds a match.

Conclusion

Although the power of scripting might not have been immediately apparent, after you have scripted a task that otherwise would be tedious, you will begin to appreciate the reliability of scripts. Scripts can save you time and headaches by automating repetitive tasks. To know Maya well is to know MEL scripting.

Just like a MEL script can make your life easier, working with the right tool can also help ease a rigger's pain. In the next chapter, we'll cover a new tool designed to make the process of UV mapping easier.

UV Mapping and UVLayout

Before we get started, we would like to express our appreciation to the creator of UVLayout, Phil Dench, for helping with the editing process on this chapter.

16

UV mapping is like 3D taxidermy. Consider a bear rug. The taxidermist needed to make particular cuts and then add seams to allow the pelt to lie flat. You can treat 3D surfaces in a similar fashion. UV mapping creates a 2D representation map for painting on the 3D surface. However, it can be a time-consuming chore if you don't know what you are doing or if you have only basic tools. With some of the tools we will cover in this chapter, you can lay out an entire surface by defining seams and using only one command. We'll also show you some efficient ways to represent a 3D surface on a 2D space.

Chapter Contents
UV mapping applications
Using UVLayout
The UVLayout workflow

UV Mapping Applications

Good UVs are essential for great textures. Many applications and robust toolsets are available for you. However, here are a few that can really be of benefit to learn. Here are some amazing UV editors:

UVLayout UVLayout was created by Phil Dench at Headus (Metamorphosis). This powerful package features great tools for relaxing, pelting, and mirroring and is our recommended choice for UV editing. It supports subdivision and polygon relaxing algorithms. It also has brushes for local usage of the algorithms. We will talk more in-depth about how you use UVLayout throughout this chapter.

Modo The folks at Luxology really are pushing the boundaries. Modo is built for speed with its "click, drag, done" philosophy. You can select a portion of the geometry in the UV editor and then drag your mouse to the left, and it will unwrap quickly and efficiently. It also has other tools to refine from there if the initial pelt unwrap does not meet your needs. If you want a very fast and reliable tool, Modo is an excellent choice.

DeepUV Right Hemisphere has done a great job in putting together this package for UV editing. DeepUV combines multiple relax algorithms with greed tolerances. This allows you to relax proportionally to the current UV layout or to the actual 3D surface. You also have the ability to relax in specific areas and with falloff.

UVMapper Professional Developed by Steve Cox, UVMapper Professional has a good deal of the UV-editing capabilities you want at a fraction of the price. Although this application doesn't have some of the more complex relaxing algorithms, it holds its own with great projection tools and quick manipulation and organization tools. It also creates amazing antialiased templates. It is neat to see a program like this in a cost-effective package.

UV editing can be simple if you research the tools that are available and use each for its strengths. There are a few crucial functions to look for as you evaluate UV editing programs. Look for programs that have efficient tools such as pelt mapping, relax algorithms, moving with falloff, pinning, material and group selection, packing, and mirroring. Lets talk about pelt mapping and relax algorithms and why they are important.

One of the more recent movements in UV mapping is the process called *pelt mapping*, which basically takes a mesh and divides it by having you select the seam to be used to separate the model. The selected sections are then isolated and flattened. If you can pick sections of the mesh by isolating certain loops or sections, break them off, and then relax them, you have the basic workflow down. The ability to define sections for a pelt cut should be at the top of your requirements list.

Relax algorithms, simply put, are methods for creating smoothed surfaces of a UV map. They are powerful tools that save time and create UV maps that accurately represent the 3D surface. Not all relax algorithms are equal. Each application relaxes surfaces in 2D space differently. You want an application that offers multiple relax options and perhaps has a greed tolerance per the 2D or 3D surface. DeepUV has excellent tools for performing this function. UVLayout also has multiple UV relaxation algorithms and is very fast.

Using UVLayout

UVLayout has become one of the best UV editors available. With its role in film, video games, and general 3D capabilities increasing, as well as its low price point, it is an amazing tool for the price. At first glance its layout is somewhat simplistic, but once you acquaint yourself with its many options and hotkey combinations, you will find it to be an efficient UV editor.

One of our favorite features in UVLayout is the symmetry. Texture artists love to work with symmetry when they can, and UVLayout excels here. It even tries to get symmetry on nonsymmetrical models, and it does a pretty good job. It also has smoothing brushes that relax UVs with a falloff. This provides isolated control with the click of a button. Being mostly hotkey driven, UVLayout has a slightly longer learning curve than other tools, but once you learn it, you will see that it is very powerful. To help shorten your learning curve, the Headus website hosts example videos at www.uvlayout.com. Viewing these videos is a good way to see how the the power of the program and how it operates. A little later this chapter, we will run through some of the tools that make this package so powerful and show an example workflow.

Hotkeys

As you already know, hotkeys are great for efficiency. You can quickly execute commands without having to navigate through menus. Within Maya, you use hotkeys for viewport settings and other common operations, such as modeling selection and animation control. UVLayout was basically created for speed and efficiency, so it has hotkeys for almost every command. Once you learn them, UVLayout comes alive with its captivating way of relaxing and its informative color representation of stretch and compression. As you work through the tutorials in this chapter, we will provide you with hotkey information each step of the way.

Table 16.1 lists a few of the standard viewport hotkeys you'll find most useful.

▷ **Table 16.1** Standard Viewport Hotkeys

Shortcut	Action
View	
1	Toggles view to UV
2	Toggles view to Edit
3	Toggles view to 3D
3D Window	
Left mouse	Orbits
Middle mouse	Pans
Left mouse and middle mouse	Zooms
UV Window	
Alt+middle mouse	Pans
Alt+left mouse and middle mouse	Zooms

Maya Plug-In

You can use UVLayout as a stand-alone application or as a downloadable plug-in for Maya. The plug-in, shown in Figure 16.1, allows you to easily move between Maya and UVLayout without having to run the exporter and importer.

Figure 16.1 The UVLayout plug-in UI

The UVLayout plug-in for Maya download page at www.uvlayout.com/maya has complete instructions for installing and opening the plug-in. After you install the plug-in, use the Info UVLayout shelf icon to open the plug-in user interface. Select your mesh, and send it to UVLayout.

While running the plug-in, make sure your objExport plug-in is loaded. Without it, UVLayout cannot transfer automatically. Also, be sure to incrementally save your work by sending your model and its UVs back to Maya and saving the .mb file. If you are editing from a mesh that has existing UVs, make sure Edit is selected in the UVLayout interface if you want to retain the existing UV data when the file imports.

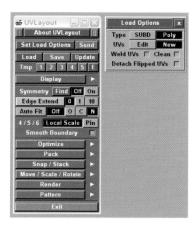

Figure 16.2 The UVLayout initial UI

General Interface

For Windows users, the UVLayout interface, shown in Figure 16.2, may look daunting. With a little usage you will find that the interface is really quite functional. The Display, Optimize, and other buttons hide and reveal options you can use while editing. Figure 16.3 shows the items you can access through the Display, Symmetry, Optimize, Snap/Stack, and Move/Scale/Rotate buttons. The only differences between the plug-in and the stand-alone application are the file import and export capabilities. With the plug-in, the import and export functions were built to run specifically with Maya.

Figure 16.3 The UVLayout expanded UI

Table 16.2 describes the functions you'll find when you click the buttons and expand the UI.

Button	What You'll Find
Display	In the Display panel, you will most likely use the View (3D/UV editor view) options.
Symmetry	The Symmetry options are used for keeping your UVs symmetrical across the V-axis. We will talk about the symmetry options a little later in the chapter.
Optimize	The Optimize tab provides lock options and for the length of time for autorelaxation.
Snap/Stack	The Snap/Stack tab has tools for snapping like shells (contiguous UV surfaces) together.
Move/Scale/Rotate	The Move/Scale/Rotate tab has tools for manipulating your UVs. Scale is especially useful, since you can numerically adjust the size of the shells and keep them in numerical multiplications of the original size.

Tip: Using UVLayout, you can scale the hand UVs to proportionally twice the size of the arms, and then the hands will hold twice the information they would have held before. The little arrows to the right of each tab will float the tab in a new, separate interface window. This is great for working with minimal space, or it can come in handy with multiple monitors.

The UVLayout Workflow

UVLayout has a really great workflow. However, it may take a little getting used to, and you need to do some hotkey memorization to reach maximum efficiency. In the sections that follow, we'll show you a typical workflow. But first, here are some tips that will help you on your way to great UVs:

- Periodically save your work. You can do this by sending your UVs back to Maya and saving the Maya file. You may need to keep all the UVs inside the UV bounds for the transfer.

- Be aware that when you send the file to Maya, the plug-in creates a copy of your mesh. Watch for this in the Outliner (Windows > Outliner), and delete unneeded copies as necessary.

- If your geometry is part of a group, you may want to pull it out to the base file level to work on it and then move it back into the group when you're finished.

Dropping 3D Objects to the UV Editor

The word *drop* in UVLayout is used when you want to send a simple 3D surface that is ready to be relaxed to the UV editing window. You will want to drop all your simple, one-sided surfaces, such as fingernails. Drop objects that don't need to have seams, such as the eyes and the hair, shown in Figure 16.4. You can drop a surface by mousing over the separate surface and hitting the D key at the same time. If you are in the UV editing window, you can bring objects back to the 3D window by mousing over the surface and pressing Shift+D.

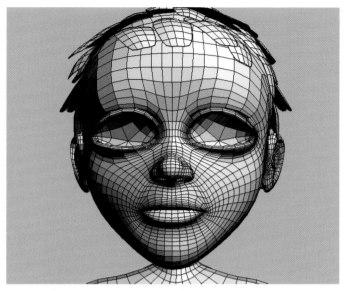

Figure 16.4 The eyes have been dropped to the UV layer.

Cutting the Pelt Seams

The ability to cut apart seams is one of the functions that defines a good UV package. But, before you cut anything apart, drop all the flat, one-sided pieces of geometry into the UV Edit window (mouse over them, and hit D). Then, establish seams on your figure. For instance, you want the front of the face to have lots of real estate in the UVs. You may want to cut the ears away from the face to allow for better relaxing. (The ears usually hold the sides of the face tighter than they would without them.) You will also want to spread the UVs of the eyes, nose, and mouth after the initial relax and then perform a secondary relax on them. Most artists have their own favorite approaches in splitting a model. Each model requires individual attention to seam placement. Be cognizant of areas where there is higher-resolution mesh next to lower-resolution mesh. The ear/head and hand/arm transitions are areas where you need to decide, on a character-by-character basis, whether to create a seam or leave the part attached. Once a surface is split, the individual pieces are referred to as *shells*.

In your efforts to create optimal seams, think about what each shape will look like when it is unwrapped. For instance, the best way to flatten the torso, neck, and arms is to split the figure vertically down the back and down the underside of the arms. This keeps the seams to a minimum and places them in a somewhat hidden area. After you have moved all the simple geometry to the UV Edit window, you can go back to the head and body and select the seams by pressing the C key, as shown in Figure 16.5. You then can cut them up, by having your mouse over the piece of geometry and using Shift+S.

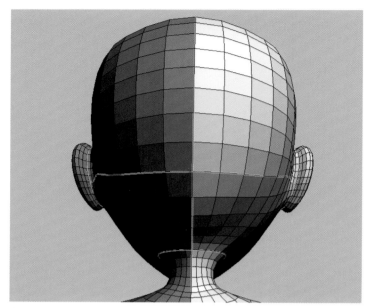

Figure 16.5 The seams of the head

You will want to put a seam on the inside of the lips, cut off the inner mouth, and do an initial relax on the head. Once you've done this, you will notice that there is some stretching on the forehead and that the nose and ears are small in the UVs, which is not good for final texturing. You can look at the model in the 3D view and use the T hotkey to apply the test textures. Figure 16.6 shows a model that requires a little more work.

Figure 16.6 Initial flattening on the head

Relaxing the Tension

In the UV edit window, now flatten the eyes and hair and all the other parts of the model that don't need to be split up. Any contiguous surfaces that would be cylindrical after they are smoothed need to be split. So, an arm or leg needs a seam, whereas a plane of hair should be dropped initially. The hands and head need seams, but eyes with a hole in the back will be OK if you drop them. If a dropped part has areas that appear in deep red, blue, or overlap, that surface can be cut in those areas to allow for better relaxing. It is usually easier to cut in the 3D Edit window, but you can also cut in the UV Edit window. If you don't have much experience determining which surfaces should be dropped and which should be cut, test some surfaces by applying a checkered texture and then see how it lays out. You want the checkered texture to lay out evenly with no stretching.

> **Tip:** Including text on the checker pattern helps you see the amount of stretching that occurs. With text, you can perceive even the slightest stretching.

After you have dropped all the initial pieces, you can relax them by mousing over them and pressing the F key. Hold the F key down for an extended relax.

You can also flatten using the brushes. The O, R, and B hotkeys access the brushes, call other flattening algorithms, and yield different results. These hotkeys are used in a similar fashion as the flatten key. The only difference is that you can direct the area of influence with your mouse while holding the brush key down.

Each brush has its own algorithm for relaxing. You can test each to see which one works best for the area on which you're working. Here's how they work:

- The O, or "old relax brush," relaxes with more regard to the smoothing of the UVs.

- The R brush relaxes according to the 3D topology.

- The B brush is reminiscent of the overall flatten command but in brush form.

If you find that, overall, your piece of surface is either deep red or deep blue, you will need to scale the shell. (Hold the spacebar while dragging the red or blue area with the right mouse button. You can see that by moving with a falloff, you can correct the stretching.) Scale the shell equally to a size where you minimize the amount of dark blue or red. To organize your layout, you can move (with the spacebar and the middle mouse button) and rotate (with the spacebar and the left mouse button) your shells. You'll really appreciate the ability to quickly change the size of your brush with the hotkeys – and = .

For additional tweaking, you can press the hotkey 4 for shrink or the hotkey 5 for stretch. This is useful in areas like those shown on the head in Figure 16.7. Don't worry about a little crinkling. It is more important to spread or shrink when needed and then relax the mesh later with the appropriate brush. You can also move with a falloff using a radius move (Shift+middle mouse drag) or a defined four-polygon radius move (Shift+Ctrl+middle mouse drag).

Figure 16.7 More proportional flattening of head

Another great tool for the relaxing of surfaces is the Bloat and Relax command (Shift+F). After the initial relax in the circular bloat, you are prompted to hit the space-bar. It then relaxes to a nice coloring that is not too red or blue. Figure 16.8 shows UVLayout working on the teeth, and Figure 16.9 shows the final relaxed process. This tool works great if you are having a hard time pulling a part from your model and relaxing it.

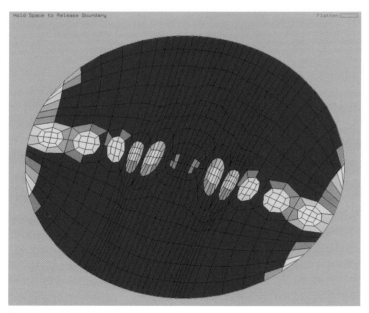

Figure 16.8 Bloated teeth for UVing

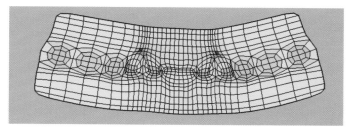

Figure 16.9 Relaxation from bloat

Pinning

You can pin selections by hitting the P hotkey. Pinning keeps a defined area still while you work on surrounding geometry. You can pin an edge by hovering over an edge UV and hitting Shift+P. Pinning an edge allows you to relax the middle of a shell without moving the border.

Symmetry

Texture artists like having the ability to mirror from one side to another when needed. So, now you need to find symmetry. This is how good UVs are made:

- If your model is symmetrical or close to symmetrical, use the UI button Find by Symmetry, and click an edge on the centerline to select it.

- If your model in contiguous, hit the spacebar to create symmetry.

You can now mirror the UVs from one side to the other by using the S hotkey. If your surface crosses the centerline, half of it will gray once you establish the midline. If you want to swap the side that is mirrored, hover over the object and use the swap mirrored selection hotkey (Shift+S). Cutting the lines in the 3D Edit window will also mirror over, as shown in Figure 16.10. Figure 16.11 shows how the borders look after being offset and cut away. This offset will not affect the actual position of the mesh.

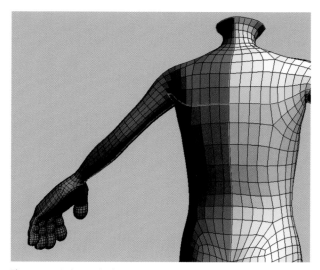

Figure 16.10 Cuts on back

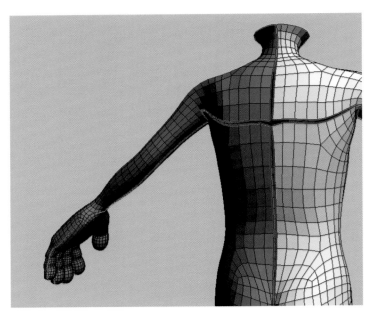

Figure 16.11 Splitting cuts

Sometimes, symmetrical objects are not contiguous geometries, like the shoes shown in Figure 6.12. To define symmetry in this case, click the Find button in the symmetry panel. Then click an edge on one side, and middle-click the corresponding edge on the other side. Figure 6.13 shows symmetry in contiguous geometries.

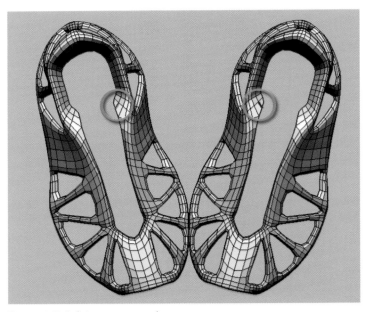

Figure 16.12 Defining symmetry on shoes

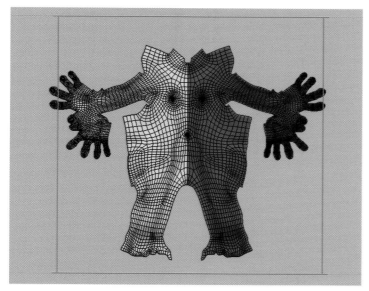

Figure 16.13 Symmetry

Overall Concerns

You will want to watch for stretching or compression of the texture when testing with the checkered textures. This is an excellent test to see whether the UVs are proportionally representative of the 3D surface. If you encounter any stretching, try to alleviate it with the methods we have discussed. Figure 16.14 shows the shorts being prepared with their seam. It is split down the back and underside so that the entire surface can lie flat. Figure 16.15 shows how to prepare a closed surface for symmetrical unwrapping.

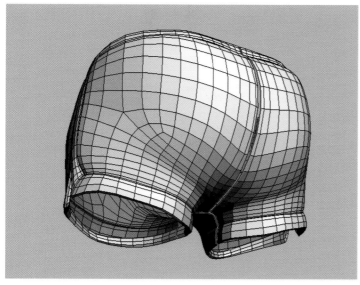

Figure 16.14 Prepping the shorts

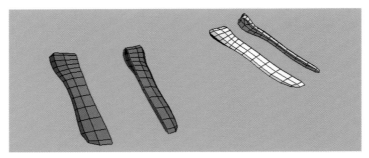

Figure 16.15 The tongues of the shoes needed to be broken apart and welded together. The cut tool works only in the 3D edit view.

Subdivision Surfaces

If you are working with a subdivision-ready surface, you can define it as such on import. In Set Load Options, you can declare whether the object is a normal poly mesh or a subdivision mesh. In the Optimize options, you can select Calc Subdivision Targets to reevaluate the way the subdivision mesh is represented on the surface. You will need this only if you have extremely low-resolution subdivision meshes. Overall, if you designate the mesh as a subdivision, UVLayout will create the appropriate surface calculations to reflect the most accurate UVs. In the Display panel, you will see a Smooth SUBD UVs option, which is for designation of linear vs. subdivision smoothed UVs. This deals with the UV smoothing and whether it is representative of the UV cage or whether it is representative of the subdivided mesh. It affects the appearance of the checker and test textures only and has no bearing on the UV flattening.

Irregularities

You will run into irregularities in the mesh like those shown in Figure 16.16. This happens during the process of creating UVs. Around the character's chest you can see deformation that needs to be corrected. If you look ahead to Figure 16.19, you can easily spot the difference. The figure was relaxed a couple more times with a brush relax and now is accurate with low distortion.

Packing

Packing is the process of arranging the unwrapped portions of the model in the most efficient way in the UV space. UVLayout has options for this. It will autopack your UVs into the main 1×1 field. This is a great option to have if you are pressed for time and do not have time to manually lay out the UVs. As an alternative, use autopack for the initial packing, and then you can edit from there. In Figure 16.17 and Figure 16.18, you can see the relax and the packing of the UVs.

You can adapt the packing preferences. UVLayout makes this easy with multiple tools for creating localized boxes that will stay together while packing. Refer to the videos for more information about this technique and the packing process in general. Select Bleed to increase the borders between objects. The tile option allows you to have models in a 2×2 pattern.

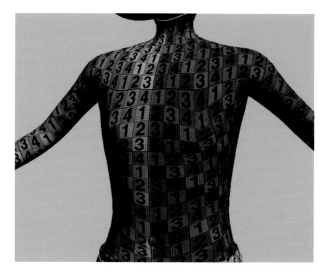

Figure 16.16 Messed-up pectorals

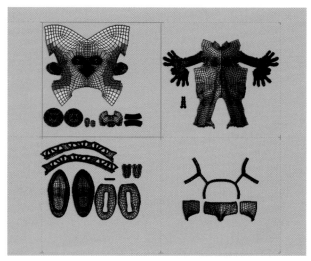

Figure 16.17 Initial relax

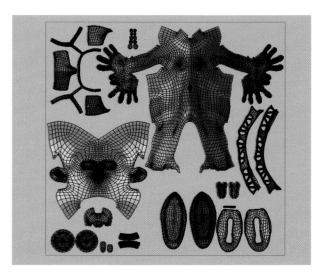

Figure 16.18 Final fitting and packing

Testing

When you're in 3D view, UVLayout allows you to see the prebuilt textures. These textures are great for seeing the result of the unwrapping. Look at Figure 16.19 to see a well-thought-out layout of a model. Use the T hotkey to flip through the textures and use – or = hotkey to increase/decrease the brush size. You can also load an image map onto the model or in the background for matching. In the display trace area, you can set opacity for both layers. You can find these options by navigating to them (About UV Layout > Preferences > Map). Click Map again to return to UVLayout checkers.

Once you have a good layout, final skinning is next. Figure 16.20 shows the results after the model was brought back to Maya.

Figure 16.19 Final checking

Figure 16.20 Final transfer to Maya

UVLayout Hotkeys Reference

Remember that the trick to utilizing UVLayout's amazing speed is getting to know the hotkeys. Table 16.3 describes some of the more common hotkeys you will use.

▶ **Table 16.3** UVLayout Hotkey Reference

Shortcut	Action
Menu Operations	
L	Locks shell
H	Hides
S	Stacks
G	Marks and pins
F	Flattens box

continues

Table 16.3 UVLayout Hotkey Reference *(continued)*

Shortcut	Action
Drop	
D	Drops (sends from 3D to UV edit)
Shift+D	Undrops (sends from UV to 3D edit)
Focus	
Home	Focuses on mouse location (if background, centers on entire model)
End	Focuses on shell
Cutting	
C	Cuts
Shift+S	Splits a loop (3D window)
W	Welds
Enter	Splits and welds
Backspace	Deselects cut loop edges
Symmetry (Click Find)	
Left mouse	Defines midline
Spacebar	Starts symmetry
Shift+S	Swaps sides
Shell Manipulation	
Spacebar MM	Moves shell
Spacebar LM	Rotates shell
Spacebar RM	Scales shell
Falloff Commands	
4	Expands
5	Compresses
Shift+MM	Dragging with falloff
Ctrl+MM	Single UV move
Relax tools	
F	Flattens entire shell
B	Flattens brush
R	Relaxes brush
0	Produces the "old flatten brush"
Shift+F	Bloats, then flattens
Mesh moving	
Ctrl+middle mouse	Moves point
Shift+middle mouse	Moves with defined radius
Ctrl+Shift middle mouse	Moves with falloff (4 poly radius)

continues

Shortcut	Action
Radius sizing	
= and −	Changes radius size
Packing	
Tile	Packs into layers
]	Packs
Spacebar mm	Moves boxes and shells
\	Rotates box 90 degrees
Del	Removes the box
}	Boxes fix position (like "I" locks)
Del All button	Deletes boxes
Selecting	
G	Selects menu
Shift+G	Unselects
GG	Selects region
G (1–9)	Makes a bigger brush
Pinning	
P	Pins UV
PP	Pins region
Shift+P	Selects border (mouse need to be on border)
K	Selects edges for arbitrary axis
KK	Selects loop edges
Shift+K	Selects edges
Ctrl+K	Unselects
Straightens on Vertical and Horizontal (Boundary Edges)	
S	Selects ends of desired straight edges
SS	Straightens
Shift+S	Straightens
Straightens on Arbitrary Angle Defined by Endpoints (Interior Edges)	
K	Selects edges for arbitrary axis
KK	Selects loop edges
Shift+K	Selects edges
Ctrl+K	Unselects
I	Makes square to grid (vert and horiz) (interior edges)
II	Connects loop

continues

Shortcut	Action
View	
1	Toggles view to UV
2	Toggles view to Edit
3	Toggles view to 3D
3D window	
Left mouse	Orbits
Middle mouse	Pans
Left mouse and middle mouse	Zooms
UV window	
Alt+middle mouse	Pans
Alt+left mouse and middle mouse	Zooms

Conclusion

As you have seen, UVLayout has many ways to get very clean UVs. The program includes some great features to expedite the process, but it also allows for ease of use. UVs have historically been difficult to handle. In the past five years or so, there has been a real effort to increase the speed by which UVs are made, and in almost every area, UVLayout is leading the pack.

In the next chapter, we'll show you a muscle system that can be used to create realistic muscular deformations.

Maya Muscle

This chapter was contributed by Jared Fong, a technical director resident currently working at Pixar Animation Studios.

17

In every rig there comes a point where the rigger wants to take things to the next level. If it's a cartoony character, adding muscle means the ability to do enormous amounts of squashing and stretching. If your project is more realistic, the idea of muscles or a "muscle system" comes to mind. There are basically two approaches: the first is fake muscles with blendshapes or other deformers, and the second is some sort of simulation. The blendshape approach can produce fantastic results, but it requires a lot of work to set up fully. In this chapter, we will introduce Maya Muscle and show you how to get started setting up industry-standard muscle simulation.

Chapter Contents
Overview of basic muscle theory
Using Maya Muscle

T-Rex

T-Rex by Ron Dollase is the opening image used for this chapter. The dinosaur was built using cMuscleSystem (now Maya Muscle). The full-featured system controls deformations in a character.

Basic Muscle Theory

Our muscles and bones are really just a complex system of levers. It makes sense when you think about it: your biceps don't connect from the base of your humerus to the tip of the humerus. There wouldn't be much point unless our biceps were trying to bend the humerus in half. Instead, our biceps connect from the end of our scapula (shoulder) to the neck of the radius (forearm), so when we flex our biceps, it pulls the radius upward.

Most of our muscles are set up in this fashion and work as third-class levers. Figure 17.1 shows a third-class lever. Think of your arm; it is set up with the fulcrum (pivot at the elbow) at one end of the beam (forearm). When the force is applied on the beam from the bicep (the red hand), the weight is lifted at the opposite end of the bar. The idea of levers will help when it comes time to attach muscles to the correct origins and insertions along our digital skeleton.

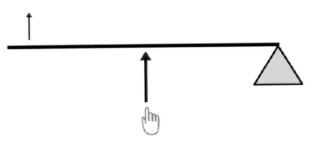

Figure 17.1 A third-class lever (http://en.wikipedia.org/wiki/Image:ThirdClassLever.svg)

An understanding of anatomy is very helpful when you are working with muscles. Although you would rarely re-create every tiny muscle in an appendage, knowing where the core muscles are located will help make your setup look realistic. Muscles are categorized as either agonist or antagonist.

An *agonist* muscle is responsible for the main movement of an appendage, and the *antagonist* provides the opposite force. For a good example in the human body, let's take a look at the arm again. The biceps brachii (biceps) are the agonists, and the triceps brachii (triceps) are the antagonists. When you bend your elbow and bring your forearm toward your shoulder (like a dumbbell curl), you are flexing your biceps. When your arm extends to a straightened position, you are using your triceps to counteract the previous movement of your biceps. If you keep this simple system in mind, you should easily be able to place muscles with some function in mind.

Introducing Maya Muscle

The current Maya Muscle Extension 1 for Maya Unlimited was originally created as a plug-in called cMuscleSystem by Michael B. Comet at Cometdigital.com. Autodesk acquired this functionality, and as of December 2007, it will be incorporated into future versions of Maya Unlimited. The muscle created by the original plug-in not only had the features expected of a commercial muscle system, but it also combined those features with an understanding of the rigging pipeline, and the integration was seamless.

Since the cMuscleSystem was a plug-in for Maya, it extended the core features of Maya to allow for more complex and specialized systems. The tutorials and samples that are included with Maya Muscle are very well done, and I highly recommend reading them and familiarizing yourself with the samples to get an intimate understanding of the features that are included. The help file in the extension is under the Muscle menu. As Maya Muscle is incorporated into future versions of Maya Unlimited, the help information will likely be rolled into the general Maya help available in the Help menu.

Creating a Muscle System

With Maya Muscle, you'll use a few general steps for creating every muscle system:

1. Create the skeleton.

2. Create the muscles.

3. Define their interactions.

Each step can be as simple or as complex as you need. Maya Muscle has a large range of options for simulation that allow for very fast simulations or slower, more complex simulations. This makes it easy to scale simulation complexity up or down, depending on the need of your production, on a shot-by-shot basis.

Creating the Skeleton

Maya Muscle skeletons are built with capsules, rather than bones. A *capsule* is an object used by Maya Muscle as a collision space for muscles. Capsules also bind the skin to the muscle system, in a setup similar to Maya's skinCluster, using sticky weights.

You can create the skeleton from scratch by creating capsules from the Muscle menu. Select Muscle > Muscle/Bones > Create Capsule to create a default capsule. If you look at the Channel Box, you'll find that you can edit the attributes of the muscle-CapsuleShape to change the radius, length, and axis of the capsule. Once the default capsule has been created, you can then create more and more capsules and parent them under one another to create a hierarchy of joints.

An easier way to create your capsules is to create your rig with joints, as you usually would, and then convert those joints to capsules using the Convert Surface to Muscle/Bone option. To do so, you must select all the joints you want to convert and then select Muscle > Muscle/Bones > Convert Surface to Muscle/Bone. A dialog box will pop up and ask which axis your joints are on. Select the correct axis for the joint chain that you are converting. Maya's default is down the X-axis.

You should now see capsules associated with all the joints you selected. If you look at your Outliner, you will see that there are new capsuleShape nodes parented below the joints. From the Outliner, you can select the capsules and adjust the values manually if you don't like the automatic results.

At this point, the capsules aren't doing anything. Select the geometry of your prebuilt character, and choose Muscle > Skin System > Apply Muscle Skin Deformer. Now select all the capsules and the geometry to be deformed; then choose Muscle > Skin System > Connect Selected muscleObjects to attach the capsules to the muscle deformer.

Unlike Maya's smooth skin, the muscle system does not automatically assign weight values to the deformer. You must now paint the weights of the each capsule by selecting the geometry and using Muscle > Skin System > Paint Muscle Weights. The paint tool that comes with Maya Muscle is similar to the method of painting weights; however, the difference is in attributes that are painted and influence objects that are paintable.

Creating Muscles

Maya Muscle has a great muscle-making utility. The only things you need to provide are the two attachment joints. Access the UI by choosing Muscle > Muscle/Bones > Muscle Builder UI. Select the first joint, and press the <<< button to load the name into the text field for Attach Obj 1. Then repeat the process for the second joint using Attach Obj 2. Once you've loaded both joints, hit the Build/Update button to create the muscle. Don't really worry about getting the settings exactly right; you can always adjust them later. Figure 17.2 shows the available settings.

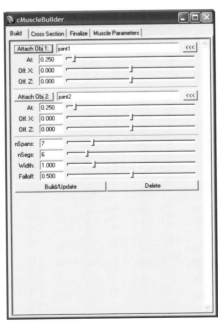

Figure 17.2 The cMuscleBuilder settings

Even after you hit the Build/Update button, you can continue to adjust parameters to get a good starting point. Pay particular attention to the At sliders. The At sliders define the attachment point of the muscle to each joint. Remember, the idea of the attachment points is based on levers. That analogy will help guide your placement of the muscles.

If you want more control over the shape of your muscles, check out the Cross Section tab. There you will find options to change individual spans and to adjust the CVs to get the exact shape you want. You can also find these curves in the Outliner. You can select and edit them in the viewport.

Once you are satisfied with the look, switch to the Finalize tab. Leave the settings at the default for now, and hit the Convert to Muscle button to finalize the muscle deformer. Figure 17.3 shows the muscle system. Once the muscle is made, you can adjust many of the simulated effects, such as jiggle and jiggle weights, on the Muscle Parameters tab to give you more control over the look of the muscle. Pay special attention to the length options, because they define the amount of squash and stretch that the muscle exhibits. Once you have the muscles, you can weight the mesh to the muscles just like a capsule.

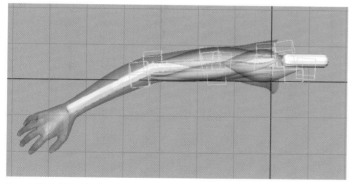

Figure 17.3 Maya Muscle after converting to muscle

Defining Muscle Interactions

After the skeleton and muscles are made, the majority of the setup is done. At this point, you need to define the interaction between the muscles, the capsules, and the skin.

Make sure that all your muscles are connected to the muscle system deformer by selecting the muscles and the skin and choosing Skin System > Connect Selected muscle-Objects. Choose Auto-Calculate Best Distance Per Muscle when the Creation window opens.

For speed reasons, not all the features you'll learn about next are enabled by default. However, each can add an extra layer of realism.

Tip: You can turn these features off until rendering to keep animators happy.

Sticky Weights

Sticky weighting is similar in function to Maya's smooth bind. Every point is weighted by a percentage to a capsule or muscle. You can paint the weights almost exactly as you would with Maya's paint weights.

A good way to paint weights is by weighting all the mesh to the bones, slowly adding influence to the muscles, and checking the way it looks as you go. This ensures that all points are at least weighted to the capsules, and everything else is extra goodness.

Sliding Weights

The sliding weights allow you to define when an influence object will slide under the skin, rather than pulling it along, like the muscles in Figure 17.4. To do this, you paint a small portion around the object that defines the range under which it will slide. This works particularly well with bones that slide under the surface of the skin, such as clavicles and hips.

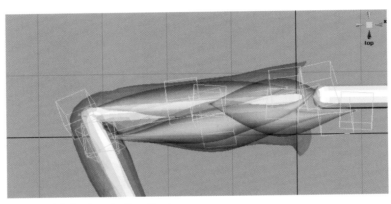

Figure 17.4 Deforming using Maya Muscle

Relax Weights

The relax attribute allows for the sliding effect to not only push mesh outward but also to have the muscle pull some of the surrounding mesh along with it. This gives the pushing a subtle falloff, as shown in Figure 17.5.

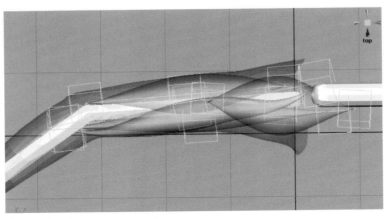

Figure 17.5 Relaxing with Maya Muscle

Per-Point Jiggle Weights

The per-point jiggle weight allows points to jiggle without being influenced by something else that is actually jiggling. This gives you more control to add subtle jiggling to regions that need to move, such as fat flaps or loose skin.

Conclusion

Try a simple setup using the Maya Muscle, and test some of the features. You will see how intuitive the workflow is once you get the hang of it.

Then, after taking a look at some innovative tools for enhancing characters, you'll look into the final step of the rigging process, skinning the character, in the next chapter.

The Skinny on Skinning: Effective Surface Attachment

Skinning *encompasses the process of binding and painting weights. The weights are attached from joints to the surface on a vertex level, and influence objects share in the smooth bind weighting. Other deformers and simulation can have weight on the surface, as well. In the past, the methods of skinning were cumbersome, but Maya now has great tools, such as smoothing and additive painting, that really help in defining those smooth falloffs that are needed for exact weighting. Be sure you test your skeleton thoroughly before you bind. In this chapter, we'll address binding the skeleton to the surface.*

18

337

THE SKINNY ON SKINNING: EFFECTIVE SURFACE ATTACHMENT

Chapter Contents

Planning your skin
Binding your skin
Painting weights
Establishing deformation order
Working with vertex weight maps
Bomb-proofing and testing your rig

Planning the Skin

Weighting your figure will not require a lot of planning. You just have to get in there and get working, especially if you are new to binding. Above all, when you set up weights, keep in mind that each vertex has only 100 percent of its weight to add, no matter how many joints that's split among, and that 100 percent is represented as a weight of 1.0. If two joints share a vertex, they share the weight. For example, a vertex may have a weight of 0.4 assigned to one joint and 0.6 to the other. If you assign only part of the full weight, Maya will try to figure out where the other part will go. Maya usually can figure this out, but sometimes it gets it wrong and there is a problem. The initial Maya smooth bind will work for testing your rig, but more often than not, you will want to start from scratch and define weights exactly to get the character to deform as you need. Plan for working through your figure joint by joint from the extremities and then inward. Paint generously inward, and then take away from the last when you move to the next joint.

Be sure to test your figure thoroughly before binding. Make sure all the switches are working and all the rotations of the joints are correct. Save your scene, and do a simple test animation. Specifically, watch your joints, and make sure they are rotating correctly. If you run into problems later after binding, you still can fix them, but it is easier to test thoroughly now. You can add a temporary simple initial bind for the sake of testing joint rotations, so plan this testing into the process. Work smart, not hard.

You should do one last thing before you start binding: go into your geometry, and delete all the nondeformer history. This gets rid of any baggage that your geometry is carrying. To delete the history, select Edit > Delete by Type > Non-Deformer History.

Binding the Skin

In Maya, *binding* is the process of attaching each vertex to one or more joints with varying percentages to achieve even, predictable deformations. The initial bind will be a good test of your surface and the joint rotations. You can see quickly whether your joints behave as you intended.

Selecting Bindable Joints

During the skinning process, you will likely need to test and rebind your rig. You will probably run through this process at least once or twice, so finding some good MEL tools for saving weights to text files is very useful. You want to be able to achieve a really good initial skin to shorten your manual work. In fact, we recommend you name your bindable joints with a suffix like BND. It can be very painful to select all the bindable joints each time you have to bind, especially if you haven't been keeping up with the organization and naming. In the process of creating the figure, we recommended renaming the joints and objects that you will need to run through different processes. For instance, joints are not added to a bind the same way that influence objects are added. So if you haven't already, use the naming tools now to clean up the naming of your rig. Try some of the name-editing tools we talked about in Chapter 3, "Rigging That's Right: Concepts You Need to Know." In addition, you can use some of the many MEL scripts online that can quickly add or replace any prefix or suffix on your joints.

Take the time to make sure all your joints are named correctly. Do this before you begin skinning and adding influence objects. MEL can be a powerful ally in repetitive tasks. If everything is appropriately named and organized, it will help you tremendously with the selection process. You also will want to deselect your end joints, which do not need to be bound. You can even name these with a different suffix and deselect them with a simple MEL script. Figure 18.1 shows the process of selecting bindable joints from the Outliner.

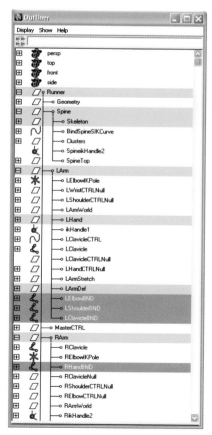

Figure 18.1 Selecting the bindable joints

Walk through your rig now. Identify the joints to be skinned and check the names. Have you named all the joints and joint chains to be bound with a simple BND suffix? (Remember in this example, we're using prefixes to identify the location of joint within the rig.) Check the spine, the floating joints of the clavicle, the shoulder and elbow, the deformable floating joints, and so on. You need to rename only the starts of joint chains. The chain, once selected, will be bound in its entirety. Be sure the BND suffix is included in the name of any that will need to be selected every time you bind. In our figure, we added the suffix INF to the influence objects for easy selection. Check yours.

You may need only one initial bind. However, you will likely need to rebind the character after fixing joint problems, and if you do, you will need to select these same joints all over again. A little later in this chapter, we'll show you a quick MEL command that, in conjunction with a consistent naming convention, can save a lot of time when you need to rebind.

Manually Selecting Joints for the Bind

Here is a partial list of joints that you will want to select for an appropriate bind. There is no specific order to the selections that follow.

- The first of a chain of joints on the spine
- The floating joints of the clavicle, shoulder, and elbow
- The deformable floating joints
- The joints of the hands and head
- The main leg chain from the ankle to the ball

All of these will need to be selected every time you bind. You then need to add the influence objects. To speed the workflow of binding, you can shorten the process by naming each applicable joint with an appropriate suffix.

Automating the Joint and Object Selection Process with MEL

Did you enjoy all that selecting? If you've named everything consistently, you can accomplish the same thing with a simple MEL command. Intelligent naming allows you to select all your bindable joints with a simple MEL script:

```
select -r "*BND";
```

The asterisk is a wildcard that selects everything in your scene with a name that ends with the suffix BND. So to select all your joints quickly, you can just copy this to the shelf, and with the click of a button, you have your joints selected.

To select all the influence objects, you can use the following MEL command:

```
select -add "*INF";
```

If you have named everything correctly, you will be able to easily select the bindable joints and the influence objects in seconds.

Binding the Figure

Here are the steps to bind in case you are unfamiliar with them:

1. Select the joints. If you have named them appropriately, use the following MEL command:

   ```
   select -r "*BND";
   ```

   Figure 18.2 shows the bindable joints before the skin has been selected.

2. Perform a smooth bind (Skin-Bind > Skin-Smooth Bind).

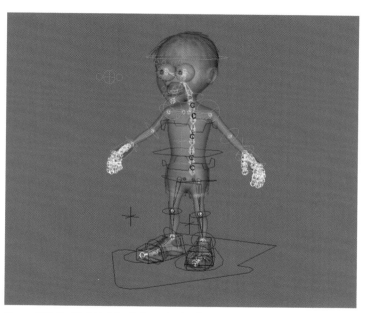

Figure 18.2 The bindable joints before selecting the skin to bind

You will want to take some time now and work with the skeleton to make sure it is deforming according to plan. If it is not, you can add secondary objects, such as lattices or influence objects, to the bind. Once the bind and rig are where you want them, save the weights. If you break something later, you'll need a known good point to start over again. We will talk about saving weights a little later in the chapter.

Adding Influence Objects

If you plan to use influence objects, you need to add them after the initial bind. Select a joint, and choose Skin > Goto Bind Pose. This will return the rig to the original bind pose. You need to be in this pose to add influences.

To use a prefix to select the influence objects in the scene, follow these steps:

1. Select the skin to be influenced.

2. Select the influence objects. If you have named them with the INF suffix, use the following MEL command:

   ```
   select -add "*INF";
   ```

3. Attach the influence objects to the bind (Skin > Edit Smooth Bind > Add Influence Object > option box). You want to make sure the weight is set to 0.0 before you add and then paint in any influence. Figure 18.3 shows adding influence objects.

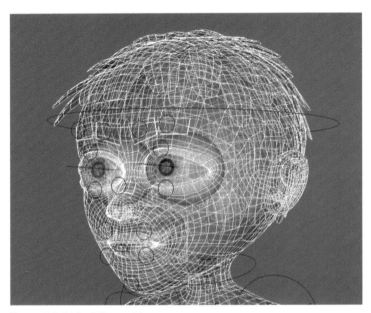

Figure 18.3 Adding influence objects

Painting Weights

Now that you have tested your joints and have a default bind that you are happy with, you are ready to move into painting the weights. *Painting* the weights is the process of editing the weighting of the vertices to the joints in an easy-to-use visual representation.

 Tip: If you have a Wacom tablet and are used to using it in Adobe Photoshop, you'll take to this method quickly. Using a Wacom tablet for weight painting is highly recommended.

The Paint Skin Weights tool is the tool you will use for your skinning. If you are not already familiar with this tool, it is an artisan-based brush that can edit the value of each joint's weight on the surface.

We'll now talk a little more about the weighting of each vertex. As we mentioned earlier, each vertex has a weight of 1.0. If all that weight isn't specifically assigned to a joint, Maya tries to find a suitable joint and assigns the rest. For example, if three joints share a vertex and you assign one joint 0.8 of the weight, Maya assigns the others 0.1 each. This is referred to as *weight normalization*. Maya always tries to normalize. So when you paint, it's a good idea to add influence so you can see it, then smooth surrounding verts, then paint some more, and then smooth with the brush until the values give you the desired results. Figure 18.4 shows the Paint Skin Weights tool.

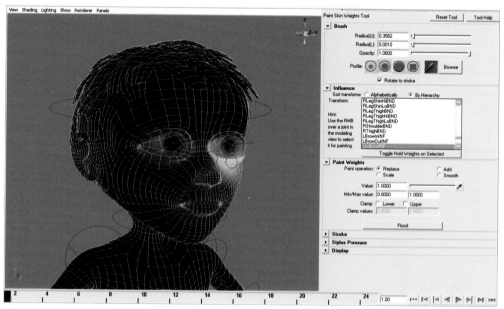

Figure 18.4 Painting skin weights

Locking weights on a joint forces Maya to pull weight from unlocked joints. This is why you work from the extremities inward, locking finished joints' weights along the way until you're left with only the torso joints. Also, if you try to paint weights to/from a locked joint, Maya will warn you in the Script Editor. Therefore, you should keep the Script Editor open while painting, in case you forget to unlock a joint. You will also see this type of warning in the Command Response field under the viewport.

Tip: Many scripts can help speed up the process of skinning. skinningTools.mel by David Walden is one of the best out there. It is a script that was created to speed up the workflow, and it helps immensely in the skinning process. You can download skinningTools.mel from http://highend3d.com. After we spend a little time with Maya's stock tools, we'll talk more about this amazing add-on.

Here are some tips and tools for working with skinning in Maya:

Clearing unused joints If your joint is not needed, you can clear its initial weighting by using the "Flood" button with the brush value set to 0. This button is shown in Figure 18.4. It will take off all weighting associated with that joint. The head placement and eye joints are examples.

Using naming for selection If the naming is correct, selection is easy. As shown earlier in Figure 18.4, the joints that are included in the bind are listed in the Attribute Editor. Use this list for quick selection.

Using the X-Ray Joints option (Maya 2008+) You can view the joints of your rig while painting smooth skin weights by turning on the X-Ray Joints option. You can find it in the Paint Skin Weights tool's settings by selecting Display > X-Ray Joints. X-Ray joints can also be used for showing the joints when you're not using the Paint Skin Weights tool. When you want to view the joints like this in a normal workflow, use the viewport camera option. This is right above your viewport in the Shading > X-Ray Joints option. Figure 18.5 shows the X-Ray Joints option in a paint weights view.

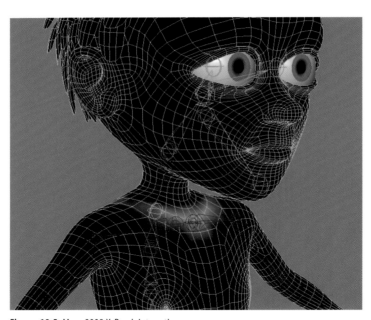

Figure 18.5 Maya 2008 X-Ray Joints option

"Adding to and taking from" and locking As we've mentioned, the best approach for painting weights is to start at the extremities and then work your way in to the torso. Use Toggle Hold Weights on Selected to lock the weights as you work inward. Test frequently to make sure your weighting is correct. You can also toggle Hold in the Component Editor, as well as in the skinningTools.mel script interface.

Using hotkeys When you are painting weights with the replace brush, if you press and hold Ctrl while you paint, the brush paints the inverse weight value. So if the weight is set to 1, press and hold Ctrl while you paint, and the brush paints 0. If you are set for .75, it paints .25. If you press and hold Shift, your brush changes to a smooth brush.

Using temporary animation You can set some temporary animation to help you in the binding process. For example, to pull down the eyelid and epicanthic fold (the loose skin right above the eyelid but under the brow), you can simply animate the lid influence object controls down. You then smooth the lid and let Maya do the rest. The smoothing causes the fold to pull apart like you want, and the animation shows how the geometry is being affected. Figure 18.6 shows painting weights with temporary animation.

> **Tip:** If you are using skinningTools.mel here, you have the ability to rotate each joint from within the interface. This, however, does not work if the joint has incoming connections controlling the particular rotation. It does not work on controls either. Still, it is handy to have this option in your weight painting toolset.

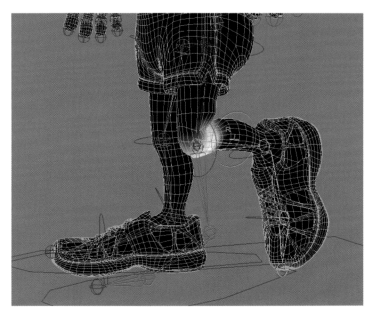

Figure 18.6 Painting weights with temporary animation

Using secondary deformers You will need to weight your lattice, influence objects, and any other secondary objects that are bound at this time. Once you add influence objects using the menu Skin > Edit Smooth Skin > Add Influence, they show up in the weight painting list. Lattices, however, only have the Edit Membership Tool for the affected vertices.

Performing additional editing You can view an individual vertex weight in the Component Editor (Windows > General Editor > Component Editor). Here, you can get in and dig through the actual values. You can modify them from the Component Editor for precise alterations or even lock the values while working. Now, you can really see normalization in action.

To paint skin weights, follow these steps:

1. Select the bound mesh.

2. Select the Paint Skin Weights Tool's option box (Skin > Edit Smooth Skin > Paint Skin Weights Tool option box). You can also double-click the Paint Skin Weights icon.

3. Select a bone from the Influence list.

4. Paint the weights onto the surface using the value, paint operation, and opacity options. The Smooth tool will help you clean up the transition from joint to joint.

5. While painting, use the hotkey (hold the B key and use the left mouse button to drag within the interface) to adjust the radius of the brush, as shown in Figure 18.7.

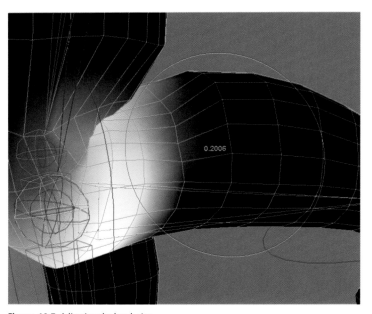

Figure 18.7 Adjusting the brush size

Using *skinningTools.mel*

We highly recommend skinningTools.mel created by David Walden. This script creates an easy-to-read UI that is compact and clean. The layout is similar to Maya's Attribute Editor with the Paint Skin Weights Tool, but it is more compact and efficient. It also adds some very useful tools for painting. Here are some of these advanced options:

Negative painting Besides having the same type of slider for Opacity and Value settings, the UI boasts the option to set the value of your brush to –1. This provides painting in the negative. This is currently not an option in Maya's default tool, and this ability is dreamy for adding small value changes to your weighting.

Influence sets Within the skinningTools.mel menu, there is an Influence Sets drop-down menu. This feature gives you the option of creating new sets of influence objects. So, say you are working on the influence objects for a face and are frustrated with running through the long list looking for face-specific influence objects. Influence Sets allows you to create sets of influence objects that include only the objects from the area on which you are working. You now can work from a subset of objects, which makes the list shorter and your life easier. Within the sets, you can right-click to toggle Hold/Unhold as well as use many other efficient options.

Stylus pressure switch This switch enables and disables stylus pressure. When you're using a Wacom graphics tablet for painting weights, enabling stylus pressure gives you the pressure sensitivity you need to optimize weights efficiently.

Joint rotation As we mentioned earlier, you now have the ability to rotate a joint within the skinningTools.mel UI (see Figure 18.8). Joint rotation is great for testing without having to jump back and forth between the joint and the skinning tools. If the joint has incoming connections, it will not work. If you are trying to move a control, you have to do so in Maya's viewport.

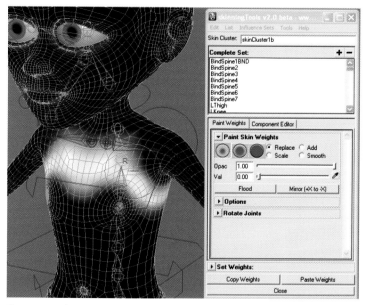

Figure 18.8 skinningTools.mel

Affected vert selection While working on a joint or influence object, you can right-click the object in the list and select the influenced vertices. If you encounter an issue—say, for example, that some of the finger vertices are weighted to your knee joint—you can select the affected verts and then zero them out in the Component Editor.

Tip: You'll find the Component Editor in the skinningTools.mel interface on a tab next to the Paint Weights tab.

Using the Move Skinned Joints Tool

With a new tool in Maya 2008, the Move Skinned Joints Tool, you now have the ability to move a joint without the bound skin following. We have not tested this tool yet, but we wanted to let you know that it exists so that you have these options, if you need them, after a bind:

- Inserting joints (you need to add the new joint to the bind)

- Connecting joints (you can connect joints into a bound system)

- Disconnecting joints

Establishing the Deformation Order

You need to be aware of how to manage the influence order for a given surface. It is a fairly big problem if, while animating, you find that as soon as you dial up a blendshape, the geometry flies back to the origin. To resolve the problem, you have to change the order of the deformations. For example, you need to make sure the blendshape gets calculated into the mesh before the skinCluster deformer. Here is how to find and manipulate this list:

1. Select the geometry.

2. Right-click the geometry, and select Inputs > All Inputs.

3. To change the order of influence, drag the blendshape deformation with the middle mouse button to below the skinCluster deformer. Be aware that you can drag an item only to a lower position in the listing. This means that you can move the item *ahead* in the calculation order only, because the order of deformation calculation runs from the bottom of the list to the top. The menu is shown in Figure 18.9.

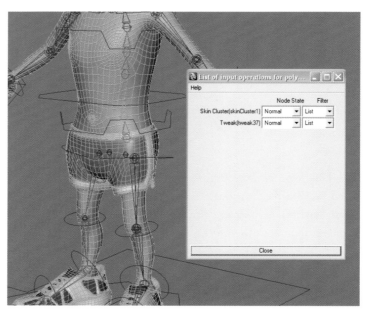

Figure 18.9 Input operations for the geometry

Working with Vertex Weight Maps

You can save vertex weighting in multiple ways. Maya has a built-in solution that works fairly well. Other solutions provide more dependable options when you're looking for the best weight transfer system. We recommend transferring weights with cometSave-Weights.mel. In the following sections, we'll discuss the tools that Maya uses, and then we will touch on cometSaveWeights.mel.

Maya's tool for importing and exporting weight maps is one option. You can find it by selecting Skin > Edit Smooth Skin > Export Skin Weight Maps. You can use Maya's tool when you need to make changes to your geometry that don't involve cutting and point order manipulation. This can be extremely helpful after you have spent a lot of time painting your weights, need to make a change, and then need to apply the weighting to the figure. Be aware that Maya's export creates weight maps that are basically black-and-white value maps per joint, so data loss can be an issue.

Saving with Maya

To save vertex weight maps from Maya, follow these steps:

1. Select the surface that has the weights applied.
2. Run the exporter on the selection by choosing Skin > Edit Smooth Skin > Export Skin Weight Maps.

Tip: You will want to save fairly high-quality maps to retain detail. Depending on how detailed your UV layout is, you may want to choose 1024×1024 or even 2048×2048. These values will return much better results than lower map resolutions.

Transferring Weights

Bringing exported weights back onto the surface is just as easy. You simply need to select your figure and choose Skin > Edit Smooth Skin > Import Skin Weight Maps. Run through your joints, and verify that there were no artifacts from the transfer. (There usually are some artifacts from the process; those you will need to clean up.)

Using *cometSaveWeights.mel*

One very good system for saving vertex weight maps is cometSaveWeights.mel. It operates by saving skin weights into a text file. It calculates the weights based on the vertices' point order, world position, or local position. To use the script, you will also need to put libSkin.mel and libString.mel into your scripts folder. The script prompts you to pick the skin cluster and to specify a filename and path. Be sure to select all the vertices from which you want weights exported.

Copying Weights

Maya includes a separate tool for copying weights from surface to surface, the Copy Skin Weights tool. The greatest advancements for skinning in Maya since version 8.0 are the options to select the Surface Association property of using the closest point on surface and the ability to define joint labels so you don't have to rename the target rig's joints. Using these features, you can take a character, place it on top of a completely different character (one with different geometry but similar structure, for example, one biped to another biped), and copy the weights from one to the other. The tool finds the nearest vertices on the source geometry and copies the values to the nearest vertices on the target geometry. So, once you paint *one* really good biped's weights, you can always transfer the weights to any other biped in seconds and have an excellent starting point for skin weights. You'll find this tool really useful for the following:

Low-resolution weighting If you have a low-resolution version of your figure, you can easily paint weights to this figure and then transfer the weights to the high-resolution figure.

Clothing The tool also works for clothing. This is how we transferred the weights from our runner character to his shorts.

Figure-to-figure As we mentioned earlier, the tool easily copies weights from one surface to another of similar topology.

Bomb-proofing Your Rig

Bomb-proofing your rig is one of the more important parts of the whole rigging process. *Bomb-proofing* is the process of locking down and hiding anything that you don't want the animators to use. Your rig should be completely driven using the controls. Even then, you likely want to allow the animators to access only certain attributes of the controls in your rig. You want to make sure that all the joints are inaccessible by hiding them. This is one of your last steps in making the rig easy to use and intuitive, but it also keeps it very powerful. This is one of the final things you will do to your rig before giving it an animator. This way, you don't have to go through and unlock and unhide a bunch of things to fix the rig if needed.

Hiding

When all is said and done, you want to present a figure with a bunch of easily found controls to the animator. All the other parts of the rig will be "under the hood." Hiding the joints is one of the ways to bomb-proof your figure. You want to guide your animators toward animating and manipulating controls and not joints. Hide nodes by right-clicking their attribute and selecting Hide Selected from the pop-up menu. Hide joints and other parts of the rig with Ctrl+H or Display > Hide > Hide

Selection. In the Outliner, you can select a hidden item and use Shift+H to show it again. To show hidden attributes, use the Channel Control Editor. To find it in the Channel Box, select Channels > Editors > Channel Control. All of the hidden and "keyable" attributes of the node are available here and can be hidden or made visible again with the click of a button. To move hidden attributes to visible attributes in the Channel Box, select the attributes, and click the <<Move button. As you may have figured, you can do your hiding in here as well. Select the nodes you want to hide, and click the Move>> button.

Hide nodes after you make sure you don't have any dependent structures. For instance, if you have a control that is a child of a joint that you want to hide, you'll need to move the control and hook it up to the rig in a different way. The joints and nodes that are to be hidden will, of necessity, either need to be the children of their controls (which can be hidden without affecting their parent) or need to be in a separate hierarchy altogether. They cannot be in the child relationship because they will be hidden with their parents.

Test your ability to hide all the joints. Make sure you can hide what you need to, and only what you need to, before moving on.

You want to hide the following:

- Joints

- Deformers (rivets, influence objects, lattices, and so on)

- IK chains (this is optional; some animators may want to see the vector)

Now you are ready to move on to locking.

Locking vs. Referencing

Tip: We have included a script, lock.mel, for locking portions of your rig. Be sure to read the comments and code in the script to know exactly what the script does before you use it.

You can now start locking parts of the rig. Be careful with what you lock, though, because connections can be stopped, which can cause real problems. Lock items that are visible and that you don't want manipulated.

You may want to change a node to a nonselectable reference object. You may have noticed in using layers that you can change any node's display to a template or reference by clicking the second check box. To do this in the object's Attribute Editor, select the Transform tab (the leftmost one), and select Display > Drawing Overrides and then check the Enable Overrides box. Now change the display type (Display Type > Reference).

Turn Display Type to Reference for the following:

- Geometry
- IK handles (if visible)

Plan carefully what you really need locked. In our character, we locked the following:

- The control visibility attribute
- Scaling attributes of master and root controls

Other than that, it is really up to you whether you want to limit the control of your rig. Remember to talk to the animators to see what they want.

One last thing that you need to lock down is the ability of the animator to pick-walk. We talked about this a little earlier in the book. Pickwalking can be an easy way for the animator to get to nulls that need to be locked.

 Tip: We have included a script for this named pickWalker.mel. It reassigns the hotkey, basically disabling it for the specified nodes. Again, familiarize yourself with the script by reading the comments and the actual code, before running it.

That should about do it for locking needs. Now that you have a figure that is prepared for animation, you are ready to do your final testing.

Final Testing

You've made it to the final testing. Nice work. For this final test, you want to push and pull on each of your controls, one last time, to verify they are set up correctly. You've done this before, as you built them, but just run through the whole figure one last time. Verify the bind. Double-check the joints and the deformers; they are hidden, but you can still check that the system is working correctly.

Go through all your UI elements, whether you have a selection of window or facial joystick controls, and check them now. Do one last sweep to make sure that all the locking and hiding is accurate. Are the controls that are visible the ones that are needed? Once you've done the final sweep and everything checks out, you are ready to animate. So, whether you are the animator or you are sending the file off into the pipeline, it is now time to do so. Congratulations, you now have the final rig.

Conclusion

With a complete figure, you are ready to move on to the next process. If you need to review and practice your artisan brush weight painting skills or need to verify files, do so now. Otherwise, your character should be fully rigged, and you should have the animator check that they have what they need. The next chapter presents a start-to-finish pipeline workflow for rigging.

Implementing a Character Pipeline: Pipeline in a Box

This chapter was contributed by Adam Sidwell. Adam has worked around the globe in a variety of studios, including Digital Domain, ILM, Sony Imageworks, and Weta, and has presented Maya Master's Classes at Siggraph.

19

To save precious hours and keep yourself from repeating work, you need a pipeline—*the tools and methods for saving your work and passing it from one stage of production to another. A good pipeline lets a select few artists (or even one artist) manage the data, from modeling all the way to final images, for the entire crew by creating a workflow that is automated and easy to use. The tools provided on the book's companion CD were written to give you a character pipeline straight out of the box. This chapter shows you how to use that pipeline. After mastering the tools and techniques, you'll wonder how you ever lived without them!*

Chapter Contents
Organizing Maya projects for a pipeline
Creating a versatile and reliable pipeline
Using some basic and essential building blocks
Extensions and further recommendations

Runners Everywhere!

The opening image for this chapter includes a small army of characters from the mock short film *The Big Race*, created especially for this book. It shows how a typical scene in the film might be set up. The Pipeline in a Box tools and techniques demonstrated in this chapter will show you how to organize your characters and their animation in a way that will let you focus more on the art and less on file management while working on shots such as this one.

Organizing Maya Projects in a Pipeline

Organizing a project with its many varied tasks is like moving into a new house. It is very exciting at first, but your life will quickly turn to chaos if you haven't planned a place for your dishes, furniture, DVD collection, books, and clothes. To efficiently move through your day, you need a place to store your things, and you need to know exactly where they are stored so you can get at them in a moment's notice. Storing data for a project is no different. Files need to reside in locations that are reasonable and, above all, consistent. You also need to establish methods for accessing that data without having to browse through folders every time.

If you are new to organizing a project, working with project settings, or referencing files in Maya, read this entire chapter carefully and follow the step-by-step instructions. If you are an experienced Maya user and have worked with character pipelines before, you can skim over the first few sections and skip right to "Special Solutions." Be sure to review the " Directory Structure" section, however, since it will be used in the tutorials, before skipping to "Special Solutions."

The tools provided on the book's companion CD are written to give you a character pipeline straight out of the box. The same tools could take weeks, even months, to plan and develop, but now you don't have to wait—you can begin using them right away. You can use the tools as they are or, for the more advanced user, adapt them to your specific needs. The ideas covered in this chapter give you a complete backbone for a pipeline, an essential part of any animation project.

An Interview with Adam Sidwell

What is your background?

I began my studies in mechanical engineering at Brigham Young University, when I saw a rotating sphere in Maya. That's where it all started. I switched my major immediately to animation and then tacked on computer science. The animation program was great, because it allowed me to hone my skills in figure drawing, storyboarding, and design. That's where I got my introduction to Renderman

and Maya as well. Computer science taught me to think more clearly and to analyze and solve problems. The algorithms I was exposed to and the practice in inductive reasoning have helped me to break down some of the challenges I've faced on the job and to invent solutions. It was like reading the Matrix.

What software do you use? What software do you prefer and why?

Most of my rigging work has been done in Maya. I've also taken on some lighting/rendering issues in Render-man. Most of the cloth work I've done has been in Syflex, which is a very quick and versatile cloth plug-in for Maya. When you're in production and pushing to achieve top quality, these programs can tax the limits of any computer. All of the cloth for *King Kong* was solved in Syflex. Syflex is great because you can do just about anything with it, and it runs quickly. I really like Maya because it has a simple and elegant underlying architecture. Everything is a node, and it's connected in one way or another to other nodes. It's just pushing and pulling the data through. It's so simple a two year old can do it. Well, a 2-year-old supergenius. It allows you to see everything that's going on under the hood and manipulate it.

What did you do on *I, Robot* and *Pirates of the Caribbean III*?

Two completely different things. On *I, Robot*, I was a general technical director, which meant that for that particular show I built a lot of the character pipeline and lighting pipeline tools. It meant that I was involved in troubleshooting animators' and lighters' scenes and making sure that all the data flowed through every step smoothly and cleanly. I wrote scripts that transferred and stored animation data, character UIs, rendering utilities, scene setup tools, crowd animation optimizers…whatever. I also did some rigging for crowd characters. Most of my work was done in MEL and Perl. I was very good at typing by the end of that show.

For *Pirates of the Caribbean III*, I was a cloth TD, which meant that I did all shot work. I'd get a shot with as many as eight fish-pirate-zombies and have to solve all the cloth for them. Sometimes there wasn't much time before the shot was due, and simulations can take a few hours to run at times. It was also a challenge because all the work was done in Industrial Light & Magic's proprietary software, and it takes time to get used to a new software package. The best part was working on Davy Jones's cloth and tentacles. I think he's the most impressive CG character to date, and the artists and TDs who built him from the ground up have my respect (as well as an Oscar).

What was the most difficult/most fun rig you've worked on?

I'd have to say the hardest rig I worked on was probably a hair rig for Naomi Watts's digital double in *King Kong*. Initially, we were having difficulty simulating hair at super-high G forces. What looks right in animation isn't always based in reality; Kong would have broken Ann's spine in the real world as he threw her from hand to hand at 236 Gs. It looked like she was in a wind tunnel. In the end, I removed all the forces from her and then used Syflex gravity to add them back in based on how much acceleration she was experiencing per frame multiplied by a scaling factor. For shots where she was being thrown or falling violently, I turned down that scaling factor to give her "movie magic" hair that looked much better. Then the hair model kept changing or would get swapped out for different hairstyles in different shots, so it had to be rebuilt multiple times. Luckily I scripted the build, so I could execute the build script and then play Stinkoman 20X6 on www.homestarrunner.com while I waited for it to finish.

Can you tell us anything about your role on your current project?

I'm working as a rigger on *Speed Racer* at Digital Domain. Before that I was working on *I Am Legend* at Sony. With that and *Pirates of the Caribbean III*, I've been making a lot of zombies these days. Some people sell cars for a living; I get to make zombies.

The Necessity of a Versatile and Reliable Character Pipeline

The idea behind a good pipeline is that a select few artists (or even one artist) can manage the data and assets for the entire crew. These savvy technicians are called *technical directors* (TDs) and have the responsibility of creating a workflow that is robust, automated, easy to use, and flexible for everyone else involved in the production. A good pipeline establishes locations for data storage and tools that transfer that data correctly and consistently so that work moves from conception to final rendered image as smoothly as possible. Tools that allow you to accomplish tasks with a touch of a button minimize user error and guarantee consistency.

Whether you have an army of animators and lighters or you're a one-person show, it is always easier to go through a process with a click of a button. Taking time to automate repetitive tasks is worth the effort. You won't have to spend time wrangling assets or chasing down data, and you can focus on making those shots look right!

Directory Structure

The most important part of your organizational process is a solid, logical directory structure. There are hundreds of different ways to design a directory structure; design yours to suit your facility and project needs. For example, take a look at the example directory structure in Figure 19.1. This type of structure is well organized and contains locations for the many assets you will need to store. It is also compatible with the methodologies and scripts we'll be showing you in this chapter.

Figure 19.1 Sample directory structure

All of the items marked with a dollar sign ($) represent variable folder names. Replace the variables with names that describe the show, sequences, shot, or asset for your particular project. Table 19.1 lists the directory variables and the folders' intended uses.

▶ **Table 19.1** Pipeline in a Box Directory Variables

Variable	Meaning
$show	Your film, commercial, short, or project name
$sequence	Sequences in your film, a series of shots linked together
$shot	A single camera cut
$asset	An item such as character and puppet rig, model, texture, light rig, or shader

You can download the sample directory structure and then modify and add the scene, shot, and asset names to suit your needs. After you have completed this chapter, you can use the newShow folder to create a directory structure for your own project, replacing the variables with ones of your own choice.

For now, keep the sequence and shot names the same as the ones in the sample directory so you can follow along as you go through the exercises in this chapter. Be careful not to replace or change the names of the other directories, or you will disrupt the organization of the pipeline. The scripts and directories included are built for Windows, but with a few simple modifications, they can be made compatible with Linux. With a few more modifications, the tools can be compatible with other types of directory structures. The pipeline tools and rest of the chapter will work within the directory structure shown earlier in Figure 19.1.

To set up the directory structure, do the following:

1. Download the characterPipeline.zip file from the book's companion CD.

2. Unzip it.

3. If you're working in Windows, copy the projects file, which contains a sample directory structure, to your root of your C:/ drive.

4. Rename the folder USER to your username. Execute getenv USER in Maya's Script Editor to be sure you and Maya are using the same name.

5. In Maya, click the black arrow in the upper-left corner to the left of the shelves. Select Load Shelf from the pop-up menu.

6. Browse to select the following shelf: C:\projects\standard\maya\shelves\ pipeline_shelf.mel. Then choose Open. The shelf was included in the folders you copied from the CD.

7. Open the script editor in Maya, and cut and paste the following line of code:

```
putenv MAYA_SCRIPT_PATH (`getenv MAYA_SCRIPT_PATH` +
";C:/projects/standard/maya/scripts/");
```

8. Execute it by highlighting it and pressing "Ctrl+Enter."

Under ideal production situations, the pipeline TD would change the permissions on the folders so that they could be modified by only a few people.

Establishing a Set of Rules

Any time you work with a team, you must establish a few ground rules. This is true for your pipeline, as well. The following sections explain how you set the basic rules for projects using tools from Pipeline in a Box.

Location, Location, Location: What and Who Goes Where

In this pipeline, text files called shotinfo.info are used to define the parameters for your scene. Information, such as frame range or characters used for the scene, is recorded here and then read and parsed behind the scenes by the pipeline tools that do the work for you. When animators publish their animations using the animationPublisher tool (it's one of the pipeline tools included on the pipeline shelf—we'll get to that later), the tool needs to know which frame range to publish. When animators or lighters are building their scenes, the characterLister tool (also included on the pipeline shelf) needs to know which characters to reference into the scene. Having a shotinfo.info file allows the coordinator in charge of this kind of information to put the proper information in these files and saves animators and lighters from constantly asking the question "What and who goes where for how long?"

Assets tree The assets tree is the place to store general show assets, such as character and puppet rigs, models, textures, light rigs, shaders, and so on. This is where you would store your hero rig or geometry.

Shots tree The shots tree is the production folder. Animators and lighters work in these areas and store their scenes in the work branch of the directory structure under individual usernames. This is where you can store items specific to a shot, such as set geometry, textures, a lighting rig specific to the shot, animation for the shot, and so forth. Here you will store, for example, a muddy skin texture for your character after he falls in a puddle.

Some Key Locations for This Pipeline

For this pipeline, assets are stored in a few key locations. Again, these are suggestions, and any number of configurations will work, but the tools in this chapter store files as follows:

- Low-resolution puppet rigs:

    `$drive/projects/$show/publish/pub/assets/[$asset]/[$flavor]/depts/char/pp`

- High-resolution character rigs:

    `$drive/projects/$show/publish/pub/assets/[$asset]/[$flavor]/depts/char/hi`

- Published animation:

    `$drive/projects/$show/publish/pub/shots/[$sequence]/`
    `[$shot]/depts/anim/anim/[$namespace]/scenes/anim.mb`

- shotinfo.info files:

    `$drive/projects/$show/publish/pub/shots/[$sequence]/`
    `[$shot]/depts/info/shotinfo.info`

- Character files:

    `$drive/projects/$show/publish/pub/shots/[$sequence]/`
    `[$shot]/depts/info/*.character`

These files are essential to the pipeline. We'll explain how they fit in and what they do later in this chapter.

Some Basic and Essential Building Blocks

All Maya projects include certain basic elements and essential building blocks. The following sections explain how to use Pipeline in a Box tools to handle those elements.

Environment Variables

Certain variables control the Maya environment and are not attached to any specific file or script. They are very useful for telling Maya where you want to be in the directory structure and what to look for. The information is not saved with your scene but is stored in your session of Maya.

You can set sequence and shot numbers using environment variables so you can know your location in the tree.

To set environment variables, in the Script Editor, type the following:

```
putenv SCENE "deathScene";
```

and press Ctrl+Enter. Then type the following:

```
getenv SCENE ;
```

and again press Ctrl+Enter. The following are the output results:

```
// Result: deathScene //
```

Setting Projects and Using Workspace Files

A project is the basic set of definitions that Maya uses so that it knows where to put data. Setting the project automatically defines for Maya the folders where renders, particles, 3D paint textures, sound, clips and other data go. Ordinarily, you set your project by choosing File > Project > Set and selecting a folder. This tells Maya where it is, and from here on out, Maya knows its own location. This information is not saved with your scene but stays with the session of Maya you have open.

Maya writes out a workspace file that is located in the folder where you set your project. It contains MEL commands that define these folders where your assets will be stored. It is a good idea to have a standard workspace for your show. The workspace used with this pipeline is located here:

```
c:/projects/$show/workspace.mel
```

You can open with a text editor to look at the details.

File Referencing

Some TDs have been reluctant to use file referencing. They are foolish and must be punished! File referencing is the grand art of taking a file from another location and making its contents part of your scene. It is *similar* to importing, but Maya remembers that the contents come from an outside scene, and if that outside scene is updated, Maya updates the current scene with the outside scene's new contents. It is an extremely powerful tool. Imagine having to somehow update and reapply animation every time the character TDs publish a new character rig. It could add weeks to your production. With referencing, your animators' scenes get updated automatically when the rig does. It's like magic!

Another huge advantage of referencing is that all the data that comes from the referenced files does not need to be written out when the current scene is saved. This can save *huge* amounts of time for animators, and it can save disk space.

To use referencing, choose File > Create Reference, and select a file that you want to reference as your outside source file.

 Note: You cannot change the hierarchy of referenced files. This is a huge advantage because it allows you to lock down the hierarchies and keep them from being modified accidentally.

Special Solutions

To illustrate a good workflow, we'll visit a mock production for a special mini-film, *The Big Race*. During the course of the film production, artists will need to perform various tasks in order move their data along the pipeline and hand it off to other departments or artists. The scenes in *The Big Race* will need to be populated by characters who will then need to have their data moved along the pipeline.

The story revolves around Bob, a fat kid who is training for a big race. In this story, Bob is joined in training by several generic boy racers who we will call Joe and two generic girl racers we will call Amy.

Bob, Amy, and Joe all have slightly different rigs. The first sequence revolves around all three characters practicing at the track. In later sequences, Bob puts in some extra training by himself for the race, so he will be the only character in those shots. As he trains, Bob loses weight. During the race sequence, we are back to all three characters. Then, in a final sequence, we see Bob back to his chubby self.

At first glance, it sounds simple enough, but really, there are a few things that would be tough to organize without a handy pipeline. Let's break it down by sequence, as listed in Table 19.2.

▶ **Table 19.2** Sequence Summary and Character Requirements

Sequence	Summary	Characters Required
001	All three racers training.	Bob, two Amys, and several Joes
002	Bob trains on his own and loses weight.	Bob, but now he's slimmer (we'll need a variation on Bob's rig)
003	All three racers training.	Slimmer Bob (also the fat rig), two Amys, and several Joes
004	Bob gains his weight back.	Bob, but back to his fat self

You'll need several instances of the same characters, a way to store the animation, and a way to define what goes where for each sequence.

Relative File Referencing

The following sections illustrate how you can use referencing to streamline the flow of *The Big Race*.

Namespaces

Since there are several Joes, you'll use namespaces to differentiate between them. You can use the name of a specific character in the namespace, so use namespaces to define separate instances of your character. You may have a whole herd of characters, but you can place namespaces on each one to differentiate it from the rest.

We'll reference Joe's rig several times into the scene under different namespaces, Amy's rig twice, and Bob's rig once. You can define them like this:

```
bob:bob
amy001:amy
amy002:amy
joe001:joe
joe002:joe
joe003:joe
joe002:joe
...
joe008:joe
```

To reference in the characters for the scene, follow these steps:

1. Set the project by clicking the projectSetterUI button (PS) on the shelf. Select bigrace shots 001 029 anim anim, the first shot in *The Big Race*. We'll explain the projectSetter tool later in this chapter.

2. Start a new scene.

3. Open characterListerUI by clicking the CL button on the shelf.

4. In characterLister, select Bob from the Characters menu, and then select Bob (the star of our show) from the Namespaces menu.

5. Click Reference.

6. Repeat the process for the characters Amy and Joe.

> **Tip:** You can select more than one namespace at a time to reference multiple instances of the characters simultaneously.

Resolved and Unresolved Referencing Paths

There's more than just your typical referencing going on under the hood of the characterLister tool. The tool creates a relative reference for each of the characters.

Maya always has specific locations where it looks for information. You set that location by setting your project. (Again, we'll go deeper into setting projects later.) In the case of the project you just set using the projectSetter tool, Maya begins looking for information here:

```
C:/projects/bigrace/publish/pub/shots/001/031/depts/:
```

So, in order to reference the character located here:

```
C:/projects/bigrace/publish/pub/shots/001/031/depts/char/pp/scenes/
[$character].mb
```

you can reference in a file by giving only the second half of the path:

```
char/pp/scenes/[$character].mb
```

Maya will combine the project path:

```
C:/projects/bigrace/publish/pub/shots/001/029/depts/
```

with the relative path:

```
char/pp/scenes/[$character].mb
```

and access the character stored here:

```
C:/projects/bigrace/publish/pub/shots/001/029/depts/char/pp/scenes/
[$character].mb
```

With all the characters still loaded, open the Reference Editor by choosing File > Reference Editor. Select each character, and look at the resolved and unresolved paths. You'll notice how Maya appends the partial, tail end of the relative path to Maya's current project location.

Besides the obvious advantage of less typing, relative referencing has some great benefits that we will explain later in the chapter.

What the *characterLister* Tool Does

The characterLister tool, shown in Figure 19.2, does all the work of referencing with relative paths of the appropriate puppet rigs for your shot, as well as showing you which characters are available for the shot. The characterLister tool displays only the puppets and high-resolution characters that are available for your scene along with their available namespaces. The availability of namespaces and puppets is based on information that is usually set by the coordinator or TD responsible for determining which characters go in each shot.

The shotinfo.info file is the primary source for defining which characters should be in which shots. It is a simple text file that you can edit to define what goes where. Open the file at C:/projects/bigrace/publish/pub/shots/001/029/depts/info/shotinfo.info, and take a look at its contents:

```
//characters and namespaces
bob,bob
amy,amy001,amy002
joe,joe001,joe002,joe003,joe004,joe005,joe006,joe007,joe008
//frame range
0,64
```

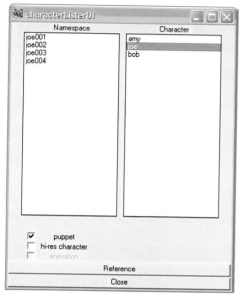

Figure 19.2 The characterLister tool

After the //characters and namespaces comment, there are three characters: Bob, Amy, and Joe. In sequence 001, shot 029, there can be one instance of Bob, named bob. There are also two Amys, amy001 and amy002, and there are eight Joes, joe001 through joe008. This is handy if you have a whole herd of Joes, as in the final sequence of *The Big Race*.

Now, let's suppose the powers-that-be have determined that you need more Amys at the big race. The coordinator can make more Amys available by editing the shotinfo.info file in any text editor:

1. Open the shotinfo.info file located here:

    C:/projects/bigrace/publish/pub/shots/001/029/depts/info/shotinfo.info

2. Change the line that reads this:

    amy,amy001,amy002

to read the following:

    amy,amy001,amy002,amy003

3. Open the characterLister tool again, and reference amy003:amy.

The shotinfo.info file gives you a simple way to define which characters and how many of each of them will be included in a shot. It stores that information for later use by the pipeline tools. The information is important for continuity issues. Suppose Joe #3 slips in the mud and gets his face all dirty. In the next shot, it is important to have that same Joe covered in sludge. Defining namespaces for the characters helps you to keep track of them, especially if you have several animators working on one shot or sequence. It is especially useful when you are dealing with hundreds of characters with several variations each. Imagine dealing with entire crowds!

Constraining the assets in a scene makes it easier for animators and lighters to know what to use. People working in your pipeline immediately know the answer to questions like "How many Amys are supposed to be in this scene?" or "Was Amy or Joe supposed to be in the background here?" Finally, it provides predictable, reliable naming for characters throughout the pipeline.

Setting Up Your Project Like Never Before

Setting up your project properly yields benefits throughout your workflow. The projectSetter tool will assist you in setting up your project so that Maya has all the information it needs to find files and set up shots in your pipeline. It also sets all the variables and information that custom tools need to place items properly. The projectSetter tool is the main organizational tool for Pipeline in a Box and must be used before you access your other tools.

The *projectSetter* Tool

Using a tool that sets up the project and environment for everyone working on the show guarantees consistency. The projectSetter tool, shown in Figure 19.3, allows the user to select from available shows, sequences, and shots in the directory structure. It also copies the common workspace file to your shot, sets environment variables, sets up multilevel search paths, and creates folders as necessary.

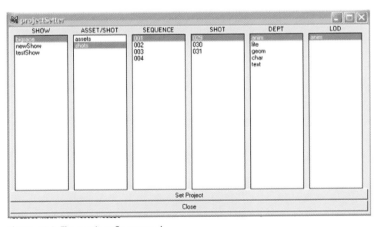

Figure 19.3 The projectSetter tool

To use the projectSetter tool, follow these steps:

1. Open the projectSetter tool by clicking the PS button on the shelf.

2. Select a show, scene, and shot. Then, select the department. For this example, select bigrace, shots, 001, 029, anim, anim. This sets your project to the animation department.

3. Open your project editor to see the changes by selecting File > Project > Edit Current.

   The resulting edit should look similar to Figure 19.4.

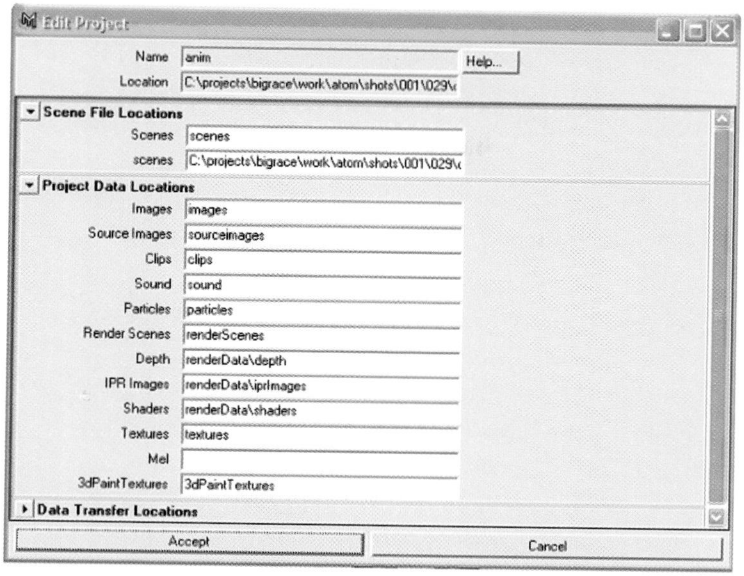

Figure 19.4 Current project locations

Setting Environment Variables

When setting your project to a shot, you should set certain environment variables so that Maya always has access to the show, sequence, and shot you're working in, as well as other information about the pipeline. These are good environment variables to set:

- SHOW
- SEQUENCE
- SHOT
- START_FRAME
- END_FRAME
- LOD (level of detail)
- DEPT (the department you are dealing with, such as lighting, texturing, and so forth)
- ASSET_SEARCH_PATH

    The projectSetter tool sets all these environment variables for you.

Setting Projects with Multilevel Search Paths

The projectSetter tool sets your project to search for assets in multiple locations, much like the Maya script path does. The following MEL call in the workspace file sets the search paths for your Maya project:

```
workspace -objectType   "scenes" `getenv ASSET_SEARCH_PATH`;
```

Consider the show bigrace, with the sequence 001 and shot 031. The ASSET_SEARCH_PATH variable, as set by the projectSetter tool, would have a value similar to the following:

```
C:/projects/bigrace/work/USERUSER/shots/001/031/depts;C:/projects/bigrace/
publish/pub/shots/001/031/depts;C:/projects/bigrace/work/USERUSER/shots/001/
depts;C:/projects/bigrace/publish/pub/shots/001/depts;C:/projects/bigrace/
work/USERUSER/shots/depts;C:/projects/bigrace/publish/pub/shots/depts;
```

Notice how the variable is really a hierarchical list of paths concatenated by semicolons (;), or colons (:) if you're on a Linux system. Maya searches the paths in the following order:

```
C:/projects/bigrace/work/USER/shots/001/031/depts/char/pp/scenes/
C:/projects/bigrace/publish/pub/shots/001/031/depts/char/pp/scenes/
C:/projects/bigrace/work/USER/shots/001/depts/char/pp/scenes/
C:/projects/bigrace/publish/pub/shots/001/depts/char/pp/scenes/
C:/projects/bigrace/work/USER/shots/depts/char/pp/scenes/
C:/projects/bigrace/publish/pub/shots/depts/char/pp/scenes/
```

Search-Level Priorities

Basically, the multilevel search path tells Maya to search through each path one at a time and, when it finds the file it's looking for, then stop.

The shot-level user area is searched first, then the shot-level published area, then the sequence-level user area, then the sequence-level published area, then the show-level user area, and finally the show-level published area.

For *The Big Race*, this means you can store modified Bob rigs for specific shots or sequences by placing the modified rig in Maya's search path. Bob is determined to win the race, so he trains hard, and finally, a newer, skinnier Bob emerges. We have to change our rig. A problem arises because we don't want to replace the base Bob with the new skinny Bob rig and change all the rigs in each shot (remember, they're referenced!). We want the skinny Bob to show up in only the shots where Bob should be skinny—where his skinny rig should be referenced. Fortunately, the pipeline is built to support this.

To see how the multilevel searches work, follow these steps:

1. Start a new scene.

2. From your file browser, copy the skinny Bob rig from here:

   ```
   C:\projects\bigrace\publish\pub\assets\bob\skinny\depts\char\pp\scenes\
   bob.mb
   ```

   and then paste it here:

   ```
   C:\projects\bigrace\publish\pub\shots\001\031\depts\char\pp\scenes\
   ```

3. Use the projectSetter tool to set your project to shots 001 031 anim anim.

4. To see the search paths, choose File > Project > Edit Current, and look at the scenes (not the "Scenes") value.

5. Open the characterLister, and reference bob:bob.

Huzzah! You have the new and improved skinny Bob, shown in Figure 19.5. He is looking sooo good.

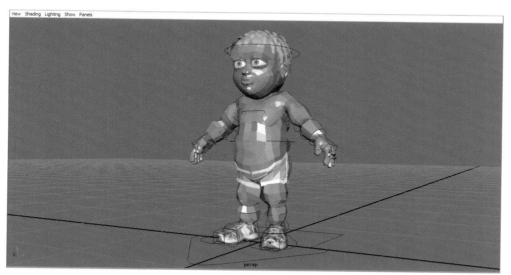

Figure 19.5 The skinny Bob animation rig

> **Tip:** Now, this is what you will want to tell all the other TDs standing around the water cooler about: you can place an asset at the shot level (as opposed to the show level), and its use will be *forced* for everyone working in that shot. One designated TD can control the usage of assets for an entire production army. The folks in production never even have to think about which assets to use where. It's automatic!

If a character or prop will be used for the entire show—a standard hero character rig, for example—place it at the show level. If you need a specific hero rig for a certain shot (he might be scaled, have extra appendages, have a larger head, or have a different IK system), you can place it at the shot level, and it will be referenced automatically. In this case, Bob's skinny rig is getting referenced for seq 001 shot 031.

To force a rig at the sequence level, follow these steps:

1. Using the projectSetter tool, set your project to shots 002 255 anim anim.

2. Open the bob_struts scene:

```
C:\projects\bigrace\work\USER\shots\002\255\depts\anim\anim\scenes\
bob_struts.ma
```

From the browser, select Current Scenes in the drop-down menu to navigate there instantly, and then click Open. Notice how the Bob appearing in the scene is corpulent Bob again.

3. Use Windows Explorer to copy the file from here:

    `C:\projects\bigrace\publish\pub\assets\bob\skinny\depts\char\pp\scenes\`
    `bob.mb`

    to here:

    `C:\projects\bigrace\publish\pub\shots\002\depts\char\pp\scenes\`

4. Now, reload Bob. Select File > Reference Editor, and then click bobRN bob.mb. Once the line is highlighted, click the Reload button in the right corner. As an alternative, you can simply reopen the scene:

    `C:\projects\bigrace\work\USER\shots\002\255\depts\anim\anim\scenes\`
    `bob_struts.ma`

You should see a newer, slimmer Bob. You just forced the use of the skinny rig on the sequence level, which will make the skinny Bob available throughout the sequence.

USER Areas

Having a USER branch for each person who works on the project is vital so that each user can test their files and see how they work in referenced scenes, without having to replace the assets that are referenced by the entire show. While you are working on your scenes, Maya is automatically set to save your scenes in the USER portion of the directory tree (remember, you replaced USER with your own username):

`C:\projects\bigrace\work\USER`

Your USER branch is also automatically included in the search paths at each level before the published area so that you can test and experiment with whatever asset you are working on before copying it to the publish area for everyone to use.

You can create a new USER branch in the directory tree by copying the USER folder from the book's companion CD, pasting it to C:\projects\bigrace\work\, and renaming USER to a new user's username.

Handling Animation Data with High-Resolution Characters

Animators want fast rigs that will allow them to scrub back and forth through the animation timeline without delay. In the final render, however, the character needs to have all that fancy skin weighting, deformation, wrinkling, and muscle influence dynamics. Rigs with all these bells and whistles are heavy and cumbersome to update while animating. Can the two be reconciled? There is hope. Read on.

Transferring Animation

You can export animation from a low-resolution, lightweight puppet to a high-resolution, skin-deforming character rig. For *The Big Race*, Joe's rig was built as two separate rigs: one a lightweight puppet and the other a higher-resolution deformation rig, as shown in Figure 19.6.

Notice that when you referenced any of the puppet rigs, you got a rig with the bound, smooth skinning removed and simplified, polygonal geometry. The lightweight geometry allows Joe's puppet to be animated quickly and easily, without being bogged down by the usual deformations. In Joe's case, it doesn't make a huge difference, since his skinning is relatively light, but imagine how complex and computationally intensive a character can be! Bob himself (or the next character you build) could have been built with a rig that includes fat jiggle and skin wrinkling, the likes of which might take several minutes or several hours to simulate for a shot!

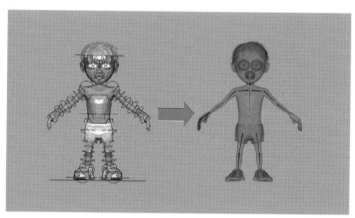

Figure 19.6 Transferring animation from a low-resolution puppet to a high-resolution character

With all the deformations pushed into the character rig, you don't have to worry about making the deformation rig scrubbable on the timeline, and you can give it the complex deformations, wrinkling skin, and jiggling muscle models needed for realistic skinning. All the heavy computation is run separately from the animation. This gives you extraordinary flexibility in your character pipeline.

Using the *animPublisher* Tool

A powerful tool, available in Maya since version 6.0, is the ability to export animation from referenced characters and store that animation as a file that contains only animation curves and their connections.

```
file -f -type "mayaAscii"  -exportSelectedAnimFromReference
destinationFilename.ma
```

Fortunately, the animationPublish tool, included with your Pipeline in a Box, takes care of this for you, so you don't have to open the Script Editor. This handy tool, shown in Figure 19.7, makes publishing animation conveniently fit into the pipeline. It does all the legwork for you by baking your animation, exporting it from your referenced character to the correct location in the directory structure, and storing it for later use.

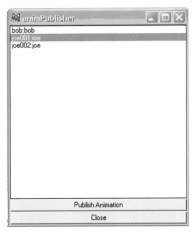

Figure 19.7 The animPublisher tool

PUBLISHING AN ANIMATION

To publish an animation, follow these steps:

1. Using the projectSetter tool, set your project to shots 003 321 anim anim.

2. Open the following scene:

    C:\projects\bigrace\work\USER\shots\003\321\depts\anim\anim\scenes\
    "joe_runs.ma

3. Launch the animPublisher tool, select joe001:joe, and then click Publish Animation.

The process will run in the background. Meanwhile, you can continue with necessary work on your scene or sit back and read the output in the window that's spawned by the command.

When you click Publish Animation, the tool saves a copy of your scene in its current state, using a different name, in a different file location. A system call is made using the MEL command exec (which runs processes in the background without taking control of your Maya scene). It starts Maya in batch mode and runs the script bakeAnimInBatchMode.mel. This script finds the .character file for your character (in this case, C:\projects\bigrace\publish\pub\shots\depts\info\bob.character) and reads the bone list from it.

When you build characters for use with the animationPublisher tool, you need to create a text file of the exact names of any nodes you want baked: blendshapes, clusters, lattices, and any other deformer for which want to transfer animation. The bone list for Joe has already been created for you.

Remember that whatever items are baked must exist in both the animation puppet and the high-resolution rig. In most cases, you bake only joint information for the body and blendshape information for the facial rig. The tool bakes animation on all the bones and exports that animation using the file command's -exportSelectedAnim-FromReference flag. The animation is stored here:

    C:\projects\$show\publish\pub\shots\$sequence\$shot\depts\
    anim\anim\$characterNamespace\scenes\anim.mb

Or, for this specific case, Joe's animation is found here:

```
C:\projects\bigrace\publish\pub\shots\003\321\depts\
anim\anim\joe001\scenes\anim.ma
```

Saving the animation in a separate, published area, away from the animators' scenes, protects it as an asset and keeps finished work compartmentalized from animators' scene files. It also allows you to repurpose the animation.

REFERENCING ANIMATIONS INTO OTHER CHARACTERS

Let's continue with the process and use the animation you exported from the low-resolution rig on the high-resolution character. To reference the animation onto the high-resolution character, follow these steps:

1. Start a new scene.

2. Open the characterLister tool, and check the boxes labeled High-Resolution Character and Animation.

3. Select joe and joe001, and click the Reference button.

    You will see the animation you published from the low-resolution puppet applied to the high-resolution character.

    Behind the scenes, the characterLister tool references the animation using a MEL call similar to this:

    ```
    file -reference -namespace "new" -swapNamespace "old" ":new" "path/file.mb";
    ```

    For characters of the same type but with different namespaces, the -swapNamespace command allows you to switch animation from one namespace to another.

REPURPOSING ANIMATIONS FOR OTHER SCENES

You can also repurpose an animation and apply it in another scene. You can do this by reopening a scene from one sequence into another project environment. Imagine that you want to reuse Bob's strutting animation from shot 002 255 again, this time in the final scene of your short film. The animPublisher tool prepares the data to make this possible.

To reuse Bob's animation in another scene on another variation of the same rig, follow these steps:

1. Using the projectSetter tool, set the project to shots 002 255 anim anim.

2. Open the file bob_struts.ma again. Choose File > Open. From the top drop-down menu, select Current Scenes. That directs the browser to the correct folder. Select bob_struts.ma, and then click Open.

3. Export Bob's animation using the animPublisher tool. Launch the tool from the shelf, select bob:bob, and click Publish Animation.

    The animPublisher tool stores Bob's animation (along with the scene you published from) here:

    ```
    C:\projects\bigrace\publish\pub\shots\002\255\depts\
    anim\anim\bob\scenes\animScene.mb
    ```

4. Start a new scene.

5. Set the project to shots 004 111 anim anim.

6. Select File > Open, and browse to open the scene you just copied:

   `C:\projects\bigrace\publish\pub\shots\004\111\depts\`

   `anim\anim\bob\scenes\animScene.mb`

   Now chubby Bob is back (using the puppet from the show level).

7. Playblast to see chubby Bob, now with his weight back but still feeling confident, strutting his stuff.

Extensions and Further Recommendations

Where do you go from here? Any number of assets on your show can use the multilevel search paths and then be referenced relatively. These include light rigs, shaders, models, environment sets, and cameras. The trick is to control the contents of your shot by what you place in the show, sequence, and shot folders. You can add whatever environment variables to the projectSetter tool with a few simple lines of MEL. You can also add subroutines in the MEL tools to parse through any kind of information pertinent to a shot by placing that information in the shotinfo.info file. You can write out information, such as which props or sets to make available, and even add other information files (such as a .camera file) that can be parsed with a bit of clever MEL. Basically, the pipeline is open to any expansions you can think of.

The following are a few extensions you might want to implement:

Remote animation publishing When you publish an animation, it is far more convenient to run on a remote network machine if you have a farm available for processing. If you have a remote system available, just launch Maya in batch mode and run the script bakeAnimInBatchMode.mel. (You'll find it in the C:\projects\standard\maya\scripts folder.) This allows artists to keep working without their machines slowing down.

Versioning system The animPublisher tool overwrites previously published animation files. For a production with any volume of animation, you can modify the bakeAnimInBatch-Mode.mel script to add a new version number of the anim.ma file in a versions folder every time it writes out an animation. That way you can store animation as you go, in case it is necessary to revert to earlier versions.

Baking skins In the same script that publishes animation, bakeAnimInBatchMode.mel, you can add a geometry-baking routine using Maya's Geometry Cache feature. This removes any deformations that may bog down your scene and be prone to errors. By the time the lighters get their assets to light, they will be fast, ultrascrubbable geo.

Compatible with .ma and .mb files Currently the scripts are written to handle .mb character files in the character lister and bakeAnimInBatchMode.mel. Scripts that support *.ma files as well are preferable so the ASCII file can be edited by the user when necessary.

Locking down the folders Change permissions on files in the publish branch of the directory tree so that only a select few can create sequences, shots, or assets in the publish areas and key folders higher in the tree.

Conclusion

If you organize all your data into an efficient pipeline, then the data can flow during each phase of project. Using the tools explained in this chapter can be a huge time-saver and will allow you to manage the many rigs and assets presented to you in this book. Now that you can organize all the data you've learned to build in *Body Language*, you are artistically unstoppable!

Appendix

About the Companion CD

What You'll Find on the CD

The following sections are arranged by category and provide a summary of the items you'll find on the CD. If you need help with installing the items provided on the CD, refer to the installation instructions in the "Using the CD" section of this appendix.

Project Files

In the Project Files directory you will find two versions of the completed character. Each version is saved out in a Maya .mb and .ma format. The files are written from and intended for use in Maya 2008 Unlimited. You may open the .ma files in older versions of Maya, but you may find that not all of the setup is available or working.

One pair is locked and ready to be animated. The other pair is the working version that you can disassemble and figure out how it works. As you go through the chapters of the book, you will be able to refer to the rig and compare the connections within the rig.

The Runner © 2008, created by Eric Allen for use in this book. The Runner geometry and rig may be used for tutorial purposes only. Distribution of this figure in any way is prohibited. See the ReadMe on the CD for more information.

MEL Scripts

Within the MEL folder you will find all of the MEL scripts referenced in the book. You will also find the complete selection UI setup as well as some of the code from Chapter 15. These MEL scripts are for use as tutorials only. They are not to be used for any other purpose.

The UISource is Copyright © 2008, written by Jared Fong and adapted by Eric Allen for use in this book. Anyone may use and modify this script, as long as credit is given to the author for the original script. Use and modify this script at your own risk. This example only works on Maya 8.5 and higher versions. See the readme.txt on the CD for more information.

Referencing

You will also find a Referencing folder in the main directory. This is the example of Adam Sidwell's Pipeline in a Box™ from Chapter 19.

Movies

Within the Movies folder you will find an example of a facial setup that uses blend-shapes driven by joysticks. You will also find a movie that demonstrates the automatic lacrimal caruncle and cornea displacement of an eye.

System Requirements

Make sure that your computer meets the minimum system requirements shown in the following list. If your computer doesn't match up to most of these requirements, you may have problems using the software and files on the companion CD. For the latest and greatest information, please refer to the ReadMe file located at the root of the CD-ROM.

- A PC running Microsoft Windows 98, Windows 2000, Windows NT4 (with SP4 or later), Windows Me, Windows XP, or Windows Vista

- A Macintosh running Apple OS X or later

- An Internet connection

- A CD-ROM drive

Using the CD

To install the items from the CD to your hard drive, follow these steps.

1. Insert the CD into your computer's CD-ROM drive. The license agreement appears.

> **N o t e :** Windows users: The interface won't launch if you have autorun disabled. In that case, click Start > Run (for Windows Vista, Start > All Programs > Accessories > Run). In the dialog box that appears, type **D:\Start.exe**. (Replace *D* with the proper letter if your CD drive uses a different letter. If you don't know the letter, see how your CD drive is listed under My Computer.) Click OK.

> **N o t e :** Mac users: The CD icon will appear on your desktop, double-click the icon to open the CD and double-click the Start icon.

2. Read through the license agreement, and then click the Accept button if you want to use the CD.

   The CD interface appears. The interface allows you to access the content with just one or two clicks.

Troubleshooting

Wiley has attempted to provide programs that work on most computers with the minimum system requirements. Alas, your computer may differ, and some programs may not work properly for some reason.

The two likeliest problems are that you don't have enough memory (RAM) for the programs you want to use, or you have other programs running that are affecting installation or running of a program. If you get an error message such as "Not enough memory" or "Setup cannot continue," try one or more of the following suggestions and then try using the software again:

Turn off any antivirus software running on your computer. Installation programs sometimes mimic virus activity and may make your computer incorrectly believe that it's being infected by a virus.

Close all running programs. The more programs you have running, the less memory is available to other programs. Installation programs typically update files and programs; so if you keep other programs running, installation may not work properly.

Have your local computer store add more RAM to your computer. This is, admittedly, a drastic and somewhat expensive step. However, adding more memory can really help the speed of your computer and allow more programs to run at the same time.

Customer Care

If you have trouble with the book's companion CD-ROM, please call the Wiley Product Technical Support phone number at (800) 762-2974. Outside the United States, call +1(317) 572-3994. You can also contact Wiley Product Technical Support at http://sybex.custhelp.com. John Wiley & Sons will provide technical support only for installation and other general quality control items. For technical support on the applications themselves, consult the program's vendor or author.

To place additional orders or to request information about other Wiley products, please call (877) 762-2974.

Index

Note to the reader: Throughout this index **boldfaced** page numbers indicate primary discussions of a topic. *Italicized* page numbers indicate illustrations.

Symbols and Numbers

* (asterisk), as wildcard in script, 306
// for comments, 290
; (semicolon) for command end, 20, 290
` (tick mark), 288
3D objects, dropping to UV Editor, **314–315**, *315*
3D Studio Max, 257
3D surface, representing in 2D space. *See* UV mapping
3D window in UVLayout, hotkeys, 327

A

A viseme, **234**, *234*
AA viseme, **234**, *234*
Adams, Mark, *Inside Maya 5*, 70
Add Attribute dialog box, *43*, 43
Add Selected to Graph command, 62
advanced foot setup, 119
    vs. classic reverse foot setup, 120
advanced rigging, planning, 3
agonist muscle, 330
AH viseme, **233**, *233*
aim constraints, 38, *39*
    for eyes, 159
ambulation
    creating torso and master controls for, **86–87**
    rigging for, **84–88**
anger, eye morph for, *183*, 183
Anghelescu, Mihai, 190, 218
Animate menu > Set Driven Key > Set, 145
animation. *See also* rigging
    handling data for high-resolution characters, **370–374**
    publishing, **372–373**
    remote publishing, 374
    repurposing for other scenes, **373–374**

requirements for rigging plan, 46
    temporary, for binding process, *345*, 345
animationPublisher tool, 360
animators
    locking down and hiding components from, 350
    requirements for rigging plan, **9–10**
    riggers and, 138
animPublisher tool, **371–374**
antagonist muscle, 330
applications
    for image map, 306
    for rigging, **4**
    for UV mapping, **310–311**
<area> tag, 306
arm, **94–96**. *See also* forearm
    creating, **103–114**
    FK/IK, constraints needed, *114*
    grouping, **114**
    mirroring, **114**
    rivet-based deformation, **274–276**
Arnold, *14*, 16
arrays, 288, **290–291**
    loops for, *295*
assets tree, 360
asterisk (*), as wildcard in script, 306
attitude, 12
Attribute Editor, *21*, **21**
    button, 20, *20*
    for eye joint, 175
    for rig information, 29
attribute fields, color of, in Channel Box, 24
attributes
    controls, *251*, **254**
    creating, **43**
    to define nodes, 42
    locking and unlocking, 24
    for morphs, 222
        list, **256**
    for set-driven keys, 144
    showing hidden, 351

Modo, 192, 196, 310
morph approach. *See also* master morphs
   and attribute lists, **256**
   attributes for, 222
   blink, *180*
   creating, **194–196**
   in deformations, 176–178, *177*
   vs. deformers, for facial expressions,
      243–247
   for eyes
      blink, 180
      LowerLidDown, 183, *183*
      LowLidUp, *182*, 182
      UpperLid Down, 181, *182*
      UpperLidUp, 180, *181*
   for jaw, **192–193**
      vs. rigged jaw or morphs with rigged
         jaw, **190–191**
   vs. jointing, 169
   list, *255*
   naming conventions for, **193–194**
   and painting weights, **191**, *192*
   in setup, **214**
   slider grouping, *255*
mouth, open between visemes, *223*, **223**
MouthCornerDepth morph, *200*, 200
MouthHeight morph, 199, *204*, **204**
MouthWidth morph, 199
Move Skinned Joints tool, **348**
movement
   constraints for, **36–39**
   goals for, **119–120**
   rigging for, **84–88**
Muscle menu
   > Muscle/Bones
      > Convert Surface to Muscle/
         Bone, 331
      > Create Capsule, 331
      > Muscle Builder UI, 332
   > Skin System
      > Apply Muscle Skin Deformer, 332
      > Paint Muscle Weights, 332
muscles. *See also* Maya Muscle
   creating, **332–333**
   defining interactions, **333**
   theory, **330**
My TMNT, 336, 338

N

N viseme, **235**, *236*
names
   for bindable joints, 339
   for controls, 41
   for hand joints, 137
   importance in organizing rig, **30–31**
   for joints
      in script for FK/IK switch, 298
      scripts for changing, 56
namespaces, for characters, 363
naming conventions, 30–31, **282**
   and conditional statements, 294
   for morphs, **193–194**
neck
   setup, **156–157**
   standard rigging, **156–157**
neck joints, **152–153**, 156
   rotation for, 153
negative painting, with script, 346
New Shelf command, 17
NG viseme, **236–237**, *237*
nodes
   changing to nonselectable reference
      object, 351
   defining, **42–43**
   information for rig, 29
   relationships between, creating, 26
nondeformer history, deleting, 338
normal constraint, 39
NoseWrinkle shape, *245*, 245
null-based controls, 40, **41–42**
null groups, 30
NURBS curve, attaching spine joints to, 55
NURBS rivets, *272*, **272–273**, *273*
NURBS surface, script to hook locator to, 270

O

O viseme, 226, *227*
objects
   adding to layer, 23
   control to lock to hand, 148
   in Outliner, parenting options, 25
OH viseme, **233**, *233*
OO viseme, **219**, **226–228**, *227*
Open Season, 224

S